The Atlantic World
in the Age of Empire

PROBLEMS IN WORLD
HISTORY SERIES

The Atlantic World in the Age of Empire

Edited and with an introduction by

Thomas Benjamin

Timothy Hall

David Rutherford

Central Michigan University

Houghton Mifflin Company   Boston New York

Editor-in-Chief: Jean L. Woy
Sponsoring Editor: Nancy Blaine
Associate Editor: Julie Dunn
Associate Project Editor: Jane Lee
Editorial Assistant: Martha Rogers
Associate Production/Design Coordinator: Lisa Jelly
Senior Manufacturing Coordinator: Marie Barnes
Senior Marketing Manager: Sandra McGuire

Cover Image: Scala/Art Resource, New York

Printed in the U.S.A.

Library of Congress Catalog Card Number: 00-133803

ISBN: 0-618-06135-5

123456789-CRS-04 03 02 01 00

Contents

Preface

In the 1930s, Herbert Bolton proposed that the history of the thirteen British colonies of North America and subsequently the United States was better understood in the context of the rest of the Americas. In the 1980s and 1990s, neo-Boltonians argued that the proper context of study was the entire Atlantic basin or what has come to be called the Atlantic world. Placing people, processes, and events in a broader geographical context reveals general trends and patterns prevailing across imperial borders and allows the historian to weigh the impact of different variables. The increasing appearance of courses, conferences, and programs of study suggests that the age of the Atlantic world, at least in the halls of academe, is upon us.

We have assembled this book in the course of creating an Atlantic studies program at Central Michigan University. Our program is part of the joint degree program of Central Michigan University and the University of Strathclylde, Glasglow, Scotland. This book has evolved from some of the courses in this program: "The Atlantic World in the Age of Empire" taught by Benjamin, "British North America," taught by Hall, and "European Discourse and the Age of Discovery," taught by Rutherford. This text consists of thematically organized selections by highly respected historians. We hope it will assist others in learning and teaching Atlantic history as well as provide an Atlantic perspective for students and professors in courses on early American, Latin American, Caribbean, European, African, and African-American history.

We are grateful for the constructive comments provided by the anonymous reviewers for Houghton Mifflin. Nancy Blaine at Houghton Mifflin also gave us encouragement and helpful advice and guidance from inception. We would like to thank our friends and colleagues at Central Michigan University for many valuable suggestions on the make-up of this book and, most of all, our students, who over the years have provided feedback on the readings we have assigned them and have challenged us to make sense of the diversity of the Atlantic world. Their interest and curiosity have inspired this book.

Thomas Benjamin
Timothy Hall
David Rutherford

Chronology of
Events

1637	The Dutch seize Portuguese Elmina Castle on the Gold Coast of Africa
1640–1660	English Civil War
1640s–1650s	French Tortuga in the Caribbean becomes the most notorious of the buccaneer strongholds
1641–1648	Dutch seize Luanda and occupy part of Angola and São Tomé
1650s	English Barbados becomes a major sugar producer and exporter
1651	First of the English "Navigation Acts," mercantilist legislation, to control colonial trade
1655	Jamaica is captured from the Spanish by England
1664	New Amsterdam falls to England and is renamed New York
1668–1670	English pirate Henry Morgan of Jamaica raids Spanish Caribbean
1670	English founding of Carolina
1674	Dutch West India Company declares bankruptcy and is dissolved
1675–1676	King Philip's War in Massachusetts
1676	Bacon's Rebellion in Virginia
1680	Popé leads Pueblo Revolt
1689	England's "Glorious Revolution"
1689–1697	War of the League of Augsburg
1690s	Gold discovered in Minas Gerais, Brazil
1697	The western third of Hispaniola, Saint Domingue, is ceded to France by Spain

The Eighteenth Century

1700–1713	War of the Spanish Succession
1702	Spanish slave trading contract granted to the French Guinea Company
1713	Spanish slave trading contract granted to English South Sea Company
1718	Jean Baptiste le Moyne, Sieur de Bienville, founds New Orleans
1720s	Saint Domingue overtakes Jamaica in the production and export of sugar

1740–1748	War of Austrian Succession
1754	Albany Congress proposes "Plan of Union" for British American mainland colonies
1756–1763	Seven Years or "French and Indian" War
1762	Colonial capital of Brazil is moved to Rio de Janeiro
1763	Treaty of Paris transfers New France to Great Britain
1776	Declaration of Independence of Thirteen Colonies
1787	American Constitutional Convention
1789	Fall of Bastille and beginning of French Revolution
1789	French Declaration of the Rights of Man and Citizen
1791	Start of slave rebellion in Saint Domingue
1791	Approval of United States Bill of Rights
1792	France abolishes monarchy and declares a republic
1799	Constitution of the Year VIII in France establishes the dictatorship of Napoleon Bonaparte

The Nineteenth Century

1804	Independence of Republic of Haiti
1807–1808	Napoleon invades Iberian peninsula: Portuguese royal court flees to Brazil; king and crown prince of Spain abdicate in favor of Napoleon
1808–1826	Revolutions for Independence of Spanish America
1812	Spanish republican Constitution of 1812
1814	Return of Ferdinand VII and suppression of Spanish Revolution
1822	Brazilian independence declared and constitutional monarchy established
1824	Federal Republic of Mexico established
1826	Spanish armies withdraw completely from the republics of former Spanish America

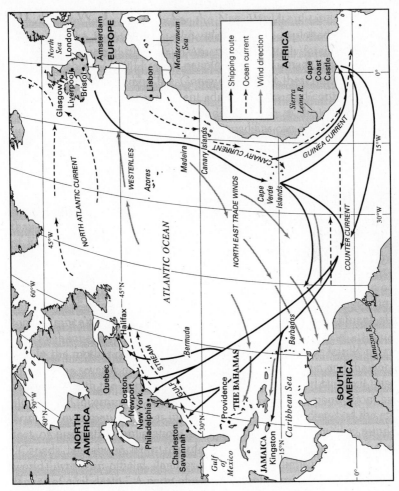

Atlantic Shipping Routes, Ocean Currents, and Trade Winds

Introduction

> Traffic in goods, ideas, and people made it possible to think of a
> single civilization spanning the ocean.
>
> Felipe Fernández-Armesto

The European navigations of the fifteenth and sixteenth centuries
brought four continents and three branches of humanity into interaction where there had been little or no contact before. This New World
was not discovered but assembled by sailors, traders, mapmakers, soldiers, natives, colonists, slaves, missionaries, bankers, monarchs, and
many other varied participants. Since 1492, the Atlantic has provided
the corridor for fundamental exchanges of people, crops, animals,
products, diseases, technology, and ideas. Those exchanges transformed
existing societies and created new communities and peoples within the
vast Atlantic arena. The new civilization that was built from this fer-
ment, one centered around and tied together by the Atlantic Ocean,
would shape the destiny of Europe, Africa, and the Americas—indeed
the entire globe itself—for five hundred years and more.

The formation and development of the Atlantic world in the age of
empire (1415–1825) is the subject of this volume. Its overarching
theme is a dramatic departure and revision of the traditional Eurocen-
tric perspective. That long-held view assumed that the age of discovery,
the conquest and settlement of the New World, the African slave trade,
and the creation of an Atlantic world were first and always European
projects. Recent research, in ethnohistory primarily, has demonstrated
that Africans, Amerindians, and Europeans together made the Atlantic
world. This is not to say that these three peoples were equal in power
and influence, but rather that each in its distinctive ways was critical in
its participation and contribution to the construction of an Atlantic
world tied together by trades, alliances, empires, experiences, and marriages. Within this theme, five topics are explored in the readings.

Part I considers the origins of the Atlantic world in the fifteenth
century. Part II is about the interactions among Amerindians, Africans,
and Europeans, and how those interactions and adaptations shaped
Europe, West Africa, and the Americas and the empires that brought
them together. Part III addresses the creation and evolution of the colonial Atlantic economy. There are readings about Spanish treasure
fleets, the North American fur trade, and the Atlantic slave trade, and
how all of these parts fit together to create wealth and poverty, both in
the past and today. Part IV deals with the flow of peoples who crossed
the Atlantic to create new societies. Finally, Part V considers the age of

Atlantic revolutions from 1775 to 1825 with readings on the American and French revolutions, the revolution of French Saint Domingue in the 1790s, and the Spanish and Spanish American revolutions of the 1810s and 1820s.

Origins: Creating the Atlantic World

The creation of the Atlantic world in the fifteenth and sixteenth centuries was a joint European, African, and Amerindian enterprise. The newly consolidated states of western Europe, equipped with sturdy caravels and carracks and recently borrowed or invented instruments of navigation, first mastered the sea. As the fifteenth century began, European navigators believed the great Ocean Sea—the Sea of Darkness, or the "Great Green Sea of Gloom," as Arab geographers knew it—unknown and certainly too vast to cross, confined the continent and its people.[1] A century later, the Atlantic had become a circuit of highways taking Europeans to the Gold Coast of Africa, the West Indies, the fisheries of the Grand Banks, and the rest of the world. After four thousand years of primacy, the western world no longer revolved around the Mediterranean Sea.[2] The peoples the Europeans encountered on the west coast of Africa and throughout the Americas contributed significantly (sometimes willingly, oftentimes not) to the formation of the Atlantic colonial world. Their knowledge, trades, wealth, and labor constituted the foundation of the entire project, one that often denied them any hope of advancement save salvation in the next life.

Iberians led the way. Portuguese mariners opened the difficult gate to the west coast of Africa, beginning in 1419. Throughout the century, expeditions overcame obstacles and reached distant shores and peoples. Only three years before Bartolomeu Dias passed the Cape of Good Hope and opened the passage to the Indian Ocean, the banner of Castile was carried across the Atlantic by a Genoese mariner. The four Columbian voyages from 1492 to 1506 sought the shores of

---

[1]Donald S. Johnson, *Phantom Islands of the Atlantic: The Legends of Seven Lands That Never Were* (New York: Walker and Company, 1994), p. xvii.

[2]"Until about 1600," writes William H. McNeill, "the Mediterranean zone of Europe remained culturally dominant." *The Shape of European History* (New York: Oxford University Press, 1974), p. 46.

Cathay (China) or at least Cipangu (Japan) but found gold in Hispaniola. Subsequent Andalusian expeditions — the so-called minor voyages — sketched the outlines of new continents previously unknown and unimagined. Mexico and Peru were integrated into the new Atlantic world as Spanish kingdoms. Portuguese, Spanish, English, and French voyages in the North Atlantic sought but found no Northwest Passage to the Orient.[3] They further filled in the outlines of what would become the Atlantic world in the sixteenth century.

European mariners and traders at the same time crossed the Indian and Pacific oceans. The precious spices, silks, and other exotic luxuries of the East were carried home from widely scattered toeholds on the coasts of India, China, Japan, the Philippines, and Indonesia. In Asian waters, Portuguese, Spanish, Dutch, French, and English trading factories were little more than parasites on vast and powerful societies that tolerated them.[4] In the East, Europeans had gained access to great and ancient civilizations and with it much wealth. In the West, they created a new civilization with Africans and Amerindians.

The delineation of the Atlantic Ocean emerged within a generation following the first voyage of Columbus. Even Amerigo Vespucci in 1501 believed he was cruising somewhere off the Asian coast. Yet, based on Vespucci's letters, Martin Waldsemüller in 1507 published a map that pictured two continents, the southern one named America, separated from Europe by the "Oceanus Occidentalis," the Western Ocean also called the North Sea by contemporary cartographers.[5] This and other maps of the early sixteenth century, however, portray the New World as an extension or close neighbor of Asia. Even after Balboa saw the "South Sea" — the Pacific Ocean — and Magellan crossed it, this vision persisted. It was not until the Diogo Ribeiro world map of 1529, from the top secret Spanish "Padrón Real," that the modern shape of the Atlantic basin appeared on paper. The Flemish map-

---

[3] It would not be until 1903–1906 that the first successful voyage through the real Northwest Passage was made, by the Norwegian explorer Roald Amundsen.

[4] The King of Portugal, "the Lord of Guinea and of the Conquest of the Navigation and Commerce of Ethiopia, Arabia, Persia and India," possessed more than fifty forts and factories on the Indian Ocean and the South China Sea.

[5] The name "Oceanus Atlanticus" appeared on some early sixteenth-century maps, usually off North Africa, so named after the Atlas mountains and the story told by Plato of the continent of Atlantis that had disappeared beneath the ocean.

makers Gerardus Mercator and Abraham Ortelius represented the newly discovered world—and the Oceanus Atlanticus—in widely publicized atlases in the 1560s and 1570s. Allegories often decorated Renaissance atlases and portrayed semi-naked female figures representing "Africa" and "America" submitting themselves and their products before a regal "Europa."[6] The world the Renaissance cartographers designed was literally and figuratively an Atlantic-centered world.

Encounters: Amerindians, Africans and Europeans

Never before in human history had so many different people connected and interacted, invented arrangements to live together, commingled so widely and at the same time so intimately. On the coast of West Africa, invisible microbes as well as fierce warriors protected the continent and its peoples from European invasion and conquest, at least for some four centuries. As a result relations between blacks and whites in Africa were on a fairly equal footing until the late nineteenth century. It was in the Americas, where slavery distorted and complicated every relationship, that the African-European connection created so many unhappy or unhealthy patterns. On a larger scale, plantation societies developed customs and codes as well as complex caste systems that regulated and ranked every shade of color. Under the most difficult circumstances, nevertheless, elements of African culture were transplanted in the Americas. African spiritualism today is widely practiced from Brazil to the Caribbean. "Brazilian Candomblé, like Haitian Voodoo, is at bottom the religion of African villages transported to American plantations."[7]

The European encounter with Amerindians began with much promise. Native Americans in the Caribbean naively welcomed Columbus. They freely traded dyewood with the Portuguese in Brazil and beaver pelts with the French, Dutch, and English in North America. European appetites expanded exponentially and met resistance.

---

[6]Jose Rabasa, "Allegories of Atlas," in *Inventing America: Spanish Historiography and the Formation of Eurocentrism* (Norman: University of Oklahoma Press, 1993), pp. 180–209.
[7]Peter Winn, *Americas: The Changing Face of Latin America and the Caribbean* (New York: Pantheon, 1992), p, 388.

The military conquests by the Spanish of the Mexicans and the Andeans, the Aztecs and Inkas, were rapid but hard fought. The subsequent conquests in Yucatan, Chile, Florida, and elsewhere were both long and hard. Everywhere, native peoples fought two enemies: the European warrior and his invisible allies, smallpox, influenza, and the other diseases, which produced "the worst single demographic disaster ever to have befallen mankind."[8] Amerindians survived nevertheless. Those who faced the main onslaught of the Spanish empire were engulfed and incorporated, taxed and worked, and superficially Christianized. Those beyond the pale, in South and North America, learned how selectively to avoid, resist, fight, trade, and negotiate with the intruder.

Europeans everywhere in the Americas benefited from Amerindians' knowledge of the land and its products, their military assistance against European as well as Amerindian enemies, their "irregular" style of warfare, their technology in canoe making and techniques in corn farming, and not least, their women. Europeans in New Spain and New France sought to "civilize" their native subjects or neighbors with little success. Native life, however, seemed to hold an attraction to Europeans, thus affirming the adage, "It is very easy to make an Indian out of a white man, but you cannot make a white man out of an Indian."[9]

The European encounter with the African and the Amerindian produced wealth, misery, and new peoples: mestizos, métis, mulattos, and other hybrids. Although despised by the colonial classifiers, their descendants today comprise entire nations, societies, and cultures. This blending is highly valued by the Mexicans, "the cosmic race," but also deplored and disguised in some American societies.

Trades: The Atlantic Economy

The Atlantic world from the beginning was an expanding network of trades linking long-established consumers with long-established pro-

---

[8]Felipe Fernàndez-Armesto, *Millennium: A History of the Last Thousand Years* (New York: Scribner, 1995), p. 276.
[9]Quoted by James Axtell, *The European and the Indian: Essays in the Ethnohistory of Colonial North America* (New York: Oxford University Press, 1981), p. 281.

ducers, while creating new wants and whims supplied by new providers. Again, it was a joint enterprise of Europeans, Africans, and Amerindians, each bringing into the mix their particular skills, resources, and consumer demands. European merchant capitalism provided the framework that integrated the distinct parts into one ever-expanding system. This surprisingly sophisticated yet unregulated economy utilized techniques and institutions such as commercial partnerships, double-entry bookkeeping, bills of exchange, maritime insurance, and more. "Trading in merchandise is so necessary," the merchant Tomé Pires wrote in 1515, "that without it the world would not go on."[10]

Integrated into this structure were Africans and Amerindians as producers and consumers. Most textbooks emphasize Europe's voracious appetite for "worldly goods": precious metals, sugar and spices, silks, porcelain, furs, dyestuffs, hardwoods, tobacco, ivory, gemstones, chocolate, and more. Africans and Amerindians, however, purchased as well as produced and therefore were vital participants in Atlantic markets. "Africa's trade with Europe," writes John Thornton, "was largely moved by prestige, fancy, changing taste, and a desire for variety—and such whimsical motivations were backed up by a relatively well developed productive economy and substantial purchasing power."[11]

Africans and Amerindians are best remembered for their coerced contribution to the Atlantic economy—their labor. The mines and haciendas of Spanish America and the sugar plantations of the tropical Atlantic produced great wealth because of, more than anything, such ingenious forms of exploitation as the encomienda, the Andean mita, peonage, and—most tragically—chattel slavery. The European downtrodden also provided their labor under contracts little better than slavery. But it was African slavery more than anything else that joined together the interlocking economies of the Atlantic world. "What moved in the Atlantic in these centuries," notes Barbara L. Solow, "was

---

[10]Quoted in Lisa Jardine, *Worldly Goods: A New History of the Renaissance* (New York: Doubleday, 1996), p. 327.

[11]John Thornton, *Africa and Africans in the Making of the Atlantic World, 1400–1680* (Cambridge: Cambridge University Press, 1992), p. 45.

predominantly slaves, the output of slaves, the inputs to slave societies, and the goods and services purchased with the earnings on slave products."[12]

The Atlantic economy was a vast, complicated network of mines, haciendas, fisheries, trading posts, plantations, shipyards, and industries, which governments vainly attempted to monopolize. The political economy of the Atlantic world was as ruthless as the traders, consumers, and producers of all nations were cooperative when profit so demanded. Governments and their allied chartered companies thought nothing of stealing cargoes, ships, convoys, factories, ports, and entire colonies and empires. The stakes were enormous for everyone involved, from princes to pioneers: never had the world seen such wealth created, transported, exchanged, won and lost. The late seventeenth-century Bristol merchant John Cary was right on the mark: "the wealth and Greatness of the Kingdom of England is supported by its Trade."[13]

Newcomers: The Flow of Peoples

The creation of the Atlantic world entailed the transfer of peoples, crops, livestock, technology, institutions, and ideas to the Americas. Of greatest significance was the peopling of the New World in the wake of the holocaust of its native inhabitants. For most of the imperial age, the largest flow came from Africa. Of the more than six million souls who traveled to the Americas from 1492 until the American Revolution of 1776, only one million were "pale-faced" Europeans. The Atlantic slave trade, fueled by the sugar plantations' insatiable demand for expendable labor, ultimately transported something in the range of nine to eleven million people over the course of four hundred years. The cost in lives was staggering: it is estimated that more than 400,000 perished in the crossing. Those who survived populated the tropical and

---

[12]Barbara L. Solow, "Introduction," *Slavery and the Rise of the Atlantic System*, Solow, ed. (Cambridge: Cambridge University Press, 1991), p. 1.

[13]Quoted in David Harris Sacks, *The Widening Gate: Bristol and the Atlantic Economy, 1450–1700* (Berkeley: University of California Press, 1991), p. 341.

semitropical regions of the Americas: Brazil and Guiana's "Wild Coast," the islands of the West Indies, certain coastlines of Spanish America, and the southern colonies of North America.[14]

European immigrants came by their own will for the most part, seeking wealth, power, adventure, souls to save, and religious freedom. The greatest waves over the longest periods came from Spain and England. Little Portugal and Holland contributed more than their share, while giant France parted with very few of its own. The New World, however, was attractive to all. Scots, Irish, Welsh, Italians, Scandinavians, Germans, Austrians, Swiss, Poles, Russians, Hungarians, Ukrainians, and others found new homes. New Spain, New England, and New France are well known today but what about the Irish colony in the Amazon in the 1620s, the Scottish colony in Darien in 1700, or the Austrian Lutheran colony in Georgia in 1740? These untypical settlements underscore the numerous ties, some wide and many narrow, linking the continents bordering on the Atlantic.

Catholics, Protestants, Jews, and Muslims came with their ideas about one God, Biblical stories, sectarian conflicts, and occasional tolerance. Europeans not only carried religious ideas but also influences from the classical Mediterranean age, such as Roman law, as well as the new "experimental philosophy" we today call science. American conditions and European misbehavior, and criticism of such behavior, led to the invention of new ideas such as universal human rights. Europeans organized themselves in the only ways they knew how. They transplanted and multiplied their institutions throughout the Atlantic world. Churches were fundamental. Of no less importance were companies, towns and cities, guilds, militias, and universities. All were essentially European, although they acquired American characteristics.

Europeans also brought their crops and livestock. Wheat was planted across the plains of the Americas; vineyards sprouted; and sugarcane invaded. A "plague of sheep" engulfed Mexico, while Amerindians welcomed swine and chickens. Cattle and horses colonized every region as surely as did people. Institutions, crops, and livestock were accompanied by technology such as the plow, water mills, and

[14]Until the late nineteenth century, writes David Eltis, the Americas were more an extension of Africa than of Europe. See Eltis, "Free and Coerced Transatlantic Migrations: Some Comparisons," *American Historical Review*, 88, No. 2 (1983), p. 255.

windmills, foundries, spinning wheels, printing presses, and more. While empires may have divided Americans and created fissures across the Atlantic, the spread of European peoples and their religions, ideas, institutions, crops, animals, and technology established the foundation of an Atlantic civilization that exists still.

Revolutions: The Great Transformation

In less than two generations, from 1775 to 1825, twenty fragments of four empires in the Americas separated from their motherlands.[15] This dramatic end of the age of empire along the western shores of the Atlantic did not end, or even break up, the Atlantic world. The ties of people, trades, technology, and ideas that created the Atlantic world survived the age of empire. Revolution created a new American world within the older Atlantic civilization, one now composed of independent nation-states.

The American colonies began as attempts to recreate the distinct European homelands in new environments. Although small, weak, and dependent at first, there came a time when many of the colonial societies could stand on their own and defend themselves. Eventually European Americans—Creoles—lost their sense of fellowship with the mother country and developed different sentiments, values, and identities.

The age of revolution was part and parcel of the "second hundred years war," the titanic struggle for European, Atlantic, and global supremacy between Britain and France. The all-embracing struggle motivated the intrusive imperial reforms of Britain, France, Spain, and Portugal that alienated Creole elites and incited downtrodden Amerindians, provoked free mulatos and black slaves, and inspired American rabble-rousers from Buenos Aires to Boston. In one way or another, the conflict helped ignite every American revolution from that of the Anglo-American thirteen colonies to the slave revolution in

---

[15]Consider the Adams family of Massachusetts. Father John Adams participated in the thick of the American revolution from its beginning to its end. His son, John Quincy Adams, as Secretary of State in the James Monroe administration, wrote the Monroe Doctrine in 1823, which formulated American foreign policy with respect to the new nations of the former Spanish American empire.

Haiti, the Hidalgo revolt in Mexico, the liberation of Spanish South America, and the civil divorce of Brazil from Portugal. We need to remember, as well, that revolution was a European as well as American movement, with liberal republican upheavals in France, Spain, and Portugal as well as in their colonies.

The selection of readings that follow reflects the spirit of Herbert E. Bolton's call for an epic of greater America. "There is need of a broader treatment of American history," he wrote in 1933. "Each local story will have clearer meaning when studied in light of the others."[16] But where Bolton and his colleagues saw primarily a European project, the present generation of historians have probed beneath the surface of colonial impositions to discover that Amerindians and Africans were active participants and vital contributors to the construction of an Atlantic civilization. Atlantic history is not simply a story of European pioneers building a new world out of the wilderness or even one of European usurpers destroying the lives of Amerindian and African victims. Despite inequities of power and wealth, Amerindians and Africans acted as much as they reacted, invented as well as adopted, and built new lives and societies under the most difficult circumstances. Their stories are integrated with those of the Europeans in the readings of this volume and that perspective must force us to rethink the origins of our modern Atlantic world.

[16]Herbert E. Bolton, "The Epic of Greater America," *American Historical Review.* 38, No. 3 (April 1933), pp. 448–449.

I Origins: Creating the Atlantic World

The selections presented here seek to establish a historical context of the initial formation of the Atlantic world and to analyze, in part, the early constellation of ideas and patterns of thought that, for good or ill, have formed the notion of the Atlantic world. Janet Abu-Lughod's reading takes us back to an earlier "world-system" centered on the Middle East and the Indian Ocean, known commonly as the Silk Road. This "Old World" system set the stage for those who encountered each other, intentionally or unintentionally, in the new Atlantic world, especially insofar as it shaped aspirations and expectations. Abu-Lughod's examination of the Silk Road trading networks also provides important paradigms for understanding the formation of the Atlantic world and demonstrates some fruitful ways to analyze developments that span time, geography, culture, and commerce on this scale. This earlier system not only shaped European notions about the sources of wealth and commerce, but also, as she points out, influenced the relationships of the other players in the system.

Prior to the appearance of the Atlantic world here under discussion, the patterns of life around the Atlantic can only be reconstructed in the most hit and miss way, although archaeologists and ethnologists continue to recover the record. This earlier Atlantic may have had "darkness upon the face of the deep," but we should not imagine that it was completely "without form, and void" when the *Santa Maria* "moved upon the face of the waters."

Accordingly, John Thornton examines trading networks of the peoples of sub-Saharan and central West Africa, but begins with the very period when Abu-Lughod shows that the Silk Road networks, for a variety of reasons, unraveled. These areas of Africa had remained peripheral to the Silk Road system in much the same way as Abu-Lughod describes Europe as peripheral in that system. That is, the Silk Road was important to sub-Saharan and central West Africa and Europe, but Europe and central and sub-Saharan West Africa were not of great importance to the Silk Road.

Thornton also analyzes the physical and technological limits that had kept Africa, Europe, and the Americas separate: limits that contributed to other separating factors of both cause and effect, such as language, culture, religion, commerce, and disease. By taking the reader back to the early Atlantic world, ordered by prevailing winds, ocean currents, tidal estuaries, and riverine kingdoms, Thornton provides an analysis not only of what happened and how, but also of what could not happen and why not. The Portuguese and others, as he shows, worked their way down the coast of Africa, not to settle scientific questions about the earth's geography (although they were keenly inquisitive about such matters), but moved by aspirations more base and financed by means most evil.

While Thornton concentrates largely on the Portuguese voyages in the African Atlantic, D. W. Meinig explores the Spanish voyages to America. Meinig sees this expansionism as a continuation of the expansion of Christian Europe extending back to the High Middle Ages. Meinig's geographical perspective offers an interesting model for understanding transatlantic exploration and colonization, which involved seafaring, conquest, and planting. These three activities and phases were adopted by all Europeans who came to America although not in exactly the same way. Analyses of the similarities and differences, Meinig writes, "provide the basis for a set of geographical generalizations about the whole process of transoceanic transfer and the interactions involved."

We must realize, finally, that the age of European exploration and discovery was also a time of intellectual and cultural discovery. Europeans came into direct contact with unfamiliar peoples with very different appearances and habits. Olive Patricia Dickason examines the first reactions Europeans had of Amerindians and that Amerindians had of Europeans. In the Americas and Africa, there was mutual discovery and mutual accommodation.

Janet L. Abu-Lughod

Before European Hegemony

Studying a System in Formation

The second half of the thirteenth century was a remarkable moment in world history. Never before had so many regions of the Old World come in contact with one another—albeit still only superficially. At the beginning of the Christian era, the Roman and Chinese empires had been in indirect contact, but the connections between them declined when both empires fragmented. In the seventh and eighth centuries, Islam unified many parts of the central region that lay between the European and Chinese extremities, reaching out in both directions, but the peripheral areas of this reviving world economy still remained relatively isolated from one another. By the eleventh and, even more, twelfth century, many parts of the Old World began to become integrated into a system of exchange from which all apparently benefited. The apogee of this cycle came between the end of the thirteenth and the first decades of the fourteenth century, by which time even Europe and China had established direct, if decidedly limited, contact with each other.

The thirteenth century was remarkable in another way. In region after region there was an efforescence of cultural and artistic achievement. Never before had so many parts of the Old World simultaneously reached cultural maturity. In China, the most glorious pottery ever produced, Sung celadonware, was being created, and in Persia glowing turquoise-glazed bowls constituted the only serious rival. In Mamluk Egypt, craftsmen were fashioning elaborate furniture inlaid with complex arabesques of silver and gold, and in western Europe, cathedral building reached its apex. The gem-like stained glass window-adorned Saint Chapelle of Paris was built in mid-thirteenth century, just before St. Louis departed on crusade. The great Hindu temple complexes of south India climaxed at this same time. Almost everywhere there was evidence of a surfeit of wealth being devoted to ornamentation and symbolic display. The era was equally productive intellectually, suggesting that the surplus was used not only to produce things but to support scholars as well.

These two qualities of the thirteenth century, increased economic integration and cultural efforescence, were not unrelated. Technological and social innovations produced surpluses, which were, in turn, traded internationally to further intensify development. Parallel advances in navigation and statecraft facilitated contact among distant societies, which generated even more surpluses. In all areas, prosperity—at least at the top—yielded high culture, and Europe, hitherto the least developed region, perhaps had the most to gain from the new links being forged.

In this book we explore the thirteenth century "world economy" which facilitated such pandemic prosperity for its rulers, and examine how it was forged. We also examine why this promising start faltered by the middle of the fourteenth century. How much of it remained when, in the sixteenth century, Europe took the lead in forging what Wallerstein (1974) has termed the "modern world-system"? In *that* world system, which has persisted for some five hundred years, the West was clearly hegemonic. But to understand its roots it is necessary to examine the period *before* European hegemony. That is the descriptive task of this book.

There is an analytic task as well. The world economy of the thirteenth century is not only fascinating in itself but, because it contained no single hegemonic power, provides an important contrast to the world system that grew out of it: the one Europe reshaped to its own ends and dominated for so long. This contrast suggests that the characteristics of world systems are not invariant. There is no unique way for the parts to be organized. Furthermore, world systems are not static. They evolve and change. At this moment in time, the particular world system that originated in the sixteenth century is in the throes of change. Understanding the system that preceded it may help in better comprehending what lies ahead. . . .

The Thirteenth Century: A World System?

Between A.D. 1250 and 1350 an international trade economy was developing that stretched all the way from northwestern Europe to China; it involved merchants and producers in an extensive (worldwide) if narrow network of exchange. Although primary products (including but not confined to specialty agricultural items, mostly spices) constituted a significant proportion of all items traded, particularly over short distances, manufactured goods were surprisingly central to the system, which probably could not have been sustained over long distances without them. The production of these goods had to be sufficient to meet domestic needs as well as those of export. Thus, all the units in the system were producing surpluses, impossible unless the methods of mobilizing labor and organizing the work process were quite advanced.

Furthermore, the trade involved a wide variety of merchant communities at various points on the globe. These merchants did not necessarily speak or write the same languages, although Arabic covered a wide area, as did Greek and the vernaculars of Latin, and Mandarin Chinese was a lingua franca for the many nationalities in the far east. Nor were their local currencies the same. Silver was highly valued in Europe, gold was used in the Middle East, whereas copper coins were the preferred specie in China. Distances, as measured by time, were calculated in weeks and months at best, but it took years to traverse the entire circuit. And yet, goods were transferred, prices set, exchange rates agreed upon, contracts entered into, credit—on funds or on goods located elsewhere—extended, partnerships formed, and, obviously, records kept and agreements honored. . . .

Of all the comments I have read, those of Fernand Braudel seem to be the most sensible. He acknowledges that world-economies existed in various parts of the world long before the thirteenth century and that certainly a European world-economy had taken shape before the sixteenth century, singled out as so crucial by Wallerstein and in certain writings by Marx. . . .

. . . Although [Braudel] readily acknowledges that "the first world-economy ever to take shape in Europe [was born] between the eleventh and thirteenth centuries" (1984: 92) and that "several world-economies have succeeded . . . each other in the geographical expression that is Europe," or rather, the "European world-economy has changed shape several times since the thirteenth century," he fails to make what to me is the essential point. Before Europe became *one* of the world-economies in the twelfth and thirteenth centuries, when it joined the long distance trade system that stretched through the Mediterranean into the Red Sea and Persian Gulf and on into the Indian Ocean and through the Strait of Malacca to reach China, there were numerous preexistent world-economies. Without them, when Europe gradually "reached out," it would have grasped empty space rather than riches. My plan is to examine this world system as a whole, treating Europe at that time as it should be seen, as an upstart peripheral to an ongoing operation.

This book is less interested in identifying origins and more in examining a crucial moment in history. It takes the position that in terms of time, the century between A.D. 1250 and 1350 constituted a fulcrum or critical "turning point" in world history, and in terms of space, the Middle East heartland region, linking the eastern Mediterranean with the Indian Ocean, constituted a geographic fulcrum on which West and East were then roughly balanced. The thesis of this book is that there was no *inherent historical necessity* that shifted the system to favor the West rather than the East, nor was there any inherent historical necessity that would have prevented cultures in the eastern region from becoming the progenitors of a modern world system. This thesis seems at least as compelling as its opposite. The usual approach is to examine ex post facto the outcome—that is, the economic and political hegemony of the West in modern times—and then to reason backward, to rationalize why this supremacy *had* to be. I want to avoid this.

It is not that I do not recognize that the outcome determines the narrative constructed to "lead inexorably" to it. This indeed is the real methodological problem of historiography. . . .

Not only were there great variations in the European periphery, but there were also substantial differences within the countries in the Old World core—in the Middle East, India, and China (at that time the leading contender for hegemony). Although the Middle East was generally more developed than Europe, it contained large areas relatively unintegrated with the central places that controlled empires. Cairo and Baghdad stand out as dual imperial centers, but their linkages through overland and sea routes tied them selectively to an "archipelago" of hinterlands. . . .

Nor was China a simple and unchanging monolith. That vast zone was differentiated on at least three axes: north and south, coast and interior, and along rivers or off their pathways. In general, times of expanding prosperity were associated with movements of population from north to south, from interior to coast, and from alluvial valleys to more peripheral places.

The Indian subcontinent was similarly complex and divided into subregions subject to very different imperatives. Northern India prospered when links to the Muslim world were strong and when the land routes to Russia on the north and to China on the east were open. The condition of south India, on the other hand, was contingent more upon the sea trade through the Indian Ocean, and there was often a clear differentiation between coastal and interior zones. . . .

[T]he key actors [were] in the Asian circuit (and indeed in the entire world system, as we shall show) but, as was true with respect to the Italians in the Mediterranean, we cannot leave the Arabs and Persians behind when we examine trade in the Indian Ocean. Three interwoven subsystems were involved: the westernmost circuit that linked the Arab world to western India; the central circuit that linked southeast India to the zone flanking the Strait of Malacca; and the easternmost circuit between the straits and China.

But Chinese merchants were present in Srivijaya (at the Strait), and Muslim traders—Arab, Persian, and Indian—were present in what might be termed the Chinese "treaty ports" (an older version of what came later). . . .

This book explores . . . the processes by which international connections were forged, expanded, and strengthened during the course of the thirteenth century, and describes the roles—cooperative, conflictual, or symbiotic—the varied participants played in the ongoing commercial exchanges. Each gained from the system but not to the detriment of others. When the system reached its zenith in the opening decades of the fourteenth century, no single power could be said to be hegemonic; the participation of all was required for its perpetuation.

In spite of these promising beginnings, however, during the middle decades of the fourteenth century the system fragmented and many parts went into simultaneous decline. By the end of that century, what had previously been a circulation system with many alternate routes had been reduced to a narrower set of links and numerous gaps had appeared. The economic difficulties experienced almost universally during the second half of the fourteenth century symptomized the break up of the system. Much of it was already gone by the time Portugal, a new player, entered the Indian Ocean at the beginning of the sixteenth century to set in motion the next phase of world integration.

One of the major questions this book seeks to answer is why the thirteenth-century system unraveled. The answer will not be a simple one; there are no monocausal explanations. No single overwhelming factor accounted, like some deus ex machina, for the fraying of the complex net of interrelationships among these various subsystems or for their transformation into a new balance, as world hegemony shifted westward. Rather, the cumulative effects of more modest alterations within and between subsystems undoubtedly contributed to a new weighting of the whole. If the fulcrum tipped its balance, it was because many of the subsystems were simultaneously but cumulatively shifting in the same direction.

John Thornton

The Birth of an Atlantic World

The Shape of the Atlantic Zone

The European navigations of the fifteenth century in the Atlantic opened up a new and virtually unprecedented chapter in human his-

John Thornton, *Africa and Africans in the Making of the Atlantic World, 1400–1800*, excerpts from pp. 13–42, Chapter 1 "The Birth of An Atlantic World." Reprinted with the permission of Cambridge University Press. Copyright © 1992 by Cambridge University Press.

tory. Not only did European sailors provide direct ocean routes to areas that had been in contact with Europe through more expensive and difficult overland routes (such as West Africa and East Asia), but the ships reached areas that had had no previous sustained and reciprocal contact with the outside world. Of course, this was obviously true of the American continents, and historians have rightly focused their attention on this immense new world in their discussions of the period. But it was not just the Americans who came into outside contact, for virtually the entire region of west central Africa, south of modern Cameroon, was also without outside contacts, in spite of the fact that it was geographically a part of the landmass whose eastern and western parts had long-standing connections to the Mediterranean and Indian Ocean. Thus, in addition to easing and intensifying relations between various parts of the Old World (which in this case also included West Africa), the European navigations opened up connections between the Old World and two new worlds—the two sections of the American continent and the western part of central Africa.

The French historian Pierre Chaunu has argued that perhaps the most significant consequence of European navigation was what he calls "disenclavement"—the ending of isolation for some areas and the increase in intersocietal contacts in most areas. This allowed an increased flow of ideas as well as trade throughout the world, ultimately leading to a unified world economy and potentially, at least, to higher levels of economic development. As such then, the opening of the Atlantic was crucial in this process, all the more so because it was only here that true isolation was broken.

More than this, however, the birth of an Atlantic world also involved a gigantic international migration of people, certainly without precedent in the Old World and undertaken nowhere else in the field of European expansion. Not only did thousands of Europeans move to the Atlantic islands and the Americas, but literally millions of Africans crossed to the Atlantic and Caribbean islands and the Americas, becoming the dominant population in some areas. This demographic fact was not lost on early residents and visitors: Gonzalo Fernández Oviedo y Valdez described Hispaniola as a "New Guinea" in the mid-sixteenth century when slave imports for its burgeoning sugar industry had changed its demography; Ambrósio Fernandes Brandão used exactly the same term to describe Brazil's sugar-rich northeast in 1618. In the Atlantic, disenclavement meant much more than it did elsewhere in the world; it was not just increased communication but a reshaping of whole societies and the literal creation of a "New World." Moreover, it was a reshaping that involved Africa quite directly, for by 1650 in any case, Africans were the majority of new settlers in the new Atlantic world.

Understanding the origin and direction of this gigantic episode in intersocial relations requires a knowledge of the basic geography of the areas involved—areas in which transport by water defined for most purposes the entire region. One must always remember that in the age before rail and air travel, waterborne travel was immensely cheaper and more practical—despite the risks of storm and shipwreck—than overland travel. Not only could boats and ships average fairly good time, but they were energy efficient in an era that had few energy resources, and they could, moreover, carry heavy and bulky goods easily. Thus, creating a geography of the Atlantic area must take areas accessible by water transport as its first dimension, for use of the water would greatly alter other considerations of space and distance, linking regions that were apparently distant more easily than regions that apparently lay close to each other.

The first of these great water routes was the Atlantic itself, opened for practical use in the fifteenth and early sixteenth centuries. But the Atlantic was also linked to riverine routes in both Africa and the Americas, which formed a vital supplement to the ocean, bringing societies and states that often lay hundreds of kilometers from the coast into contact with the ocean and, thus, with other societies and states. Even the rivers that did not allow ocean-going vessels to pass into interior regions (because of falls, narrows, or sandbanks) served as connections to extensive travel and commercial networks in the interior. The combination of ocean and river routes defined the shape of the Atlantic zone.

But one must not simply look at a map of the Atlantic and imagine that it was equally penetrable and that those who sailed it had equal access to all parts of the zone. In many ways, in the days of wooden sailing ships, the ocean was as much channeled as were rivers, whose direction of flow is clearly defined. No sailor could ignore the patterns of prevailing winds and currents on the ocean. This was crucial for the development of Atlantic navigation, for the winds and currents created barriers to traffic for thousands of years. They limited contact between the Mediterranean and Africa for a very long time and thwarted whatever potential Africans might have had for effective navigation into the

Atlantic beyond their coastal waters, just as it would act as a brake on American ventures to Africa and Europe.

Raymond Mauny has shown that the constant north-to-south flow of the Canary Current along the Saharan coast made it possible for ships from the Mediterranean to sail southward as far as West Africa but prevented a return voyage. For Mediterranean sailors, Cape Bojador, just south of the Canary Islands, represented a point of no return, and even if voyages, intentional and unintentional, went beyond it, they did not pioneer any route with practical significance. Arabic accounts cite several voyages made by accident beyond this point. al-Idrisi (1154) cites one that left from Lisbon, ibn Sa'id heard from a Moroccan traveler named Ibn Fatima of a similar voyage sometime before 1270, and al-'Umari heard of another one from Almeira in Spain made by Muhammad b. Raghanuh in the early fourteenth century—all were forced to return to the Mediterranean area by overland routes. It was only in the fifteenth century, and then using routes leading back through the Canaries, Madeira, and the Azores and risking a high-seas voyage, that Europeans were able to finally conquer the difficulties of the Bojador on a regular basis.

If the problems with the winds and currents off the Saharan coast checked Mediterraneans from entering the African portion of the Atlantic, a similar problem hampered African navigators. Of course, Africans would have been just as interested in going to North Africa and Iberia by sea as the Mediterranean people were interested in reaching Africa, given the knowledge that each area had of the other through the overland trade, but the constant current that prevented return trips to the Mediterranean also frustrated African efforts to go to the Mediterranean from the very start. The extent of northward sailing by African vessels seems to have been the saltworks of Ijil on the Mauretanian coast, at least according to al-Idrisi's twelfth-century account.

On the other hand, Africans faced the strongly prevailing westward-flowing Equatorial Current from the Senegambian region into the Caribbean basin. Although this current may have made African voyages to the Americas possible, it required fairly well developed techniques for high-seas navigation to even begin, and Africans could not develop such technology on short voyages in calm seas. Thus, Ivan van Sertima, who has championed the idea that Africans made frequent voyages to the Americas since around 800 B.C., has had to acknowledge that these voyages, if they occurred at all, were accidental and initiated no transatlantic commerce. However well such African navigators may have fared in long crossings in craft not designed to sail in the high seas, they faced insuperable barriers to making return trips to any familiar point on the African coast.

Of course, some of the Caribbean peoples developed sufficiently large craft to sail regularly in the Caribbean, and such ships might well have traveled to the Old World. Historian Aurelio Tió has shown how important the native people of the Caribbean were in guiding early European voyages from Florida to the Orinoco, and how they knew the regime of wind and current throughout the basin well. He suggests that they also knew a good deal of the oceanic geography of the western Atlantic. But for them, as well, the problem of a return voyage was similar to that the Europeans faced in their own early Atlantic navigations. Indeed, not until the late fifteenth century, when the entire system of Atlantic winds and currents was understood and European sailors knew all the potential landfalls on either side of the Atlantic, was a truly practical round-trip navigation achieved.

But even when the system was understood and European ships could travel (at least in theory) to every point in the Atlantic, they were nevertheless forced to respect the wind and currents. . . .

If water routes were the earliest form of travel, then the streams of the ocean must be joined to land streams if we are to see the full dimensions of the Atlantic world. This is abundantly demonstrated by the connections of the western Sudan to the Atlantic. Riverine routes going deep into West Africa connected points quite distant from the coast to the Atlantic. Although narrows and sandbars blocking the mouths often obstructed the travel of large, sea-going vessels on African rivers, smaller craft designed for river travel navigated them easily, and portages reduced the obstructions caused by falls. . . .

European Motives:
The Prevalence of Short-Range Goals

Whatever their dreams or fantasies, whether it was encircling and isolating the Moslems or reaching the spices of Asia or the gold of West Africa, these long-range plans were largely restricted to kings and intellectuals, and neither group proved particularly willing to actually finance the voyages they considered, and private or small-scale ventures (such as those of the Vivaldis and Ferrer) failed. Thus, whatever contemporary writers may have said about motives, or how much rulers may have desired the results of such schemes, the progress of Atlantic exploration ultimately depended on financial considerations. Financial considerations must ultimately force us to agree with the Portuguese historians on the prevalence of short-range, unromantic, step-by-step exploration as the principal method of European expansion.

It is also important to note that another romantic fantasy—that the Iberians were the sole leaders of the exploration—is untrue. The exploration of the Atlantic was a truly international exercise, even if many of the dramatic discoveries were made under the sponsorship of the Iberian monarchs. The people who undertook the voyages gathered the human and material resources from wherever they were available. English, French, Polish, Italian people, ships, and capital joined Iberians in this effort. If the Iberians were pioneers in anything, it was that monarchs of these countries were quick to claim sovereignty (or to offer their protection to the earliest colonists) and to make the effort necessary to enforce these claims, usually after the economic benefits were clearly revealed by an international group of pioneers.

We can conveniently divide the expansion into two "wings," or two directions. The first of these was an African wing, which sought mainland products such as slaves and then gold as the means to finance short voyages along the coast, and whose leaders expected to find people to raid or to trade with all along the route. The second was an Atlantic wing, which sought exploitable but not necessarily inhabited land in which to collect valuable wild products or to begin agricultural production of cultivated products in high demand in Europe. The colonization of these lands began with cutting timber or gathering wild honey, but its real profitability was ultimately realized by producing wheat, sugar, or wine in rich tropical and volcanic soils.

In many respects, the Canary Islands, rediscovered by Malocello in the early fourteenth century, provided the common starting point for both wings and combined in itself both sources of profit. The islands were inhabited and could thus be raided or support commerce, they possessed wild products of interest, and ultimately they became a center for the production of both wine and sugar. Moreover, because traveling to them was fairly easy and profitable, they provided financial security to those who sought more profits on the adjacent Saharan coast or the uninhabited Atlantic islands farther out. . . .

An early voyage to the Canaries (under Portuguese auspices, but with a mixed crew and an Italian captain) in 1341 went both to trade and to raid, buying hides, dyestuffs and wood products, but also carrying weapons for raiding, and King Afonso IV of Portugal reported that slave raiding was under way at least as early as 1346. Catalan merchants joined the Portuguese at an early date in both raiding and trading with the Canarians. Attempts to colonize grew out of these ventures. . . .

But whether visited for conquest and raiding or trade, the islands were seen as a source of profit, and much attention was paid to navigation to them throughout the fourteenth century. . . .

The African Wing of Expansion

The raiding and commerce of the Canaries provided the base and the motives for European activities farther down the Atlantic coast of Africa. . . .

Thus, the actual motivation for European expansion and for navigational breakthroughs was little more than to exploit the opportunity for immediate profits made by raiding and the seizure or purchase of trade commodities. It was these more limited objectives that ultimately made possible the voyage to the Senegal that geographers and thinkers contemplating longer-range commercial or geopolitical schemes had dreamed of since at least the fourteenth century. It was more or less an extension of these same sorts of motives that eventually allowed the Portuguese to attain that even more distant long-range goal — so important both to commercial and to geopolitical thinking — the rounding of Africa and the discovery of a sea route to India and Ethiopia. The predominance of limited aims in the voyages of reconnaisance and expansion explains why the necessary exploration took so long — from 1434, when the major navigational obstacle was overcome, until 1488, when Dias showed that the Cape of Good Hope was the end of the African continent.

In the Senegal region the profits were made from gold and slaves (first captured in raids, later purchased). Gold was available from many points along the coast, and sailors expanded rapidly southward until they reached the coast of modern Sierra Leone around 1460. Much of the energy of traveling even during those years, however, was spent on commercial or military voyages intended to consolidate and explore the possibilities of the areas already known or to establish bases. The uninhabited archipelago of Cape Verde Islands was crucial to further expansion and was colonized in the 1460s.

But there were other commercial possibilities to be found further on, and perhaps the prospects of the next stretch of coast to produce the pepper known as malaguetta pepper were known to Fernão Gomes when he petitioned the Crown for exclusive rights to the trade of West Africa exclusive of the areas earlier granted to the settlers of Cape Verde in 1469. In any case, his grant included a provision that he explore further sections of the coast, and his expeditions rapidly began exporting the pepper. Shortly afterward (perhaps about 1471), to his infinite good luck, Gomes's sailors reached the gold-producing region of the Gold Coast (modern Ghana), an unexpected find that paid off handsomely for both Gomes and eventually for the Crown. His sailors located another pepper-producing region at Benin the next year, although it was only in 1485–6 that regular trade began there. They also discovered, on the island of São Tomé, another potential base for operations in the region.

Thus, for a long stretch of time, between about 1340 and 1470, European expansion proceeded slowly along the African coast. It paid off handsomely for the private parties who had sponsored most of it, and in 1482, for the first time, the Portuguese Crown decided to sponsor its own expedition into the Atlantic rather than to charter other people, who raised their own capital. Unlike the earlier voyages, the royal voyages of Diogo Cão had a clearly geopolitical goal. . . . Cão made the first attempt at expansion cast in the romantic mold, but he discovered only that the African continent turned south and ran thousands more kilometers before eventually turning. But fortunately for the Crown, Cão did come to the kingdom of Kongo, whose export products helped recoup the cost of the voyages and contributed to the success of the colony on São Tomé. Undeterred . . . the Portuguese Crown continued sponsoring exploration. . . .

Oceanic Navigation and Political Domination

Scholars have argued that this domination of the seas gave Europeans insuperable political and commercial advantages over local people in Africa and the Americas. This claim, although possessing some merit, overlooks the complexity of the situation, especially on the coasts of the continents, and when studied in detail is not as persuasive as it first appears. Although Europeans did make some conquests in both Africa and the Americas, it was not naval power that secured the conquests. Their failure to dominate local coastal commerce or overwhelm coastal societies, most pronounced in Africa but also the case in some parts of the Americas, means that we must amplify our estimation of the role played by these societies in the shaping of the Atlantic world. Domination of high-seas commerce is significant, to be sure, but perhaps not as significant as domination of the mainlands.

Naval encounters and Afro-European commerce. Europeans clearly hoped that their maritime abilities would give them military advantages that would result in large profits and perhaps conquests. They were prepared to take over territory and enslave people, and their actions in the Canary Islands bore witness to that desire. However much some visitors to the Canaries might have wanted to engage in peaceful trade, it was ultimately the slave raiders and conquerors who won out. Control of the seas allowed Europeans to land freely on the islands, resupply their forces when necessary, and concentrate large forces for their final battles—and thus maritime superiority could arguably have been the cause of their success.

The earliest sailors who reached the African coast in the fifteenth century naturally hoped to continue this tradition, as apparently did the Spanish sailors who began the conquest of the larger Caribbean islands in the late fifteenth and early sixteenth centuries. But in Africa at least, their confident approach was rebuffed. Unlike the Canarians, who possessed no boats at all, the West Africans had a well-developed specialized maritime culture that was fully capable of protecting its own waters.

One of the first expeditions to the Senegal River, led by Lançarote de Lagos in 1444, brutally seized the residents of several off-shore islands. The inhabitants, although they managed to inflict some casualties, had little other recourse than to try to flee to areas of difficult access. Other expeditions that followed did more or less the same, but it was not long before African naval forces were alerted to the new dangers, and the Portuguese ships began to meet strong and effective resistance. For example, in 1446 a ship under Nuno Tristão attempting to land an armed force in the Senegambian region was attacked by African vessels, and the Africans succeeded in killing nearly all the raiders. Likewise, in 1447 Valarte, a Danish sailor in Portuguese service, was killed along with most of his crew when local craft attacked him near the island of Gorée.

Although African vessels were not designed for high-seas navigation, they were capable of repelling attacks on the coast. They were specialized craft, designed specifically for the navigational problems of the West African coast and the associated river systems. From the Angolan coast up to Senegal, African military and commercial craft tended to be built similarly. Generally, they were carved from single logs of tropical trees and only occasionally had their sides built up. Consequently, they tended to be long and very low in the water. They were almost always powered by oars or paddles and thus were maneuverable independent of the wind. They drew little water and could operate on the coast and in rivers, creeks, and inland estuaries and lagoons. Craft that were designed to carry soldiers could, according to contemporary witnesses, carry from fifty to one hundred men.

These specialized craft presented a small, fast, and difficult target for European weapons, and they carried substantial firepower in their archers and javelinmen. However, they could not go far out to sea, and the larger, high-sided Portuguese vessels were difficult for them to storm. Alvise da Mosto, a Venetian trading in Africa with a Portuguese license, records an encounter he had with an African flotilla in the Gambia in 1456. Da Mosto was mistaken, with justice, for being another raiding party from Portugal and was immediately attacked by seventeen large craft carrying about 150 armed men. They showered his ships with arrows as they approached, and da Mosto fired his artillery (bombards) at them, without, however, hitting anything. Although the attackers were temporarily stunned by this unexpected weapon, they nevertheless pressed the attack, at which point crossbowmen in the upper rigging of the Venetian ship opened fire, inflicting some casualties. Again, although impressed by the weaponry, the Africans continued fighting until da Mosto eventually made it known he did not mean to attack them, and a cease-fire ensued.

The Africans were unable, in most circumstances, to take a European ship by storm, and the Europeans had little success in their seaborne attacks on the mainland. As a result, the Europeans had to abandon the time-honored tradition of trading and raiding and substitute a relationship based more or less completely on peaceful regulated trade. Da Mosto attempted this in his voyage, and the Portuguese

Crown eventually dispatched Diogo Gomes in 1456 to negotiate treaties of peace and commerce with the African rulers of the coast. As a result, Portugal established and maintained diplomatic relations with a host of African states. Already in 1494, Hieronymous Münzer, a German visitor to Lisbon, noted that the king sent frequent presents to the rulers of African states to win their favor, and as a result Portuguese could travel freely in Africa under the protection of these rulers. These diplomatic and commercial relations easily replaced the raid-and-trade or raid-and-conquer patterns of other parts of the Atlantic, especially because the Portuguese soon discovered to their pleasure that there was also a well-developed commercial economy in Africa that maritime commerce could tap into without engaging in hostilities. . . .

Not only did African naval power make raiding difficult, it also allowed Africans to conduct trade with the Europeans on their own terms, collecting customs and other duties as they liked. For example, Afonso I, king of Kongo, seized a French ship and its crew in 1525 because it was trading illegally on his coast. It was perhaps because of incidents such as this that João Afonso, a Portuguese sailor in French service, writing at about the same time, advised potential travelers from France to Kongo to take care to conduct trade properly, explaining that when a ship enters the Zaire, it should wait until the officials on shore send one of their boats and do nothing without royal permission from the king of Kongo. . . .

By the middle of the sixteenth century, then, the Atlantic world had begun to take shape. European sailors, who had come to understand the winds and currents of the Atlantic, had established a system of navigation that bound Europe, Africa, and the Americas into a single system of commerce. European rulers and the more powerful of their subjects had come to see the system as being of great significance and holding potential for wealth and were well on their way to wresting political and economic control away from the pioneers who had created it. But if the powerful of Europe controlled the commerce of the seas, in Africa they were unable to dominate either the coast or coastal navigation, and in the Americas the subdued regions were surrounded by hostile and sometimes aggressive unconquered people. Thus the African role in the development of the Atlantic would not simply be a secondary one, on either side of the Atlantic. In Africa, it was they who would determine their commercial role, and in America they were often the most important group among the early colonists. Even when they played no particular political role, they often could capitalize on the incompleteness of European domination.

D. W. Meinig

America as a Continuation

In A.D. 1492 the last Muslim hold upon Iberia was broken and Columbus sailed forth and discovered America. After seven centuries of grinding effort the Spanish had burst through the final barrier and in an explosion of energy spanned an ocean to begin the conquest of a new world.

Such a statement is at once misleading and usefully symbolic. The fall of Granada and the voyage of Columbus were not deeply interdependent events. Granada was a mountainous remnant that had no essential bearing upon Christian ventures out into larger realms. If there was indeed a "burst through the barrier" it had come centuries earlier with the Castilian conquest of Andalusia when warriors from the lean highlands seized control of the richest lowlands, the very seat of Islamic civilization in the west. So too was the Columbus voyage the culmination of a long prelude of Iberian Atlantic reconnaissance and island conquests. Yet this superficial coincidence can be given significant meaning, for it was in thanksgiving for the fall of Granada that Isabella equipped Columbus's expedition, and it is quite appropriate to see the *reconquista* in Europe and the range of the *conquistadores* over the Americas as successive phases in the same broad movement: the powerful outward expansion of Western Christian society. Viewed at such a

D. W. Meinig, *The Shaping of America: A Geographical Perspective on 500 Years of History. Volume I: Atlantic America, 1492–1800*, pp. 4–11. Copyright © 1986 by Yale University Press.

scale these events of 1492 do mark an ending in the Old World, a beginning in the New, and a convenient symbolic concatenation in the larger structure of history.

American beginnings of course involved more than Iberia, and to the north we can see a vaguely similar pattern wherein Cabot's voyage from Bristol in 1497 and the English and French enterprise that followed can be regarded as an overseas thrust by these peoples beyond their centuries-old Celtic frontiers. Viewed more closely, here too the actual patterns fail to sustain so simple a relationship, or indeed, any close similarities to Iberia. The British Celts had become Christians before their adversaries, and although their own rather different version of the faith had long ago been brought into basic conformity with the dominant Western pattern, in 1497 they were still a group of distinctive peoples holding out on the rainy rugged edge of Europe against the chronic pressures of the Normans and Anglo-Saxons; their conquest was not a prelude but a later integral part of this larger Atlantic history. Furthermore, the long delays and difficulties in getting anything firmly under way in the New World from this part of the Old hardly represent an explosive expansion but rather contrast starkly with the Iberian conquest of half the Americas in half a century.

Nevertheless, it is best to begin with the broader view: to see those first Spanish and Portuguese, French and English explorers, conquerors, and settlers as the vanguard of a common movement, the cutting edge of a powerful Romano-Germanic Christian culture that had burst out upon the World Ocean and would eventually bring the coastlands of every continent under siege.

It is also pertinent to see these two great Italian seafarers as emblematic of another important dimension within this broader context. For several centuries this Western Christian culture had also been thrusting eastward into Byzantine, Arabic, and Turkish waters. Now this variable Mediterranean combination of crusade and commerce was being redirected westward to lands beyond the Ocean Sea. Columbus, a Genoese financed in large part by fellow Genoese residing in Seville, and Cabot, a Genoese native and Venetian citizen long experienced in the eastern trade, were only the most famous figures among the thousands of seafarers and entrepreneurs who turned from the Mediterranean to the Atlantic and thereby forged a deep and complete continuity between the earlier and later phases of this great European outreach.

All Atlantic-bordering European societies were advantageously located for the outreach to America. The general conformation of the North Atlantic and its circulations of water and winds lay open a very extensive and complicated coastline—reaching from the corner of Brazil to Labrador—to relatively ready access from any of the Atlantic ports of Europe. Within that broadly elliptical basin the ocean currents move clockwise, accompanied by relatively steady northeasterly trade winds on the south and the much more variable but prevailing westerly winds in the north. Mariners quickly learned to make use of this natural circulation: southwesterly outbound directly into the American Indies, returning northeasterly, arching parallel with the trend of the North American coast. Therefore this entire continental seaboard and the attenuated archipelago shielding its tropical seas became a single arena of action for the competition of Atlantic Europe. For more than two centuries events in one sector might ramify into others with important impact thousands of miles away on this western rim. Thus, even though we are concerned ultimately with the United States, this entire North Atlantic littoral is the necessary beginning framework.

But position is only a potential. Transatlantic operations called for unprecedented vision and vigor, initially from a few score persons, eventually from a much larger body if anything significant was to be sustained. Although news of the discoveries quickly reverberated through the maritime systems of western Europe, not all societies were equally well prepared for American adventures.

Clearly the first requisite for transatlantic operations was *seafaring*. All Atlantic European societies made use of the sea, but not all were equipped to extend the range of their operations so drastically. Still there were at least half a dozen local maritime districts, from Andalusia to the Bristol Channel, which had the seaworthy vessels, the skilled mariners and craftsmen, the facilities and hinterland resources, and the commercial connections to undertake ventures across the ocean. Those long engaged in the North Atlantic fishery as far north as Iceland could readily extend their reach to the Grand Banks, for this required no major alteration of routine practices. Transatlantic exploration, seasonal bartering, and coastal plundering could be carried out by individual entrepreneurs and small corporate associations backed by no more than local home resources. Such parties may have sought state approval, carried the flag, and laid claims in the name of the Crown, yet they were not essentially dependent upon state support.

But although the American seaboard was visibly empty along many stretches, it was not uninhabited. A European foothold, a trading post or exploration base, might be negotiated or even forced upon local Indians without great effort but anything larger would eventually meet strong resistance. Most of these European Atlantic societies were deeply predatory, quite ready to push in upon and plunder anything to their advantage. But again, not all had so institutionalized predation as to apply it toward effective control. Buccaneers might win a battle but the security of a large area required garrisons of soldiers under orderly administration, which in turn required (even if indirectly) the participation of the state much more critically. *Conquest*, the forced imposition of European rule upon American peoples, marked the initiation of true imperialism and represented a marshaling of far greater resources and more elaborate institutions than did sporadic bartering and plundering. The possibilities for such a successful extension of the state itself were obviously dependent upon a far greater complex of factors. We might well assume that those societies most freshly and extensively experienced in the conquest of territory and the governing of captive peoples would be the most likely to have eager visions of new conquests and proven institutions ready at hand, and thus be the most likely to seize upon and make the most of American opportunities.

Conquest may yield plunder and some exaction of tribute but it does not insure long-range returns. And of course the common American experience was that a coastal territory might be conquered only to have the native people withdraw into the interior, or die from new diseases introduced unwittingly by their conquerors, or disintegrate as a society and quickly diminish as a population from forced labor and brutal treatment. When such was the case, the only hope of realizing a benefit from conquest was to bring in a new labor force to work the land. Whether making use of African slaves, European bondsmen, or wage laborers, such an economy required local subsistence and support that could only come from the *planting* of settlers to cultivate the land, establish industries, and provide essential services. This true colonization demanded an even greater range of resources, institutions, and appropriate states of mind than mere conquest. Initial success in such transplantations had little to do with size or any assumed "surplus" of populations in the home country. All these European societies had potential colonists, but the recruitment of settlers and the support of an expanding European society overseas were fraught with enormous difficulties, and here again we may assume that experience counts, that those societies which had recently been involved in the colonization of new ground would be in the best position to make the first effective implantation of European civilization on American shores.

Seafaring, conquering, and *planting* may be taken as convenient labels for three kinds of activities undertaken by various European societies overseas. They can also be taken as three phases in the European encroachment upon the American seaboard, for seafaring is the obvious first essential and conquest a necessary prelude to any extensive planting. And since the planting of European settlers is clearly the most direct and effective means of rooting European culture onto the American seaboard, we may take seafaring, conquering, and planting as three essential components in the accomplishment of that end. We can expect that those European societies best equipped with the facilities, institutions, and attitudes of mind appropriate to these three components would be the earliest successful agents of that transfer, whereas a deficiency in any one would cause serious delays and difficulties.

This simple formulation is offered as a useful guide through a complex history, helping us to account for the great variations in responses and results in the decades following the discoveries. The variation that most attracts our interest at this point can be illustrated very simply: whereas only five years separate the voyage of Columbus out of Palos from that of Cabot out of Bristol, more than one hundred years separate the founding of Santo Domingo by the Spanish from that of Jamestown by the English. A quick review of these and some intervening ventures will not only illustrate the utility of our formulation but demonstrate some patterned interrelationships and provide the basis for a set of geographical generalizations about the whole process of transoceanic transfer and the interactions involved.

Columbus's sensational triumph of discovery and his dismal failure to accomplish anything substantial with what he discovered offers a telling application of our formulation, for the Columban voyages were an extension of seafaring and nothing more. That prior to his voyage Columbus was given such an extraordinary panoply of titles, authority, and rights to revenue over all that he discovered suggests that he was not expected to discover anything really extraordinary—a few more islands in the Ocean Sea perhaps, well beyond the Canaries and Azores. His expedition was capable of no more than limited barter or local plunder on encountering inhabited lands.

But of course discovery led to visions of conquest and exploitation. On his second voyage Columbus founded Isabella, an elaborate design for the first European town in the New World. It was not a success. As Carl Sauer noted, "He wished a capital befitting his new station and ordered the building of an unneeded town in a wrong location." His attempts to exploit resources and establish a sound polity and society were little more successful, and Columbus died without having laid the foundations for the empire he so strongly desired. Much of this failure may be laid to the man's own vanities and personal limitations, but it also illustrates the more general proposition that successful imperialism is not simply a ready extension from discovery. Columbus was an experienced seafarer but a novice at conquest and colonization.

Once the Spanish Crown came to realize that there really was a New World to the west instead of a few new islands, and as the failures of Columbus as an individual entrepreneur became manifest, all the experience and institutions of a heritage of conquest, resettlement, and orderly administration were brought to bear upon these fresh opportunities. Which is to say that after the Columban ten-year prelude the reconquista, which after the fall of Granada had been carried by its centuries-old momentum on southward across the straits to Melilla and the Barbary Coast, was now redirected and projected westward across the Atlantic. It should be noted that Iberians had been gaining experience in combining seafaring, conquering, and planting for some years before Columbus in their subjugation of the Canary Islands. In this "trial laboratory of colonial matters," the indigenous people, the Guanches, resisted conquest, and Castille, which eventually obtained exclusive rights, had to replace various entrepreneurial efforts with more formal procedures. Parry notes that "in the Canaries, Spaniards served their first apprenticeship in the arts of colonial empire and had their first experience of converting and exploiting a primitive subject people." The apprenticeship was not in conquering and converting per se, but in doing so a thousand miles overseas against a people far different from the highly civilized Muslims. And the results were ominous. The liberty of baptized Canarians was recognized in law, but not always in fact. Those who resisted were fair game; thousands were sold into slavery and their lands taken by mainland opportunists (some of whom were themselves *conversos* who sought to escape the enmities and suspicions of home localities).

Thus the really firm beginnings in America date from Ovando's arrival in Santo Domingo in 1502 with a fleet of thirty vessels and twenty-five hundred men. Nicolas de Ovando, the experienced commander of a religious-military order in Spain, was sent as deputy of the Crown to be the governor general, the *adelantado* of the new *frontera*. He relocated and rebuilt his capital city (it had been destroyed by a hurricane shortly after his arrival) and founded a network of towns, all "a transplantation in general of the old Castilian municipality of the Middle Ages." Having administered large grants of conquered land and people in Spain, "he became the principal architect of the *encomiendo* system in the New World." The Church was an integral partner in the process, founding missions, building churches, and, in 1512, forming the first American bishopric. Within a few years there were perhaps ten thousand Spaniards living in Hispaniola, a colony supported by local produce and wealth extracted through the forced labor of the conquered population, administered through the Audiencia (established 1511), and connected routinely by commerce with the Casa de la Contratación (formed in Seville in 1503 to control this new Atlantic traffic). The vigor of this Hispaniola establishment soon faded as a result of the destruction of its Indian base and powerfully centrifugal attractions toward the mainland. But it does illustrate how the limitations of the individual entrepreneur were quickly overcome by experienced leaders working with tested tools and acting with the strong support of an old imperial society long involved in conquest, resettlement, and the administration of newly acquired ground.

The Portuguese sequence was not in general dissimilar. Oceanic seafaring developed only after the capture in 1415 of Ceuta, a Muslim stronghold on the African shore of the Strait of Gibraltar. Here, too, there was a strong historical logic in support of expanding such a foothold upon the Moroccan coast, but Prince Henry, who "made discovery an art and science; and . . . voyaging a national interest," directed explorations far to the south to tap the trans-Saharan gold trade nearer its source. These led to the discovery of Madeira and the Cape Verde Islands, as well as the Azores lying directly west, all of which were colonized.

About 1470 the Portuguese discovered Fernando Po, Principé, and São Tomé, uninhabited islands near the equator in the Bight of Biafra, which were quickly developed for sugar production by Portuguese entrepreneurs. Meanwhile they established trading stations and a few strong forts at key points along the African coast. Some attempts were made to evangelize the natives and to open diplomatic relations with African princes. But any hope of colonization was thwarted by the high mortality of Europeans due to African tropical diseases. Thus the Portuguese mainland venture remained primarily a coastal trading operation dealing in gold, slaves, and ivory. In this Atlantic and African prelude to their American enterprise the Portuguese displayed their superior skills in seafaring and an efficiency in planting without having to undertake much conquering.

Brazil had been discovered about 1500, but with more attractive commercial opportunities in Africa and India the Portuguese engaged in no more than occasional coastal bartering. When colonization was initiated in 1532, out of fear of French encroachment, it was done under the auspices of the Crown according to a comprehensive plan modeled on the "captaincy system already successfully tried in the Atlantic Islands." But the American mainland proved a rather more formidable environment than those benign Atlantic islands. The Indians often vigorously resisted their invaders and refused to provide a reliable labor force. Most of the *donatarios*, the proprietary landlords who were granted extensive hereditary powers in return for carrying out conquest and colonization, found the demands far beyond their skills or means. Some were repelled by the Indians; others failed for lack of colonists and profitable exports. The major early successful venture, in Pernambuco, drew upon fresh Portuguese tropical experience by the direct transfer of the sugar plantation and slave system from the Cape Verde and the Biafran islands. But in Brazil as in Hispaniola, more general success came only after the replacement of individual overlordship with a much larger measure of state control. The arrival in 1549 of Martin Afonso de Sousa, appointed to the new post of governor general and accompanied by several members of the new Jesuit order as well as a thousand colonists (many of them exiles), marks the beginning of much more direct initiative by the Crown and the Church, a shift analogous to that carried out by Ovando in Hispaniola nearly half a century earlier.

We can see this emergence of Brazil, therefore, as the culmination of more than a century of Portuguese seafaring, conquering, and planting, and a direct geographical extension of operations on the Atlantic islands and the African coast to this easternmost promontory of America. We can also see that the firm founding of Portuguese America lagged several decades behind that of Spanish America. This was certainly in part due to the greater commercial attractions of Africa and Asia. But their early Brazilian efforts also suggest that perhaps the Portuguese were less well prepared than the Spanish for conquest and planting on a continental scale. Their reconquista was further back in history, their recent colonization had been mainly on empty islands, and their national policies were more geared to overseas commercial adventuring than to systematic conquest and incorporation of land and people by state and church.

Nevertheless, both powers displayed an ability to carry forward a prodigious imperial enterprise, and that surely was related to their common Iberian and Atlantic experiences, which had given them a cast of mind and a set of institutions, military, civil, and ecclesiastical, by which they could implant their versions of civilization firmly on American shores long before their northerly neighbors in Atlantic Europe.

Olive Patricia Dickason

Some First Reactions

Early in 1493, the Spanish court received unexpected news. Christopher Columbus, the Genoese captain whom the Spanish monarchs Ferdinand and Isabella had sent in search of a sea route to the Orient the previous summer, had discovered a land inhabited by "immense multitudes" of strange non-Christian people. These people were not dog-headed, as might have been expected if Columbus had reached the Far East, where such a race was reputed to live in the mountains. On the contrary, these unknowns were reported to be well formed and good-looking, an easily verifiable observation as they were largely innocent of clothing. In view of his initial belief that they were inhabitants

Abridged and reprinted with permission from Olive Patricia Dickason, *The Myth of the Savage and the Beginnings of French Colonialism in the Americas* (Edmonton, Alberta: The University of Alberta Press, 1997), pp. 5–11, 13–25.

of the Asiatic subcontinent, Columbus called them "Indians"; but in his last will and testament, he referred to them as "cannibals," by which appellation they were widely known at the time of his death in 1506. Columbus wrote in his letter announcing his discovery:

> *The people . . . all go naked, men and women, just as their mothers bring them forth. . . . They have no iron or steel, nor any weapons; nor are they fit thereunto; not because they be not a well formed people and of fair stature, but that they are most wondrously timorous . . . they are artless and generous with what they have, to such a degree as no one would believe but him who had seen it. . . . And whether it be a thing of value, or of little worth, they are straightways content with whatsoever trifle of whatsoever kind be given them in return for it. . . . They took even pieces of broken barrelhoops, and gave whatever they had, like senseless brutes; insomuch that it seemed to me ill. I forbade it, and I gave gratuitously a thousand useful things that I carried, in order that they may conceive affection, and furthermore may be made Christians; for they are inclined to the love and service of their Highnesses and of all the Castillian nation, and they strive to combine in giving us things which they have in abundance, and of which we are in need . . . they are men of very subtle wit, who navigate all those seas, and who give a marvellously good account of everything.*

Columbus's announcement caught Spain's immediate interest, not so much because of its revelation of a new world, inhabited by a people previously unknown to Europeans, but because he reported there was every indication that it harbored immense and largely unexploited wealth. This was quickly seized upon, although the full implications of Columbus's landings on Guanahari and other West Indian islands were to be a long time in being fully realized. In the short term, news of the New World had to compete with the much greater interest aroused by the opening of the Orient as well as with Europe's rediscovery of its own classical antiquity. The difficult task of sorting out and assessing New World information in the light of Christian orthodoxy and of practical political ideology would be long and arduous. Conflicting reports did not help matters: initial impressions of timorous, gentle people, anxious to accommodate, were soon confused by accounts of monstrous men and bestial customs. If, in the meantime, Columbus's letter was disseminated with unheard-of speed, thanks to the new technology of the printing press, it was largely among an elite whose interest was sharpened by the prospect of economic opportunity.

Columbus's letter dated 15 February–14 March 1493 was published in its original Spanish in Barcelona in April. Latin versions appeared in Rome, Antwerp, Basel, and Paris that same year. Because of the international standing of Latin at the time, these versions can be presumed to have been the most widely read. But the letter was also translated into other languages. An Italian version was published in Rome in 1493, in the form of a poem by Giuliano Dati, which also appeared twice that year in Florence, and twice again in 1495. Strasbourg saw a German translation in 1497, the same year that a second Spanish edition was issued in Valladolid. In all, twenty-two editions of Columbus's letter are known, sixteen of which appeared in the fifteenth century. It is not certain how widely they were circulated; however, news of the discoveries apparently reached Poland between 1495 and 1501, and published accounts began to appear there in 1512. The sole contemporary English-language report of Columbus's voyages, *Of the newe lādes*, was published in Antwerp by Jan van Doesborch probably between 1510 and 1515, and possibly as early as 1508. Only three other accounts of Columbus's voyages are known to have been published before 1522.

The publicity, spotty as it was, heralded a new fashion in literature, the voyage account, which was to reach its peak during the seventeenth and eighteenth centuries. Even romances lost out in this switch in reading tastes, a French chancellor noted. In France, the new fashion can be traced to the appearance in Paris in 1497 of Sebastian Brant's *Le Nef des folz du monde*, only twenty years after the publication in that city of the first book in the French language. Interestingly enough, Brant was not enthusiastic about voyages of discovery; rather, he criticized the desire to discover and describe new regions as one of the follies of mankind. When Brant's work had first appeared in German in 1494 it had been the only commentary to be published during Columbus's second voyage. In France, it appears to have been the first printed reference to the New World and its inhabitants following the appearance of Columbus's letter. It was also probably the first in French.

Brant's criticisms did not prevent the taste for travel literature from developing. When Amerigo Vespucci (1451?–1512), the Florentine merchant who in 1505 had become chief navigator for the Casa de Contratación de las Indias in Seville, wrote letters describing his voyages, they were given far more exposure than the reports of Columbus had received. Between 1502 and 1529, Vespucci's letters saw sixty editions in various cities in what is today Switzerland, Germany, France,

Italy, The Netherlands, and Czechoslovakia, but none in Spain. This suggests censorship. Thirty-seven were in vernacular, of which almost half were in German, reflecting financial as well as scholarly interest in the discoveries. One of the best-known editions appeared in the *Cosmographiae Introductio* of Martin Waldseemüller (1470–1521?) and his collaborators, published at Saint-Dié in Lorraine in 1507. Besides Vespucci's "Four Voyages," the Waldseemüller edition included a map in which the New World was labelled America. The name had found ready acceptance by geographers perhaps because it was already in popular use. Its origins are uncertain; it may have been adapted by early voyagers from aboriginal place names that had been found along the coasts of Brazil, Guiana, and Venezuela. Variations included Amaracao, Maracaibo, Emeria, and Amaricocapana. It could also have arisen from the tendency of Amerindians upon first seeing Europeans to regard them as superior beings. Among their words to express this were Tamaraca, Tamerka, and Maraca, the latter also appearing as a place name. In any event, its usage was given an added fillip by its resemblance to Vespucci's baptismal name.

In 1515, twenty-two years after Columbus's letter had been printed in Paris in Latin, and about ten years after the appearance of Vespucci's letters in that same language, a collection of voyage accounts appeared in French. They had been translated and abridged by lawyer Mathurin Du Redouer from Professor Fracanzano da Montalboddo's prototype compilation, *Paesi novamente retrovati*, first published in Italian in Vicenza in 1507. Besides the accounts of Columbus and Vespucci, it included those of Pigafetta, Cadamosto, Cortés, and others. Du Redouer's adaptation, *Sensuyt le nouveau monde & navigations faictes par Emeric Vespuce Florentin: Des pays & isles nouvellement trouvez auparavant a nous inconnuz tant en l'Ethiope que Arrabie, Calichut et aultres plusieurs regions etranges,* went through five editions after its first appearance in Paris.

The comparative speed with which news of the New World was diffused in Europe becomes clearer when it is realized that during the late sixteenth century, it took approximately ten days for news to travel from Paris to London. Before the printing press, when dependence had been greater on word of mouth, it had not only taken longer for news to be disseminated, but its acceptance had been very slow. For example, Greenland first appeared on maps during the fifteenth century, although it had been discovered during the tenth. Neither the oriental voyages of Marco Polo (1254–1323?) nor those of the Friars Minor in the late thirteenth and early fourteenth centuries had exercised the least influence on medieval cartography; until the beginning of the fourteenth century, maps were a continuation of Greco-Roman geography. It was not until the fifteenth century that the influence of Marco Polo began to be noticeable. The much more rapid assimilation of the geographical information from Columbus's voyages stemmed from the presumption of the discovery of a fabled land of great riches, as cartographers clung to the classical belief in the existence somewhere in the Orient of Cryse and Argyre, islands of gold and silver. Columbus's conviction that he had reached the Orient would have been reinforced by the sight of Amerindians wearing golden ornaments. Intensifying the excitement was the search going on at the time in Africa for the legendary Rio Doro, river of gold.

Columbus's somewhat naive vision of New World natives in a state of primordial innocence awaiting the privilege of being exploited by the "men from heaven," as they called the Spaniards, did not endure past his second voyage. To his amazement he found that the garrison he had left behind at La Navidad had been annihilated in a dispute with those very Amerindians who the previous year had been so helpful when the *Santa Maria* had been wrecked. In the interval, the Amerindians had apparently realized that the Spaniards were all too human. What Columbus had taken to be artless generosity and boundless cooperation had been actually anxious maneuvers to establish good relations with these strange new beings, whatever they might be. Spaniards were later to exploit this initial reaction on the part of Amerindians by claiming descent from the sun whenever they met new peoples. This was to simplify and accelerate the process of conquest, at least in the beginning.

Another unpleasant realization awaited the admiral on his second voyage: cannibal Caribs were more difficult to deal with than he had anticipated. In fact, he reported,

> These Islanders appeared to us to be more civilized than those we have hitherto seen; for although all the Indians have houses of straw, yet the houses of these people are constructed in a much superior fashion, are better stocked with provisions, and exhibit more evidence of industry, both on the part of the men and the women.

"Cannibal" derives from a Carib word meaning "valiant man," an appellation which soon turned out to be apt from the European point of view. Even when captured after a brush with the Spaniards, Caribs maintained an "atrocious and diabolical regard" that inspired fear in the beholders. "I spoke with a man who told me he had eaten 300 men," Vespucci later reported, adding that fathers ate their children and husbands their wives. He had seen preserved human flesh hanging from the beams of houses "as we hang pork." He insisted on the veracity of his observations: "Of this be assured, because I have seen it. I tell you also that they wonder why we do not eat our enemies, as they say human flesh is very tasty." If Columbus was horrified when he first encountered the practice, he was also pragmatic: he sent captured Caribs to Spain as slaves in order, he said, to get them to abandon their bad habits.

Vespucci agreed with Columbus that Americans lived in "great multitudes," that they were generally good-looking and remarkably free from deformities. But he found that although they had "honest" faces, they destroyed them by piercing cheeks and lips, nostrils and ears. "I have seen as many as seven holes in one man's face, which holes they fill with colored stones as well as other objects. It makes them look like monsters." He calculated that the stones in one man's face weighed "sixteen ounces," adding, apparently with some relief, that the women did not indulge in this custom.

There was some uncertainty as to the color of these new people, which Vespucci saw as "pulling toward red." Being naked, they were tanned by the sun. According to Columbus, however, they were "the color of the people of the Canaries, neither black nor white." Antonio Pigafetta (1480/91–c. 1534), a gentleman from Vincenza who sailed on the three-year voyage around the globe headed by Ferdinand Magellan, reported on his return in 1522 that the natives were olive-hued. Official Spanish historian Gonzalo Fernández de Oviedo y Valdés (1478–1557) agreed that the people were all about the same color, a light brown. They were without any hair on their bodies except for their heads, men as well as women, and what they had was always black. . . .

In other aspects as well, apart from the sexual, Europeans could not at first detect order in the way of life of Amerindians, although their manner was sweet and gentle, "very like the manner of the ancients." It was "wonderful that we never saw a quarrel among them." Columbus had reported that they had no government. Vespucci also noted they were without churches, without faith, without markets, living according to nature. Neither did they have art nor order in their combat, and after battle, they ate their prisoners of war. . . .

The "great stores" of food maintained by the Amerindians afforded a point of high interest to sixteenth- and seventeenth-century Europeans, in whose homelands the spectre of famine was continuously present for the peasants. They were not slow to develop techniques for taking advantage of Amerindian hospitality, going from village to village and moving on before their welcome wore out. Antonio de Herrera y Tordesillas (1557–1625) reported that the Spanish made themselves unwelcome by billeting their men with Amerindian families because the Spaniards "eat more in a Day than the Indians in a Month." Consequently, Amerindians preferred paying tribute to having the Castillians in their houses, in spite of their lack of personal wealth and possessions.

What was more, Europeans noted with considerable interest, this sufficiency in food was achieved without much effort. Women, it was generally agreed, worked harder than the men, as they had to labor in the fields as well as look after their households; among nomadic hunters, they carried the burdens when on the move. Only later was it realized that the women's lot often went hand in hand with considerable power and influence. Europeans rarely noted, however, that Amerindian men cleared land in preparation for planting. But toil in the European sense was noticeably absent, and individuals were not worn down with excessive labor. To Europeans, the type of sustained effort needed to be a good hunter could not be classed as work, as in their society hunting was an aristocratic privilege; it was in this context, as well as that of the martial arts, that they much admired Amerindian skill in archery.

Equally appreciated was New World craftsmanship; explorer Giovanni da Verrazzano, for one, noted that Amerindian arrows were worked with great beauty. Although these men were without iron, they built canoes after the manner of rowing galleys, some of them large enough to hold eighty men. The speed of these craft was "a thing beyond belief." Columbus, in spite of regarding Amerindians as "wild" people, felt that they were "fit for any work . . . very intelligent, and who, when they have got rid of the cruel habits to which they have become accustomed, will be better than any other kind of slave."

Very early during the time of contact, Europeans attempted to show what Amerindians looked like. The first illustrations appeared with original editions of Columbus's letter. A 1493 Basel edition in Latin, *Insula hyspana*, depicted a trading scene, while Italian versions that appeared in Rome and Florence the same year represented Ferdinand seated on a throne extending his hand across a body of water to some natives fleeing on the shore. Both versions illustrated points made by Columbus in his letter: that New World people, of an "incalculable number," were naked with long flowing hair, and they tended to run away timidly at the first sight of Spaniards. Even in the trading scene, one group was fleeing as another timorously made its offerings to the reciprocating Europeans.

The best-known early pictorialization is the so-called Augsburg woodcut by Johann Froschauer, believed to date from 1505. It illustrates a cannibal scene of the sort Léry had in mind when he criticized the tendency to represent Amerindians in the midst of hanging pieces of humans, as at a butcher's, observing that the artists had never seen what they were trying to depict. The men looked not unlike Roman centurions with plumed crowns. The women also had feather headdresses, and all wore small feather capes over their shoulders. These figures set the pattern for European representation and became the stereotype for Amerindians, such as those shown in cartographical illustrations. A collection of engravings of the New World, published in 1638 under the title *L'Amerique historique*, begins with a feather-skirted couple symbolizing America, complete with a cannibal scene in the background. A less favored early method of portraying Amerindians showed the men with curling locks and full beard, as in the seventh Latin edition of Vespucci's letter, *De novo mundo* (c. 1505). Another well-known example is the initial family group in the "bas-relief du Trésor" of St. Jacques church in Dieppe, believed to have been sculpted about 1530. A Portuguese painting from about the same date, called "The Adoration of the Magi," has one of the wise men looking like a Tupinambá from Brazil, with feathered crown. He also wears a European shirt and breeches.

The first known actual portraits of Amerindians by a European were done in 1529 by Christoph Weiditz, a German artist who saw the Mexica brought to the court of Charles V by Hernán Cortés (1485–

1547). Les successful in this regard was Alejo Fernández, painting a panel entitled "Virgin of the Navigators" about 1535 for the chapel of Casa de Contratación in Seville. He depicted a group of rather negroid-looking Amerindian converts in the background. François Deserpz, in his work on fashions around the world published in Paris in 1567, included a pair of naked Brazilians, the woman with a large flower coquettishly placed on one thigh, and a *sauvage en pompe* in feathered cloak, as well as a hairy man and woman labelled l'homme sauvage and la femme sauvage. The latter two figures did not represent Amerindians at all, although they were frequently confused with them.

Another popular subject for illustration showed Brazilians collecting dyewood for waiting ships. One of the most effective of these is a bas-relief in wood dating from the middle of the sixteenth century. The figures resemble those of classical antiquity rather than of Amerindians, and display a striking vigor and vitality. This period's most accurate, if rather sketchy, representations of New World life are considered to be those illustrating Hans Staden's account of his captivity among the Tupinambá. A mid-sixteenth century Portuguese painting entitled "Inferno" has the Devil sporting an Amerindian feather headdress.

Some of the works of two artists who actually visited the New World have survived. Jacques Le Moyne de Morgues was in Florida with the Ribault-Laudonniére expedition (1556–58); and John White was in the Arctic with Martin Frobisher in 1577, and in Virginia intermittently between 1585 and 1590. Drawings by both of these artists were engraved by Theodor de Bry and his sons in de Bry's thirteen-part series published at Frankfurt am Main between 1590 and 1634 under the general title *Grands Voyages*. It is generally acknowledged that White's drawings are the only ones that catch something of the characteristic postures of Amerindians; Le Moyne, while providing a wealth of detail, did not differentiate Amerindians from Europeans, except to make them bigger and more athletic-looking, rather as if they had stepped out from the Coliseum. The de Bry engravings accentuate this tendency, which is also evident in the illustrations for Thevet's *Cosmographie*. In the latter case, the figures are treated in the manner of the school of Fontainebleau. Such difficulties in depicting Amerindians were not unrecognized at the time. In the words of Léry, "because their gestures and countenances are so different from ours, I confess it is difficult to represent them properly in words or even in painting. In order to see them as they are, one must visit them in their own country."

The best representations of New World men are found in the genre painting of England and northern Europe. In France, such art was at the bottom of the hierarchical ladder, a position endorsed by the Royal Academy of Painting and Sculpture, founded in 1648. Consequently, despite France's reputation for accommodation with Amerindians, they appear comparatively rarely in her art during the sixteenth and seventeenth centuries.

Neither did Amerindian art influence European art. Albrecht Dürer might have exclaimed in delight at the wonders of Moctezuma's treasure, but neither he nor any other European artist appears to have been affected by these creations. An exception to this is found in certain capitals in the Palais des Princes-Evêques (c. 1526) in Liège, which display Mexica influence. (Interestingly enough, the map of Tenochtitlan brought by Cortés to the Spanish court had also shown Mexica influence in its execution.) On the other hand, New World fauna were readily incorporated, and were rendered in prevailing European styles.

New Ideas in Old Frameworks

As European voyages increased so did the "rage to know" about strange people and strange customs; an urge usually satisfied by collecting curiosities. Ferdinand of Hapsburg owned Mexican carvings and feather work that Cortés had brought to Europe; a feather mosaic in the possession of Polish King Sigismond III Vasa may have had the same provenance. Montaigne owned Tupinambá items such as a hammock, a sword club, a wrist guard, and a stamping tube. Although it is far easier to collect objects or information than it is to put them into context, at least one early collector began to put objects into series. Michele Mercati of San Miniato (1541–93), keeper of the botanic garden of Pius V and museum organizer for the Vatican, was among the first to establish that flint arrowheads were man-made. Noting that they had been used by ancient Jews as well as contemporary Amerindians, he speculated that they had also been employed by early inhabitants of Italy.

Mercati's effort was unusual. Generally, during the sixteenth and seventeenth centuries, information and objects were collected fervently but with comparatively little analysis. In the material published during the sixteenth century, the only New World culture to receive much attention was that of the Tupinambá of Brazil, as it was principally in their territory that dyewood was obtained; in the seventeenth century, it was the Huron of Canada, and for a similar reason, the fur trade. Even though it was to their economic advantage to learn about these peoples, Europeans did not systematize the information they collected about the Tupinambá or the Huron until the present century.

The accepted model for describing people of other lands was provided by ancient authorities such as Pliny (A.D. 23/24–79) and Herodotus (fifth century B.C.)—a model constituted largely of sweeping generalizations. In spite of this, a good deal of first-rate ethnographic information was collected during the sixteenth and seventeenth centuries. Much was done by the Spaniards; but their interest was in conquest and administration rather than in learning about New World people as such. Spanish imperial considerations reinforced a penchant for secrecy; this, combined with strong doubts as to the advisability of publicizing pagan customs and beliefs, inhibited the publication of ethnographic material. Some of it did not appear until comparatively recently. This was particularly true for information concerning the peoples of Mexico, Central America, and Peru.

Thus the authority of the ancients continued to maintain its grip even after they had been proved to be incompletely informed, if not completely wrong, about the nature of the world, a situation that was reinforced by the fact that some classical geographical ideas were vindicated. Still, reason, to be effective, had to take into account the findings of experience—an array of strange new facts that did not accord with some cherished beliefs. Writers of the sixteenth and seventeenth centuries apparently never tired of pointing out that Aristotle had erred when he had argued against the habitability of the Torrid Zone, as had Lactantius Firmianus (c. 260–c. 340) and St. Augustine of Hippo (354–430) when they had maintained that it was absurd to think of man living feet above head in the Antipodes. Reason had its pitfalls— witness the logic of Lactantius's arguments against rain falling upward—so experience should not be ignored. When Cartier, in his report on his second voyage (1535–36) wrote that the ancients had theorized about the habitability of the world without testing their statements by actual experience, he was repeating a point that had been made again and again since the time of Columbus. But it was easier to prove authorities wrong than it was to change patterns of thought, and the ancients were still relied upon even while their errors were reported with undisguised satisfaction.

Where Europeans had been reluctant to believe in the existence of unknown races of men, they willingly (even eagerly) conceded the existence of monsters. During his first voyage to the West Indies, Columbus, while admitting that he did not actually see any monsters, accepted without question a report that on another island he did not visit, "the people are born with tails." Such an easy acquiescence could well have been based on the legendary existence of people with tails — descendants from an era when men and apes mated. He also repeated that on still another island the people were said to have no hair. From his own observations he reported that sirens were not beautiful, as was commonly believed, but had faces like those of men. While he did not consider sirens to be monsters, cannibals were traditionally classed as such, and had inhabited European geographies since classical times. Columbus never did find that favorite variety supposedly inhabiting the Orient, the dog-headed man; but more than half a century later, a stranded English sailor wandering up the North American Atlantic seaboard reported that cannibals "doe most inhabite betweene Norumbega & Bariniah, they have teeth like dogs teeth, and thereby you may know them." Belief in such creatures was not easily shaken; had not even St. Augustine discussed whether the descendants of Adam had produced monstrous races of men? However, the church father had been careful not to equate strangeness of appearance with non-humanity: "let no true believer have any doubt that such an individual is descended from the one man who was first created." Conversely, Vadianus (1484–1551) was not convinced by reports from Africa of men who had nothing human about them except their physical form and ability to speak. He denied the existence of monstrous men: "Homines monstrosos non esse." But folklore would have it otherwise; a popular tale of the late Middle Ages told of Adam warning his daughters against eating certain plants that could make them conceive *semi-homo* monsters with plantlike souls.

Learned physicians of the Middle Ages and Renaissance thought that monsters were generated because of the influence of the stars, which in certain conjunctions prevented the fetus from assuming human form. Others believed that an abnormal quantity of semen was responsible, or perhaps illicit intercourse. Cornelius Gemma (1535–79), professor of medicine of Louvain, pointed to sin in general as the cause, although he indicated that the universal cataclysm and confusion of Babel also had been factors.

The process of eliminating notions of men with one foot, faces in their chests, without mouths or anuses, or with ears so large they could use them for blankets, was to take the better part of three centuries. In fact, the immediate effect of the New World discoveries produced an efflorescence of monsters; new varieties were reported faster than the obviously unverifiable ones died out. For example, years in Cuba did not prevent Governor Diego Velasquez from instructing Cortés to look for men with great flat ears and dogs' faces during his projected expedition to Mexico in 1519. One seventeenth-century historian extolled the bravery of those who crossed the seas and fought monsters. Later in the same century, Pliny's pygmies were reported living in seclusion in mountainous regions of coastal New Spain; and in the Arctic, a tribe of Inuit was said to consist of persons equipped with only one leg and foot, and could truly be called half-men. As late as 1724 Joseph-François Lafitau (1681–1746) included a drawing of an *anecephale* (man with his head in his chest) among illustrations of Amerindians, despite some reservations on the subject. Earlier, another had written that he did not believe there were Amerindians who lived on odors, but such defiance of general belief was rare. Credulity, however, had its limits; some huge bones found in the Dauphiné in 1613 and exhibited in Paris as those of the giant Theutobochus were finally pronounced to be fraudulent, in spite of widespread belief in giants at the time.

Monstrous men receded from the popular imagination as the slow intrusion of other worlds on the European consciousness revealed peoples with cultures diverse enough to satisfy the most developed taste for the bizarre. When Columbus met the Arawak and later the man-eating Carib, he found physical differences to be less than previously imagined, but differences in culture appeared to be much greater. For instance, it was one thing to detect classical affinities in New World nudity, but quite another to accept absence of clothing as a basic condition of everyday life. Spaniards had subdued naked Canary Islanders during the fifteenth century, and varying degrees of nudity had been observed in Africa. Even in Europe, nudity was acceptable under certain circumstances. Indeed, extreme tolerance existed alongside an excessive formalism, in an age when sartorial ostentation was approaching its climax. The much acclaimed pageantry that marked the entry of Henry II into Rouen in 1550 included a tableau featuring fifty naked Brazilians and 150 Norman sailors playing at being Brazilians, all presumably naked (at least, that is how they are depicted in illustrations of the event). The tableau was much praised without reference to the nudity. What particularly surprised Europeans about New World nudity was to see everyone, including those in authority, naked all the time. Columbus, addressed by an eighty-year-old cacique "who seemed respectable enough though he wore no clothes," was surprised when he observed "sound judgment in a man who went naked." Very often, their nudity was the only thing reported of Amerindians, as it was the most obvious characteristic that differentiated them from Europeans.

Cannibalism made an even more profound impact than nudity. The word "cannibal" (cambialle and canibali were among the various spellings) almost immediately became the appellation by which Amerindians were known in Europe. A story that became a favorite toward the end of the sixteenth century told of some Caribs who died as a result of eating a friar; after that, men of the cloth were safe, at least on that island. From the Brazilian coast about Cape Frio, came reports of men who "eate all kinde of people, Frenchmen, Portugals, and Blackamoors." The ritual aspects of cannibalism were missed at first, and it was assumed that the New World men ate each other for food, hunting each other "to eat, like savage beasts." Such a conclusion was perhaps to be expected. In Europe cannibalism was, not infrequently, a result of famine, as indeed it sometimes was in the Americas.

In spite of a general revulsion against cannibalism, and a tendency to look for monsters, the first descriptions of New World men are moderate in tone, although a note of condescension is usually detectable. Even such defenders of Amerindians as Isabella could not resist observing, on being informed by Columbus that the trees of the New World did not have deep roots, "this land where the trees are not firmly rooted, must produce men of little truthfulness and less constance." Many observers, however, seemed to agree with Pigafetta: "They are men and women disposed as we are. Although they eat the flesh of their enemies, it is because of certain customs."

Visitors from Another World

As for Amerindians, they also made queries, wondering how these strangers fitted into the cosmos. Were they gods? If so, what were their intentions? When they first saw mounted Spaniards, Amerindians presumed man and horse to be one; later, discerning man from mount, they continued to believe that the horse was a god, or at least immortal. To put this reaction into context, it should be pointed out that the people concerned had never before seen an animal as large as a horse; the fauna native to the areas overcome by the Spaniards did not include any animal of that size. Eventually, realizing their error, some enterprising Mexicans skinned a horse, stuffed it to appear as in life, and displayed it in a temple.

Two centuries after the event, Fontenelle tried to imagine what the effect had been on the Amerindians of the first arrival of the Europeans:

> *Enormous structures, which appeared to have white wings and to fly over the sea, vomiting fire from all sides, came and disgorged onto the shores men all encased in iron. They subjected their racing mounts to their will, holding thunderbolts in their hands with which they felled everything that resisted them. . . . Are they gods? Are they Children of the Sun?*

Amerindians, however, quickly displayed a well-developed spirit of enquiry in their attempts to decide whether or not Spaniards were indeed children of the Sun. In one well-publicized instance, in Puerto Rico in 1508, they held a Spaniard under water to see if he would drown, and then sat by his body for three days to observe what would happen next. Later, in Mexico, Amerindians, upon killing a Moor who was with the Spaniards, cut him into small pieces to make sure he was dead. Once they lost their fear of horses and arquebuses, and having learned that Spaniards could fall from the blow of a stone or an arrow as well as anyone, they became much bolder in armed encounters, and the Jesuit Acosta (c. 1539–1600) warned that they should not be underestimated as warriors. In a more peaceful vein is the story of the aged

Jamaican cacique (the same who had impressed Columbus with his authority despite his nudity) who, upon presenting Columbus with a basket of fruit, delivered an oration, concluding with the words: "If you are mortal, and believe that each one will meet the fate he deserves, you will harm no one."

These reactions to the confrontation reveal the universality of human nature as well as particular characteristics of the two civilizations involved. As each sought to come to terms with what was often unwelcome new information, both Amerindians and Europeans operated on the premise that they were the only "true men." Around the world and throughout time, peoples have expressed their feeling of superiority over others by uncomplimentary appellations; for instance, Eskimo comes from an Algonkian term meaning "eaters of raw meat," which explains why present-day Arctic peoples are insisting that the term be replaced with their own name for themselves, Inuit, meaning "the people." Iroquois seems to be the French version of an Algonkian term that meant "adder" or "snake"; the Iroquois in their turn named the Sioux, which has the same meaning. Naskapi means "rude, uncivilized people"; their name for themselves is Ne-e-no-il-no, "perfect people." In Africa, the Zulus called all other tribes "animals"; whites were not people, but "those whose ears reflect sunlight." Greeks rejected those who were not of their own culture as "barbarians," using a word referring to the speech of foreigners, which they thought resembled the twittering of birds. St. Augustine had been even more categoric when he said that a man was better off in the company of a dog he knew than of men whose language he did not know; he cited Pliny to the effect that a foreigner is not like a man. "Each one calls barbarous that which is not of its own usage," Montaigne wrote with his usual perception, but with more than a little touch of irony. Montaigne was well aware of the pejorative implications of the word "barbarian," which at its kindest meant "foreigner," but with suggestions of coarseness, customs that were reprehensible if not downright wicked, and lack of manners.

As Europeans and Amerindians met in the New World, this type of reaction was modified by cultural factors. Their superior technology, coupled with their belief that man was made to dominate nature, and Christians to dominate the world, did nothing to mitigate their conviction that Europeans were indeed the "true men," and that New World men were of an inferior order. Amerindians, finding themselves outclassed technologically and viewing man as a cooperative part of nature rather than as its master, wondered at first if Europeans were not more than human. Was not domination the prerogative of the gods? If one is to judge the merits of these positions on the basis of the survival of their respective cultures, the less generous response had the advantage. That the reaction of the Amerindians may have been in the nature of a self-fulfilling prophecy is suggested by the story of the bearded white-faced god they were reportedly awaiting from across the sea.

In the meantime, in Europe, information about New World men accumulated haphazardly, adding much detail to Columbus's first impressions, but without seriously modifying them.

Encounters: Amerindians, Africans, and Europeans

The process of Atlantic discovery, conquest, trade, and coloniza-tion brought together, not stereotypical "red," "white," and "black" men, but women and men from an extraordinary diversity of ethnic and cultural backgrounds. Even colonists of a single European eth-nic group who embarked on the same vessel often discovered sig-nificant differences among local customs, dialects, religions, and legal traditions. The well-known diversity among Europeans was mirrored and magnified by peoples of the Americas and Africa. These various peoples came together in a complex series of en-counters that spanned several centuries and produced a bewilder-ing variety of outcomes.

T. H. Breen views the process of cultural encounter during the sixteenth and seventeenth centuries as a "tale of human creativity." In addition to challenging the strand of colonial historiography that ignored the participation of Amerindians and Africans, he criticizes those that neglected interaction in order to treat only a single group, portrayed relations among various groups as static, or treated Amerindians or Africans as passive victims. While acknowl-edging that Europeans enjoyed substantial advantages in interracial exchanges, Breen argues that African and Amerindian peoples also possessed a voice in the cultural "conversations" that led them to adapt to changing conditions by "dropping some practices, acquiring new ones, and modifying others." In "Creative Adaptations" he helps us understand the great variety of colonial encounters and outcomes.

Early encounters among Europeans, Africans, and Amerindians were often violent, but rarely simple, conflicts pitting Europeans against Africans or Europeans against Amerindians. As Europeans quickly learned, Africans and Amerindians were themselves militarily adept and had their own interests and agendas. Africans and Amerindians sought alliances with European chiefs and warriors to further their own strategic goals, just as Europeans sought alliances with African and Amerindian chiefs and warriors to make their own conquests. Thomas Benjamin looks at the "conquest of Yucatan" of the 1530s and 1540s and reveals that it was a war between one group of Maya warriors against another group of Maya warriors. Maya conquistadores had their own battles to fight and made use of Spanish soldiers to defeat their ancestral Amerindian enemies. Europeans often inserted themselves in African and Amerindian conflicts, gaining essential allies in the process. The great "conquests" of the early Atlantic world were more interesting and complicated encounters than their names suggest.

One historian has observed that European explorers not only discovered a world new to them, but made the Americas into a "New World" for the Indians who lived there. Ramón A. Gutiérrez explores a particularly rich example of cultural conversation between the mutual new worlds of Spanish Franciscan missionaries and the Pueblos of New Mexico. Despite the vast differences between Pueblo and Franciscan systems of belief and cultural practice, the Spanish missionaries found ways to adapt certain Pueblo categories and practices to their effort of Christianizing the Indians. The Pueblos readily understood and responded to Spanish intentions by drawing on traditional forms, as well as new Spanish ideas, to fashion appropriate strategies of adaptation or resistance.

The modern categories of race have proved some of the most enduring and pervasive cultural products of the encounter period. Jennifer L. Morgan examines how gender shaped European travelers' perceptions of the non-European peoples they encountered, providing powerful tools for constructing an ideology of race to justify the subjugation of African and Amerindian peoples.

Scholars once believed that enslaved Africans endured the horror of the Middle Passage only to arrive in the New World culturally naked, victims of an "African spiritual Holocaust" that stripped them of the traditional customs, beliefs, and practices that might have sustained and empowered them to resist oppression. Sylvia R. Frey and Betty Wood refute this idea with an analysis of how, from the moment of capture, slaves drew on shared memory to recreate the past, adapting remembered religious and cultural traditions to the new task of imbuing the present with structure and meaning, while challenging the "total authority over their persons claimed by the Europeans." Within the often brutal constraints of slavery, these cultural survivals gave bondspeople the resources they needed to recreate patterns of marriage, family, celebration, mourning, and community life "after their own way." African-American culture, like that of Pueblos and other Amerindians, proved powerfully resilient and adaptable to their harsh new world.

T. H. Breen

Creative Adaptations: Peoples and Cultures

The tale of the peopling of the New World is one of human creativity. Colonization of the Caribbean islands and the North American mainland brought thousands of men and women into contact who ordinarily would have had nothing to do with each other. Whether migrants arrived as slaves or freemen, as religious visionaries or crass opportunists, they were forced to adjust not only to unfamiliar environments but also to a host of strangers, persons of different races, cultures, and backgrounds.

T. H. Breen, "Creative Adaptations: People and Cultures," in *Colonial British America: Essays in the New History of the Early Modern Era*, Jack P. Greene and J. R. Pole, eds. (Baltimore: Johns Hopkins University Press, 1984), pp. 195, 197–215. Copyright © 1983 by T. H. Breen.

These challenges were staggering. Within the constraints of the peculiar circumstances in which they found themselves, blacks and whites learned to live with each other as well as with native Americans. However cruelly some exploited others, however much they resented each other's presence, in their development these three groups became intricately intertwined. How men and women chose to interact, therefore, how much they preserved of their original cultures, how much they borrowed from the strangers are topics of considerable importance, for their decisions made three centuries ago still powerfully affect the character of modern society. . . .

. . . Close analysis of specific historical contexts directs attention precisely where it should be focused, upon particular men and women shaping their lives in response to changing social and environmental conditions. In this sense, culture is a creative process: people construct reality, spin webs of meaning, and make choices about their lives. Whenever colonial historians take a long-term, often presentist, view of cultural and racial relations, they should realize that it was only within specific contexts of interaction that freedom and slavery, dignity and degradation, and a score of other abstractions acquired social meaning. An ethnohistorian, in fact, interprets the cultural "conversations" of the past in terms that the participants themselves would have comprehended. As sociologist Alan Dawe explains, "It is the prime imperative of the sociology of conversations that we ceaselessly listen to and converse with the voices from everyday life . . . listen for detail, for every nuance, every inflection, every change of tone, however slight, in the myriad ways in which people make their lives, in order to recognize and understand and articulate human agency at work."

This creative process generated different results depending upon the social, economic, and environmental situations in which early Americans found themselves. The New World produced a kaleidoscope of human encounters. To suggest that Africans and Indians possessed the same voice in shaping cultural "conversations" as did Europeans would be absurd. Whites clearly enjoyed substantial advantages in such interracial exchanges. But it would be equally mistaken to claim that either blacks or native Americans—or the poorer whites for that matter—were overwhelmed by the dominant white cultures. Within obvious limits, these people also adapted traditional folkways to meet changing conditions, dropping some practices, acquiring new ones, and modifying others. The problem for the historian of colonial cultures, therefore, is to define with precision the constraints upon choice: What actually determined the character of specific conversations?

This essay examines several major constraints upon cultural creativity in early American societies. Examples are drawn from English colonies that developed on the Caribbean islands and on the mainland. Major elements that shaped the way people adapted to each other and to their new homes were (1) the backgrounds of migrants and native Americans before colonization, (2) the perceptions that members of the three racial groups formed not only of themselves but also of representatives of other races, (3) the motives of different white settlers for moving to the New World, (4) the timing of initial contact, (5) the physical environment in which contact occurred, (6) the shifting demographic configurations, (7) the character of local economies, and (8) the force of individual personality. This list is not exclusive; moreover, it is not intended as a model or prescription for future analyses. This approach merely provides a convenient way of reviewing a vast historical literature while emphasizing at the same time the centrality of the human agent in cultural conversations.

After examining how in particular situations these elements more or less affected the character of interaction between strangers of diverse backgrounds and different races, I maintain that it is still possible to discern certain long-term trends in early American cultural and racial relations. In many English colonies the seventeenth century was a time of openness, of experimentation, of sorting out ideas. Race was important in negotiating social identities, but it was by no means the chief determinant. People formed niches in which they created fluid, often unique patterns of interaction. But during the eighteenth century—and the timing of course varied from community to community—race became more obtrusive in shaping human relations. To understand how this change came about, we must first consider constraints upon adaptation.

Cultural Conversations: Constraints

Background before contact. Colonization in the New World brought men and women of diverse backgrounds together for the first time. These people did not greet each other as representatives of monolithic racial groups—as blacks, reds, or whites. Ethnic and class divisions, some of them deeply rooted in the history of a particular Old World community, cut across migrant populations. "Those peoples called Indians by Europeans were divided into hundreds of tribes and thousands of societies," observes Robert F. Berkhofer. "Even who was a member of a tribe at any one time and what a tribe was, changed greatly over time." Both immigrants and native Americans were products of dynamic, often locally oriented societies that were changing when the New World was discovered and would have continued to change even if it had remained unknown for centuries. The backgrounds of these peoples before initial contact affected the ways they adapted not only to each other but also to strangers of a different race.

Relatively little is known about the Indians of eastern North America and the Caribbean during the precontact period. Recent archaeological investigations suggest, however, that native American cultures were both dynamic and diverse. Tribal customs changed considerably over time in response not only to other tribes but also to environmental demands. The once accepted notion that the first major alteration in Indian cultures occurred only after the arrival of the white man turns out to have been an error based upon ethnocentrism. The native American population of these regions actually was divided into scores of self-contained tribal groups and bands—best described as ethnic groups—that spoke languages virtually unintelligible to members of other tribes, sometimes even to those living in close proximity. These groups shared no common kinship system. The Hurons of Southern Ontario and the Creeks of the southeast, for example, were agricultural and matrilineal. Most hunting tribes of the Great Lakes area were patrilineal, but significant exceptions can be found to any relation between economy and kinship.

Ethnic differences profoundly affected the way specific tribes reacted to the European challenge. One particularly well-documented example involving the Iroquois and the Hurons reveals why someone interested in cultural interaction must understand Indian heterogeneity. Even before contact, the Iroquois were apparently a bellicose tribe, relying upon warfare to obtain animal skins and hunting territory. The neighboring Hurons gained the same ends largely through trade. "The contrasting responses of the Huron and the Iroquois [to the white man]," explains Bruce Trigger, "reflect not only their different geographical locations, but also *longstanding cultural differences* that had arisen as a result of cultural adaptation to these locations."

The various native Americans with whom the colonist came into contact represented strikingly different levels of technological development. On the eve of the European conquest many tribes living in what became the middle and southeastern mainland colonies experienced a cultural revolution. They adopted the Mississippian cultural complex, the central characteristics of which were "systematic agriculture, hierarchical social and political structures, elaborate exchange networks, and clusters of large, pyramidal mounds." The Mississippian reorganization did not make a substantial impact upon the Algonkian bands that the English and French first encountered in the far Northeast. These less developed peoples were less able to preserve their traditional belief system against the external threat than were the members of southern and inland tribes. "The more advanced Amerindian cultures," Cornelius J. Jaenen reports, "assimilated more rapidly than the less advanced tribes. . . . It was the less advanced, northern and eastern nomadic Algonkian-speaking tribes who were most disorganized in the face of contact."

The cultures of "precontact" Africa were less unified than that of seventeenth-century Europe. Only recently, however, have anthropologists and historians come to appreciate fully the diversity and complexity of West African societies. It is still common to read of a general African heritage, a single background allegedly providing slaves with a set of shared meanings and beliefs once they reached the New World. But as anthropologists Sidney Mintz and Richard Price argue, "Enslaved Africans . . . were drawn from different parts of the African continent, from numerous tribal and linguistic groups, and from different societies in any region." Black men and women were transported to America as members of specific tribes—as Ibos, Yorubas, or Ashantis but not simply as Africans. Indeed, historians accustomed to thinking of European migrants in terms of national origin often overlook African ethnicity, overestimating perhaps the difficulty of obtaining evidence for the heterogeneity of African culture.

African ethnicity is not a modern invention. Colonial planters who purchased slaves recognized distinctions between various West African peoples, and in South Carolina and the Caribbean islands whites sought blacks from specific tribes thought to be particularly docile or strong. Even if the planters had not made such demands, however, the slave population in the English colonies—at least in the earliest years of settlement—would have reflected a wide range of geographic and cultural backgrounds. Different European traders put together human cargoes in areas (usually at the mouths of major rivers) where they had gained commercial rights. Slaves acquired by Dutch merchants, therefore, came from different regions than did those transported by English vessels. Moreover, local political and economic instability sometimes affected the ability of coastal tribes to obtain adequate supplies of slaves, and during the colonial period the locus of the slave trade shifted from one region to another, each change bringing in its wake men and women of different cultural heritages. Such diversity meant that the Africans themselves were often strangers to each other's customs and languages, and if a single African background developed at all, it came into being on board slave ships or plantations, where West Africans were compelled to cooperate in order to survive.

Colonial American historians seldom describe England on the eve of colonization as a "precontact" culture. The reasons for their reluctance are clear. Elizabethan society seems politically sophisticated, economically expansive, and, by the standards of the seventeenth century, technologically well developed. For the purposes of this essay, however, it is salutary to consider another perspective: to conceive of the earliest migrants as coming not from a well-integrated culture but from localized subcultures scattered throughout the kingdom. English people shared assumptions about the meaning of daily events—just as the eastern woodland Indians or West Africans did—but the lost world of the Anglo-Americans was generally a specific rural area. According to Peter Clark and Paul Slack, the England of 1700 was "still very much a rural nation." Whether a colonist came from Kent or Norfolk, East Anglia or the West Country, therefore, should be a matter of considerable importance for anyone interested in cultural interaction in the New World.

This line of reasoning must not be overstated: even as men and women set out to settle the Caribbean and mainland colonies the localism that had so long characterized the English countryside had begun to dissolve. The process was slow and uneven, affecting regions near London and other urban centers more profoundly than it did outlying areas such as Cornwall and Yorkshire. Moreover, the creation of a national culture involved wealthy country gentry and affluent merchants long before it touched the common folk, many of whom traveled to America as indentured servants. Such social divisions notwithstanding, however, English colonists possessed a greater awareness of a shared culture, especially a common language, than did either the Africans or the Indians. Several historians, including Sumner C. Powell, John J. Waters, and David Grayson Allen, have argued, not that these general centralizing trends should be ignored, but rather that the story of the transfer of English culture to the New World and the attitudes of English colonists towards other Americans is richer once one knows something about the migrants' "local" as well as "national" background.

Perceptions and prejudices. Men and women involved in the colonization of North America generally regarded themselves as superior to the representatives of other groups with whom they came into contact. Such flattering self-perceptions developed long before anyone thought of moving to the New World. When Africans, Europeans, and Indians encountered individuals of unfamiliar races and cultures, they attempted to incorporate them into established intellectual frameworks, and it is not surprising that differences were often interpreted as evidence of inferiority. Early modern English writers left a particularly detailed record of how they viewed blacks and Indians, not to mention the Irish. Historians drawing upon this material concluded that ethnocentric biases pervaded the white colonists' world view. Only recently have scholars become aware that members of other cultures could be just as ethnocentric in their outlook as were the English. To the extent that these ideas and prejudices shaped the ways that persons of different race and culture actually interacted in the New World, they obstructed open, creative adaptation, especially by people of dependent status.

The study of white attitudes about blacks and Indians is flourishing, largely in the area of intellectual history. The writings of David Brion Davis and Winthrop Jordan represent the idealist tradition at its best. Within somewhat different contexts, Jordan and Davis trace European perceptions of black people, and they provide masterful analyses of the ways in which whites subtly and often insidiously developed the justification of slavery. By the time that English colonists set out for America, they had come to equate Africans with evil, paganism, bestiality, and lust—traits that seemed to deny blacks any chance of obtaining freedom and dignity in the New World. Whether these attitudes amounted to full-blown "racism" is a question yet to be resolved. To be sure, blacks became slaves in America in large numbers. There is considerable evidence, however, that the English regarded almost anyone

who was not English as inferior and that at least during the early seventeenth century Africans were just one of several groups whom they saw
as inferior.

The image of the Indian in the so-called white mind also contin-
ues to fascinate early American historians. They have discovered that
even as white settlers drove native Americans from the Atlantic coast,
exterminating many in the process, they held ambivalent ideas about
the Indian, some favorable, some derogatory. How much these complex attitudes affected Indian policy is not entirely clear. Indeed, general intellectual histories may reveal very little about the character of
race relations in specific environments. That, however, may not be
their goal. According to Roy Harvey Pearce, such accounts tell us a
great deal about white fears and obsessions, about self-perceptions
threatened by the American "savage." "The Indian became important
for the English mind," Pearce explains, "not for what he was in and of
himself, but rather what he showed civilized men they were not and
must not be."

Whites were not alone in their prejudice. West Africans possessed
an image of the white man that was extremely unflattering. Blacks
seem to have associated the color white, at least on human beings, with
a number of negative attributes, including evil. In one magnificent
Danish account compiled in the mid-eighteenth century, it was reported that an African ruler thought "all Europeans looked like ugly
sea monsters." He ordered an embarrassed Danish bookkeeper to strip
so that he could definitively discover if this was so. After examining the
naked Dane, the African exclaimed, "You are really a human being,
but as white as the devil." When William Bosman visited Guinea in
the late seventeenth century he was surprised to learn from local blacks
that while God "created Blacks as well as White Men," the Lord preferred the blacks. How much such ethnocentric attitudes carried over
to the New World and affected relations between blacks and whites is
not known. There is no reason to believe, however, that Afro-Americans viewed the English any more favorably than the English viewed
the blacks.

Reconstruction of native American ideas about Europeans presents a formidable challenge. Our only knowledge of Indian attitudes is
derived from white sources, especially those compiled by unsympa-
thetic missionaries and traders. "We are completely ignorant," Trigger
admits, "or have only the vaguest ideas about what the majority of Indi-

ans thought and felt as individuals and know little about what they did, except in their dealings with Europeans." Despite these obstacles, we have reasons to believe that while Indians were eager to obtain manufactured goods, they maintained a critical, even derogatory, stance towards the whites and their cultures. The northern tribes, for example, regarded Europeans as ugly—too hairy for their tastes. In fact, Jaenen reports that "on a wide range of points of contact . . . the Amerindian evaluation of French culture and civilization was often as unflattering as was the low regard of Frenchmen for Amerindian culture." Indians of tidewater Virginia were as ethnocentric in their outlook as were the first English planters. In fact, there is almost no evidence that native Americans wanted to live in stuffy cabins, attend white schools, give up traditional religious practices, copy English government, adopt European medicines, or, much to the white colonists' amazement, make love to white women.

Once historians have catalogued these ethnocentric biases— white, black, and red—they still do not know much about race relations in specific historical contexts. Recent studies indicate that general attitudes were often modified, muted, or dropped altogether when peoples of different races and cultures came into contact. As James Axtell points out, "Breezy generalizations about 'English' attitudes are much less helpful than distinctions between the attitudes of stay-at-homes and colonists, city folk and frontiersmen, tourists and locals, saints and sinners, and fighters and lovers."

The difficulty of studying race relations from the perspective of intellectual history may be even greater than Axtell admits. Sociologists have found no direct connection between stereotypical notions about other groups and actual discrimination. "It is quite possible," observes George Fredrickson, "for an individual to have a generalized notion about members of another race or nationality that bears almost no relation to how he actually behaves when confronted with them." In other words, if we are to understand the creative choices that people made in the New World, we must pay close attention not only to what they said and wrote but also to what they did. Whatever racial images may have inhabited the "white mind," Englishmen certainly did not treat blacks and Indians the same way throughout the empire.

Ideas that people held concerning members of other groups are best regarded as loose, even inchoate bundles of opinion. These perceptions tended to be ambivalent, and it usually required a major event such as war or rebellion to trigger outbursts of hatred. In themselves, however, popular attitudes about race and culture did not determine the character of human interaction in the English colonies.

Motives for colonization.   English men and women moved to the New World for many different reasons, not the least of which was escape from personal misadventures. However, by concentrating narrowly upon economic and religious incentives for transfer, we can argue plausibly that the further north the colonists settled, the less obsessed they were with immediate material gain. As historians constantly reiterate, Puritans journeyed to New England for more than the reformation of the Church of England, but religious purity was certainly a matter of considerable importance in establishing a "city on a hill." By the same token, some English people undoubtedly thought they were doing the Lord's work in Virginia. The major preoccupation of these settlers, however, was making money—a great deal of it very quickly. As Edmund S. Morgan has pointed out, the Chesapeake colony in the early seventeenth century took on the characteristics of a "boom town," a place where powerful persons were none too particular about the means they used to gain their ends.

These scrambling, greedy tobacco planters look almost saintly when compared with the individuals who crossed the "line" into a Caribbean world of cutthroats and adventurers. "The expectations the English brought with them," writes Richard Dunn, "and the physical conditions they encountered in the islands produced a hectic mode of life that had no counterpart at home or elsewhere in English experience." In these tropical societies organized religion failed to make much impact upon the colonists' avariciousness. Sugar producers could not possibly have comprehended the communal controls over private gain that bound New Englanders together in small covenanted villages.

How much the expectations of early white leaders affected relations between persons of different races and cultures is difficult to ascertain. Unquestionably, for people of dependent status, life in the southern and island colonies was less pleasant than it would have been in Pennsylvania or Massachusetts Bay. Adventurers who demanded quick returns on investment eagerly exploited anyone's labor, whether they were black, white, or Indian. The ambition to become rich in the New World may have transformed planters into cruel and insensitive masters. But however much we recoil at their behavior, we should not confuse exploitation with racism. In early Virginia and Barbados — two well-recorded societies — the Irish, Africans, and native Americans were at equal disadvantage. In these colonies class rather than race may have been the bond that united workers, and the willingness of the poor whites and blacks to cooperate, to run away together, and in some cases to join in rebellion grew out of a shared experience of poverty and oppression.

Timing of transfer. In shaping cultural patterns, the earliest migrants, English and African, enjoyed great advantage over later arrivals. The first colonists established rules for interaction, decided what customs would be carried to the New World, and determined the terms under which newcomers would be incorporated into their societies. According to John Porter, the founders should be regarded as "charter" groups. Porter explains that "the first ethnic group to come into a previously unpopulated territory, as the effective possessor, has the most to say. This group becomes the charter group of the society, and among the many privileges and prerogatives which it retains are decisions about what other groups are to be let in and what they will be permitted to do." A double challenge confronted men and women relocated at a later date. They had not only to adjust to an unfamiliar environment but also to accommodate themselves to the people already living there, to members of their own race as well as to other colonists. Timing of transfer, therefore, functioned as an important constraint upon cultural adaptation.

English "charter" groups exercised considerable influence over subsequent generations. They did so by making decisions about institutional forms, about the treatment of other races, about the allocation of natural resources. And in New England especially these decisions were then published. They became permanent guides to a specific social order. The *Laws and Liberties of Massachusetts* was such a document, as was the *Cambridge Platform.* Even in the southern colonies, where people died like flies and printing presses were scarce, "charter" settlers established customs and traditions, exploitative labor systems, and normative patterns of behavior. The men and women who flooded into Virginia after mid-century, for example, however wealthy and powerful they may have been, were forced to channel their ambitions through existing institutional structures. They were not free to abolish slavery or staple-crop agriculture: these had become expressions of a regional way of life. To be sure, newcomers could tinker with what they found —

make modifications, clarify procedures—but the hand of the past restricted the choices available to them. In every English colony white Creoles—persons born and raised in America—came to accept local folkways without question. New immigrants adjusted not to a single English culture transferred to the New World but to a particular creole culture that had developed over time.

Timing was a factor of profound importance in shaping distinct Afro-American cultures. Tensions between black Creoles and newly arrived Africans affected not only the development of specific slave communities but also the ways black people interacted with whites. The fullest evidence comes from the Caribbean islands, especially from Barbados and Jamaica, but similar frictions seem to have occurred in all English possessions south of New England, beginning with the landing of the first African slaves in the early seventeenth century. Frightened and ill, often separated from family and members of their own ethnic groups, these men and women found themselves thrown together with black strangers on ships and later on plantations. Since they spoke different languages, even casual conversation was difficult.

But as Sidney Mintz and Richard Price have argued so provocatively, these early blacks successfully created new cultures that were part African and part American. They transferred some customs familiar to blacks throughout West Africa. The slaves also negotiated compromises, invented new rules and languages, and learned how to deal with whites; in short, they crafted complex social orders in the face of great personal deprivation. The rich oral culture that flourished on plantations transformed these ad hoc measures into viable traditions. Older men and women, particularly obeah men and women, believed to possess special medical or spiritual powers, passed on the decisions of the founders to children born in America. Obviously it took many years and much suffering to establish genuine, stable creole cultures, but they did eventually spring up throughout the Caribbean and southern mainland colonies.

These developments sometimes aggravated hardships experienced by African-born slaves. Creoles established rules for their incorporation into Afro-American plantation communities which often seemed arbitrary to men and women fresh from West Africa. These "outlandish Negroes," "salt-water Negroes," or "Guineybirds"—as they were called by Creole and whites—could barely comprehend the mechanisms that had deprived them of their freedom, much less the customs that governed exchanges between Afro-Americans. Adjustments generated tensions, even hostilities. Consider, for example, the pain of young Olaudah Equiano, who arrived in the Chesapeake region in 1757. This twelve-year-old slave declared, "I was now exceedingly miserable, and thought myself worse off than any . . . of my companions; for they could talk to each other, but I had no person to speak to that I could understand. In this state I was constantly grieving and pining, and wishing for death." In time most Africans in Equiano's position accepted the conventions of Afro-American culture, just as so many European migrants came to terms with Anglo-American culture. Newcomers, whatever their color, did not experience the possibility of creating a new culture. For them, interacting in strange situations required them to break the code—often under great pressure and quite quickly—of creole culture.

Some new African slaves simply could not adjust. Rather than become Afro-Americans, they made a different choice, one that often cost them their lives: they ran off in gangs or violently resisted their white masters. But as Gerald Mullin, Michael Craton, and David Barry Gaspar, among others, have pointed out, whatever the provocation, Creoles and "outlandish" blacks seldom made common cause. In the Antigua slave rebellion of 1736, for example, Creoles who were "assimilated blacks, proficient in English or the local patois, intelligent in bearing, sometimes literate, and usually skilled" planned the enterprise. In contrast, Mullin discovered that in eighteenth-century Virginia "only native Africans who were new arrivals and referred to as 'outlandish,' ran off in groups or attempted to establish villages or runaways on the frontier." Black Virginia Creoles generally slipped away alone and headed for urban areas, where they passed themselves off as free persons.

The timing of contact played a considerably different role in the evolution of native American cultures. The Indians, after all, were already here, and for them, the strains of creolization were not a problem. Nevertheless, the chronology of first interaction with white settlers is a matter of great significance in the native American history. Several tribes that initially encountered Europeans—the Caribs and Arawaks of the Caribbean islands and the Algonkian bands of the Northeast—were ill-equipped to deal with the massive threat presented by the white colonists. Because of their exposed position on the first frontier of settlement, they did not have time to adjust to the external challenge. Disease wiped out many bands; others were quickly dispersed or enslaved. To claim that these men and women had an opportunity to adapt creatively would be disingenuous. In comparison with these unfortunate groups, the inland tribes—many of them more highly developed—were able to adjust to change at a more leisurely pace and thus were able to preserve fundamental elements of their cultures.

Physical environment.   Colonial historians have shown no great interest in systematically investigating the connection between culture and environment. Unlike anthropologists, they seem to take such matters for granted. No one doubts, of course, that cultural relations in the New World were somehow influenced by flora and fauna, by rainfall and temperature, by soil types and natural resources. The question is, How and to what degree did these elements affect the cultural choices made by early Americans?

Certainly such factors operated as constraints upon cultural transfer, for as English colonists discovered, it was far easier to reproduce traditional ways of life in a familiar environment than in one that threatened their very survival. The obvious contrast is between the early settlements of New England and of the Caribbean. The physical environment of Massachusetts Bay was not substantially different from that which East Anglian, West Country, or Kentish migrants had known in the mother country. To be sure, they complained of the harsh American winters, but despite snow and cold, New Englanders quickly reestablished the forms of mixed agriculture that their fathers and grandfathers had practiced before them. These fortuitous similarities meant that Puritans were spared the wrenching adjustments demanded of English people who settled in the tropics. Instead of experimenting with strange staples like rice, sugar, and tobacco, New Englanders immediately turned their attention to recreating as much of English village life in America as they possibly could, and as David Grayson Allen has argued persuasively, they experienced considerable success.

The same claim could not be made for the English people who landed on Barbados or Jamaica. In the hot, damp climate of the Caribbean, colonists stubbornly attempted to recreate English ways of life. As Richard Dunn has explained, their diet and clothes were grossly unsuited for the tropics. Some men and women managed to adjust to this strange environment. Others went home or moved to areas of the New

World where they felt more comfortable. But a few unhappy souls were overwhelmed and according to Michael Craton, they "sank into a hopeless moral stupor, eating, drinking, and fornicating themselves into an early grave." It is not clear exactly how such a major culture shock—an uprooting from all that was familiar—affected relations in the Caribbean between whites and blacks, or between creole whites and later arrivals. In what must have seemed alien, exotic surroundings to the seventeenth-century colonists, the massive exploitation of African peoples may have appeared more appropriate, even logical, than it did in an environment that look much like the English countryside.

European colonists insisted, even as they watched African slaves die by the hundred, that blacks were particularly well-suited to living in a tropical environment. The West Africans transported to the Caribbean, however, found the staple-crop, plantation agriculture as alien to their experience as did the white settlers. As Michael Craton explains, "To Africans accustomed to subsistence farming, plantation agriculture was dislocatingly strange, if not unnatural. The planters' profit motive meant nothing to them, and their spirit probably resisted the forests' despoilation as much as the exploitation of themselves." These blacks, of course, exercised no choice over where they would settle and adjusted to unfamiliar surroundings as best they could.

Environmental conditions provided some Afro-Americans with opportunities denied to others. On a few Caribbean islands, but especially on Jamaica, large maroon communities developed in heavily forested, rugged regions that the white militia found impossible to patrol. These villages, populated by ex-slaves and their children, presented an appealing alternative to bondage. Rebellious men and women knew that they could slip away into the deep woods; in fact, such people ran away to the maroons so frequently that in 1740 frustrated Jamaican authorities accepted the independence of these communities in exchange for peace and assistance in capturing newly escaped slaves. This form of resistance was not available to Afro-Americans living on a small, deforested island like Barbados. However much these slaves resented their treatment, they were constrained by the characteristics of their environment to channel hostility into other forms of resistance. Why maroon societies did not flourish in the mainland colonies remains something of a mystery. Certainly the southern back country afforded many potential hideaways. One plausible explanation is that these inland areas were inhabited by powerful Indian tribes who were no more enthusiastic about the spread of black settlements than they were about those of the whites.

Native Americans adjusted to ecological niches long before Africans and Europeans arrived in the New World. To discuss these long-term adaptations is not necessary in an essay of this scope. Of greater significance in explaining the ways that peoples of different races and cultures interacted is the simple accident of location. The experience of the Iroquois provides a good example of the importance of geography. In the early seventeenth century these Indians found themselves surrounded by Dutch, English, and French colonists. The Iroquois had obviously not foreseen the commercial advantages of this particular location, but once the Europeans landed, the Indians masterfully played one group off against the others. Had the Iroquois lived in a different area, say, along the Atlantic coast, such complex trade relations with the whites could not possibly have developed.

Demographic configurations. The last two decades have witnessed a revolution in the study of historical demography in this country. We know more about seventeenth-century New Englanders than about almost any other population on earth. More recently, colonial demographers have examined other English settlements, as well as early Afro-American communities. Cultural and social historians have rushed to incorporate this growing literature into their own work, for it seems indisputable that population density, family structure, and mortality rates—just to cite obvious themes—somehow influenced patterns of cultural and racial interaction in the New World.

The relation between culture and population, however, remains fuzzy. Historians sometimes assume a connection merely because it sounds plausible. Take high mortality as an example: How exactly did the terrible death rates experienced by the earliest Chesapeake adventurers affect their attitudes about each other or about dependent peoples? Did the threat of early death make them more hedonistic, more exploitative, or more religious than they might have been in a healthier environment? Currently we do not know. Even if we recognize these interpretative problems, it is clear that historical demography provides marvelous insights into the constraints upon creative adaptation in early America.

Any demographic discussion must begin with New England. New Englander's remarkable experience, along with other factors we have considered, greatly facilitated the transfer of local English cultures to

America. Puritan migrants were unexpectedly blessed with long life. By all rights, persons who moved to the New World in their forties or fifties could not have expected to survive very long. But they did. Many even saw their grandchildren reach maturity, a rare occurrence in contemporary Europe. In fact, once they founded communities, the fathers of New England towns literally became patriarchs, keepers of tradition and symbols of stability. Since these colonists usually migrated in nuclear families, the sex ratio of the population was relatively balanced. Among other things, this demographic structure meant that people immediately had to plan for the well-being of future generations. They established schools and churches, and even in the very earliest settlements young men and women were conscious of being members of extensive kinship networks as well as cohesive farm communities.

Strikingly different demographic configurations developed in the seventeenth-century southern mainland and Caribbean colonies. These settlements drew a disproportionately large number of young males, mostly indentured servants, who generally died within a few years. Warm climates exacerbated the spread of contagious disease, but shallow wells poisoned by salt water and hostile Indians also took a sizable toll.

Continuing high mortality appears to have had a profound impact upon white cultures in these colonies. There was little incentive to plan for the future—at least, a future in the New World. Men wanted to strike it rich and return home as quickly as possible. They paid little attention to the establishment of churches and schools. After all, in societies in which women "were scarcer than corn or liquor," few children were born, and of those, most died in infancy. In the early Chesapeake, Cary Carson finds, "many of the earlier structures were not only *not* built to last, they *were* built in ways that termites could not resist." A similar sense of impermanence pervaded the Caribbean colonies. As Carl and Roberta Bridenbaugh observe, early death combined with the absence of normal family life "made for a slower transit of English civilization to the islands than to New England."

Historical demographers have discovered that mortality in these regions did not significantly improve for generations. In the Chesapeake settlements births did not outnumber deaths among the whites until the end of the seventeenth century. And in Jamaica health conditions remained wretched throughout the entire eighteenth century.

What all this means in demographic terms is that these were abnormal societies, comparable to European mercenary armies rather than to English country villages, and those people who managed to survive must have been keenly aware of the tenuousness of life, of the need to grab for as much as one could in the race for wealth. From this evidence alone, one would predict that white males in these colonies would look upon dependent blacks and Indians chiefly as convenient sources of sex and labor.

Besides high mortality, at least two other demographic factors affected the character of early American race relations. Of great importance in the staple colonies was the shifting population ratio of blacks and whites. Recent studies suggest that white attitudes towards blacks were influenced powerfully by the number of Africans with whom the whites *actually* came into contact. In the earliest years of settlement the black populations of Virginia, South Carolina, Barbados, and Jamaica were relatively small, and white planters either treated blacks with indifference—in other words, no worse than they treated everyone else—or allowed some blacks to forge independent niches as farmers or herdsmen. As the black populations increased, however, whites began to draw racial boundaries more rigidly. They also became more vocal in their protestations of black inferiority. In colony after colony demographic change produced racial fears and hostility. Orlando Patterson, in his study of Jamaican society, explains, "In the first few years after the occupation there was a favourable attitude toward Negro freemen. . . . But as more slaves came into the island this policy changed rapidly." White authorities challenged free Jamaican blacks at every turn, and those who could not prove their status were reenslaved.

A second consideration was population dispersion. In Virginia and Maryland slaves generally worked in small groups on tobacco farms scattered across the countryside. In the fields they often toiled alongside their owners. According to Ira Berlin, interaction between members of the two races was "constant and continued," and white planters, even some of the wealthiest, developed a strong paternalistic interest in the affairs of their slaves. In the Carolinas and Georgia and certainly in the Caribbean such intimate relationships over long periods of time were rare. On large rice and sugar plantations blacks were isolated; they might go days without seeing any white person. In the eighteenth century many great planters of Jamaica fled the island altogether, becoming "absentees" living in England. They left behind a skeletal staff of salaried whites to manage several hundred slaves. Since these whites were paid to maintain high production rates and since they were usually frightened out of their wits by the possibility of rebellion, they acted like petty tyrants. Race relations were cruel and arbitrary. Indeed, the whites who remained on Jamaica would probably have regarded the paternalism of a William Byrd II or a Landon Carter as foolish, if not absolutely suicidal.

The formation of distinct Afro-American cultures owes much to demographic forces over which black people exercised little control. Slave traders decided where men and women would be sent and in what numbers. During the seventeenth century, Caribbean planters who negotiated the largest purchases demanded strong, young males. Africans, therefore, faced three particularly severe handicaps in transferring local cultures to the New World: they were unfree; their sex ratios were so badly skewed towards males that normal family life and reproduction was retarded; and they died at appalling rates, either of unfamiliar contagious diseases or of overwork. Only gradually, as life expectancy improved and sex ratios became more balanced, did slaves develop stable kinship networks, as well as sustaining folk traditions. This crucial demographic transition occurred in various colonies at different times. As Allan Kulikoff argues, the slaves of Maryland and Virginia laid the foundations for a secure Afro-American society during the early decades of the eighteenth century. But in the southern, more lethal regions the process may have been slower. "As long as slavery lasted," Michael Craton notes, "West Indian slave society was demographically not self-sufficient, though the gap between deathrate and birthrate gradually narrowed."

A second demographic element in the creation of Afro-American cultures was touched upon in our discussion of the density of various white populations. In areas where the blacks worked in small units, often in close proximity to whites, they found it difficult to maintain independent customs and practices. Their situation compelled them to make subtle adjustments to the demands of a specific work routine. Again, the more southern mainland and Caribbean colonies present a sharp contrast to this experience. In these regions the size of the plantation work force was generally large, sometimes comprising several hundred men and women, and while the tropical environment endangered good health, Caribbean and Carolina slaves lived within communities composed almost entirely of blacks. Several historians suggest that the peculiarities of work culture explain why so many African customs seem to have survived on the sugar and rice plantations. "The West Indian slave," writes Richard Dunn, "barred from the essentials of European civility, was free to retain as much as he wished of his West African cultural heritage. Here he differed from the Negro in Virginia . . . who was not only uprooted from his familiar tropical environment but thrown into close association with white people and their European ways."

For native Americans race relations represented demographic disaster. Smallpox, influenza, and measles swept through Indian peoples, who possessed no natural immunities, and in some areas, particularly in the northeastern and Caribbean colonies, entire tribes were wiped out within a few years of conquest. The impact of lethal epidemics upon Indian cultures varied from region to region and from tribe to tribe. Among some woodland bands of the far North inexplicable suffering called into question the efficacy of traditional religious beliefs. In other places death so eroded their cultures that Indian survivors lost tribal identity and joined remnants of other shattered groups or inland tribes not yet decimated by the contagious killers. The Indian population fell so rapidly that few English colonists seriously regarded native Americans as a potential labor force. As George Fredrickson remarks, "There are several reasons why Indians never became a significant part of the agricultural or industrial labor force in the United States, but the most important is the sheer lack of numbers resulting from the ravages of disease." Removal of native Americans from English work cultures, particularly in the staple economies, meant that Indians developed quite different patterns of relations with the whites than did the plantation blacks.

The story of white-Indian interaction has another, often overlooked demographic dimension. Population density influenced relations between these two races throughout the colonial period. Disease, however devastating its effects, did not hit all tribes with equal intensity. Indians who inhabited the Atlantic coast of New England, for example, suffered major demographic setbacks *before* the Puritans arrived, and as a result of these earlier epidemics, whites outnumbered local native Americans in this region almost from the very beginning of contact. But in central and western New York, in tidewater Virginia, and along the Georgia–South Carolina frontier, Indians presented a formidable challenge to white expansion. To be sure, the colonists eventually dispossessed most of the eastern tribes, but this displacement should not obscure the occasions in which large numbers of reasonably healthy native Americans more than held their own.

Economic constraints. While Europeans largely determined patterns of work and trade in the New World, everyone possessed a voice, however faint, in economic affairs. In fields of sugar, rice, and tobacco or at trading posts where Indians brought food or furs, people carried on subtle forms of cultural bargaining. In these settings they forged mutual dependencies and developed understandings about the limits of cooperation. Not surprisingly, therefore, in early America cultural borrowing and technological exchanges were most frequently associated with work and trade.

The character of the local economies, however, was quite fluid. Colonial agriculturalists switched crops and, depending upon where they lived, substituted staple crops for livestock or livestock for cereals. Moreover, as whites demanded different items from native Americans, the nature of the Indian trade changed. These shifts had a major effect upon the ways that local peoples interacted, for each change affected the exploitativeness of work, the size of the labor force, and, most significantly, the ability of men and women of different races and backgrounds to engage in creative "conversations."

The most dramatic economic transformations—for blacks as well as whites—occurred in the southern mainland and Caribbean colonies during the seventeenth century. Englishmen arrived in the regions filled with ill-conceived notions about how to become rich. They dreamed of finding passages to the Orient, of gold and rubies by the seashore. The harsh realities of the New World dispelled such fantasies, and during the early decades of settlement colonists experimented with different crops. Barbadians did not immediately see the advantages of sugar over cotton and tobacco. Only after years of economic misadventure did tobacco catch on in Virginia, and in South Carolina the planters seem to have stumbled upon rice, and later upon indigo, quite by accident. In each colony, the staple crop radically changed the structure of regional societies. Local gentry demanded, and eventually obtained, large numbers of African slaves, who replaced white servants.

Staples not only created greater reliance upon black laborers but also exacerbated economic inequalities within the English population. As the marquis de Chastellux noted in 1783, "Agriculture which was everywhere the occupation of the first settlers, was not enough to cast them all in one mold, since there are certain types of agriculture [mixed agriculture] which tend to maintain equal wealth among individuals, and other types [staple agriculture] which tend to destroy it." Many poor whites left Barbados, for example, after the switch to sugar, a crop that required a large initial capital investment for machinery. Those who remained were reduced to desperate marginality, the ancestors of modern "redshanks" (the Caribbean equivalent of rednecks in the American South). The effects of staple agriculture on the mainland societies were less striking than the effects on the island societies. Nevertheless, rice and tobacco—and the particular work routines associated with these crops—helped redefine relations between whites, as well as between whites and blacks.

As the world market for American staples expanded, the slave's life became much harder than it had been during the earliest years of settlement. Of course, Africans had always suffered discrimination, but during the first stages of economic development the line between slave and freeman and between black and white seems to have been loosely drawn in some colonies. In South Carolina, for example, slaves worked as "cowboys" along the frontier with only minimal white supervision. In this period even the black's exact legal status remained vague. Once white planters began to realize large profits, however, they pushed their slaves harder, eager to obtain full return on their human investment. Agrarian schedules settled into a dull, mindless routine. As Craton explains of one plantation on Jamaica: "With the clearing of trees and the beginning of sugar planting, the quality of life for those working in Lluidas Vale inevitably deteriorated . . . a herd of tractable blacks was needed, with no more skills than were called for in the West African agriculture of slashing, burning, and hoeing." Unskilled, often unpleasant work became part of the circular justification for slavery. Slaves performed nasty jobs, and because blacks did them, they obviously made good slaves. Other factors were operating in this process, but it is instructive to compare the experience of Jamaican blacks with the experience of those who worked on small Pennsylvania farms. Jerome Wood reports that the latter were treated relatively well, escaping much of the personal hardship connected with staple agriculture.

Economic change affected white-Indian relations in different ways. At first, English settlers required foodstuffs, and since their needs were obviously desperate, native Americans could drive hard bargains, something Powhatan learned very early in his dealings with the Jamestown adventurers. Both sides profited from these exchanges; both maintained their cultural integrity. But it was not long before the colonists demanded furs and skins. Those tribes that could not generate adequate supplies of pelts were either pushed aside or ignored. Coveted manufactured items went to inland Indians who had access to regions where the animals had not yet been hunted to extinction. Gradually, however, the European market for furs dried up, styles changed, and the Indians, now dependent upon European commerce, had little to offer in exchange for guns and cloth, kettles and knives. Under these conditions, Indians were easily exploited, abused, and cheated out of whatever they still possessed. In a none too subtle fashion, therefore, commercial relations along a moving frontier shaped native American economic behavior. These constraints on interaction did not inevitably produce tragic results. Some Indians developed skills highly marketable in certain white communities. The native Americans on Nantucket and far eastern Long Island, for example, were renowned for their ability to catch whales, and long after many woodland bands had disappeared, these people flourished.

Individual personality. During the colonial period certain persons occasionally broke the rules governing race relations, defied economic trends, and by sheer strength of personality forced other men and women to deal with them on their own terms. Whether these people possessed special genius or courage or luck is impossible to determine. Their existence, however, is not in doubt, and in areas scattered throughout English America they had a considerable influence upon local cultural conversations. Anthony Johnson was such an individual. He arrived in Virginia a slave, and by hard work and good fortune he purchased his freedom, becoming eventually a successful planter on the Eastern Shore. Johnson's story is clearly exceptional; that is the point: in a small pond he was a very big fish—a shark—and while the Virginia House of Burgesses was busy passing laws restricting black freedoms, he persuaded his white neighbors to treat him and his family with respect. Thomas Mayhew, Jr., a Congregational minister on Martha's Vineyard, helped local Indians preserve many traditional ways of life, and when external authorities threatened his work, he held his ground. Like Johnson, Mayhew set his own standards. Any analysis of creative adaptations that overlooks these special cases will fail to capture the full richness of human relations in early America.

Cultural persistence and white dominance.   Before hazarding a general interpretation of cultural and racial relations in colonial America, I should offer two mild caveats. First, for anyone studying cultures over long periods of time, there is an understandable tendency to stress change over persistence. In fact, however, most early Americans were conservative, trying to preserve as best they could familiar customs and traditions, a known way of life. Sometimes what appears to have been a radical cultural reorientation turns out upon closer examination to have been a shrewd compromise, a superficial adjustment masking the survival of a deeper, often symbolic cultural core. The native American experience provides good examples of this process. Under certain conditions, Indians converted to Christianity, a decision that would seem to have threatened the entire fabric of traditional culture. But appearances may have been deceiving. As James Axtell argues, "Even though their conversion entailed wholesale cultural changes, it preserved their ethnic identity as particular Indian groups on familiar pieces of land that carried their inner history." In other words, native Americans used "elements of European religious culture for their own purposes." Historians tracing English and African migrations to the New World report similar creative efforts, often against great odds, to protect at least the main elements of a former cultural system.

Second, while emphasizing human choice in shaping patterns of human interaction, I am fully aware that white people possessed tremendous economic, military, and technological advantages in defining cultural conversations. They often set the terms: they provided foils against which native Americans and Afro-Americans reacted. That much seems self-evident. What colonial historians have generally overlooked is the potential within specific social contexts for creative response.

Thomas Benjamin

Alliances and Conquests

The opening of the Atlantic brought the Portuguese and Spanish into the lands of Africans and Amerindians. Before these encounters Portugal and Castile had coexisted alongside, occasionally made alliances with, and often struggled long and hard against a people different in race, culture and religion who were close at hand, the Moors of the Iberian peninsula and the Maghrib. Alliances were made with Moorish states to gain temporary respite and advantage in fighting other Moorish or Christian states as conditions in the peninsula and the Western Mediterranean dictated. Conquest was also deeply ingrained in Portuguese and Spanish culture as the reconquista demonstrated, a worthy endeavor in the eyes of man and, it was firmly believed, God. The Iberians entered the Atlantic world seeking partners and allies but also finding and making enemies and subjects.

Africans and Amerindians were generally approached at first in peace. If Europeans could not attain the wealth they sought through cooperation, they were always willing to use force. Like the Moors, these newly "discovered" peoples were subject to "legitimate conquest" through just war, an important concept in Iberian thought. Unlike the Moors, however, Africans and Amerindians were generally pagans, people ignorant of the "one true faith" (not infidels who were knowledgeable of Christianity but had rejected it). Their subjection to Christian kings and ultimately the Pope through conquest was justified on the basis of evangelization rather than heresy. The Spanish and Portuguese also believed conquest was justified by virtue of superior culture: they believed they were more refined, advanced, learned; in short, they were civilized.

Although one finds alliances and conquests on both sides of the Atlantic, the Portuguese generally made alliances and collaborated with

Thomas Benjamin, "Alliances and Conquests: Forging the Iberian Empires in Africa and America," Chapter 3 from *The Atlantic World: Its Peoples and Empires* (unpublished manuscript).

local states, chiefs and traders on the coast of Africa while the Spanish generally conquered native kingdoms and chiefdoms in the Americas. These differences were not due primarily to national characteristics: the Portuguese conquered and the Spanish collaborated when circumstances made such actions appear to be advantageous or necessary. Nevertheless one senses that the Portuguese were inclined to make deals and the Spanish were predisposed to make war. In Africa the Portuguese found networks of trade and, more often than not, cooperative rulers who worked with traders in the mutual pursuit of profit. They also found societies willing and able to defend themselves. Alliances with Africans made the most sense. In America the Spanish found no such readily exploitable business environment. Wealth had to be squeezed and forced from native hands in the Caribbean and looted and plundered from rich kingdoms on the mainland. Amerindian societies also defended themselves but, generally although not entirely, without success. Superior European war making technology (and cavalry) and native rivalries in America permitted Spanish and Portuguese war bands to divide and conquer. John Hemming's comment about the Portuguese in Brazil applies to all of the European conquests in America: "All the Indian wars exploited fatal rivalries between tribes. No Portuguese ever took the field without masses of native auxiliaries eager to attack their traditional enemies."

On the coast of Africa and throughout the Americas, the Portuguese and the Spanish made alliances and conquests with African and Amerindian cooperation and assistance. The Portuguese and Spanish empires which were forged in the fifteenth and sixteenth centuries were not exclusively Portuguese and Spanish constructions. The Portuguese were on the coast of Africa with the forbearance of local African rulers and they traded in gold and slaves with the cooperation and participation of African societies. The Spanish achieved dominion over powerful Amerindian empires thanks to alliances with other Amerindian states. They ruled and taxed vast native societies through the native nobility. From the very beginning the Atlantic world was an ethnically diverse world.

The Conquest of Yucatán

From the thirteenth to the fifteenth century the northern region of the Yucatán peninsula, a vast limestone shelf with much scrub but little good farmland, had been unified by the powerful city state of Mayapán and its Cocom clan lords. Its collapse by a civil war fought between opposing clans approximately fifty years before the arrival of Spanish expeditions on the coast produced about sixteen provinces dominated by city states and controlled by rival noble clans. The Spanish therefore found no centralized Maya empire in Yucatán. They were able eventually, however, to pursue the successful strategy employed by Cortés and Pizarro: divide and conquer.

For twenty-five years, beginning in 1502, Spanish expeditions had touched various points along the coast and clashed with local communities and towns. Most of the time Maya warriors were able to drive Spanish soldiers back to their ships. During this time the Spanish had unknowingly unloosed a devastating "weapon," smallpox, which had swept through the peninsula killing tens — perhaps hundreds — of thousands and preparing the way for conquest later.

Francisco de Montejo, a member of one of the early coasting expeditions and one of Cortés' lieutenants for a short time, initiated a campaign of discovery and conquest in 1527. He followed the example of Cortés by scuttling the ships that brought his expedition to Yucatán. He failed to imitate the conqueror of Mexico, and revealed his arrogance, by not bringing an interpreter. He apparently believed Indian allies were unnecessary; in this he was proved to be quite mistaken. This expedition wandered through the eastern part of the peninsula finding little more than poor villages and hostile people. This first *entrada* encountered continuous resistance for two years until Montejo finally withdrew in order to acquire more recruits and supplies. He returned in 1531 with a larger force and achieved some victories but also suffered some painful defeats. This expedition explored most of the peninsula and forced Montejo to recognize that his future prize held no golden cities or mountains of silver. When news of the discovery and riches of Peru reached Yucatán in 1533–34, many of his men abandoned the campaign which again forced Montejo to withdraw from the peninsula.

In the first years following the departure of the Spanish, Yucatán was forced to suffer a severe drought, a plague of locusts and the inevitable famine that resulted from these calamities. Hardship then led to war. Rival clans, the Xiu of Mani and the Cocom of Sotuta, the same clans that brought down Mayapán, fought each other and thus prolonging a feud that had continued for at least a hundred years. When the Spanish returned to Yucatán it was said they hardly recognized the country.

The third and final *entrada* was led by Montejo's son, Francisco de Montejo the Younger from 1540 to 1547. His Spanish soldiers, approximately 400 of which some fifty were mounted, were accompanied by Nahua fighters and porters from central Mexico. Montejo's most important allies, however, were found in the peninsula. In western Yucatán the conquistador made an alliance with the noble Xiu and Pech clans of the northwestern towns of Chicxulub and Yaxkukul as well as a few other noble clans. To the Xiu and the Pech, their traditional rivals in the peninsula—particularly the Cocom and Cupul clans of Sotuta in the east—were of far more concern than the small party of Spaniards who were perceived as yet another lineage, a new player in the complicated politics of the peninsula and one they believed they could use to their advantage.

The Pech lords in their post-conquest annals, perceived themselves as conquistadores no less valiant or noble than the Spanish. They saw the struggle as: "the history . . . of how much suffering we went through with the Spaniards because of Maya people who were not willing to deliver themselves to God." To the Pech lords the pertinent division was not that between Indian and Spaniard but those between noble and common and between conquistador and conquered. Nakuk Pech and Mecan Pech each referred to themselves as: "Yax hidalgos concixtador en," meaning, "I the first of the noble conquistadores." According to a Xiu account, their lords brought to the war "provisions, warriors, and servants for conquering and pacifying other provinces."

Other Maya, however, perceived the Spanish as Manco in Peru and Cuauhtemoc in Mexico did, as conquerors who brought bad things. One Maya book described the invaders and the invaded: "They [the Maya of Chumayel] did not wish to join with the foreigners; they did not desire Christianity. They did not wish to pay tribute. . . . The foreigners made it otherwise when they arrived here. They brought shameful things when they came. . . ."

The campaign of the 1540s was, like the previous ones, hard fought. For the most part it was a war of west (where the Spanish found clans who would be allies) against the east (where other noble clans resisted their Maya enemies and Spanish allies). Federations of Maya towns organized armies of tens of thousands when the Spanish settled permanent cities, Mérida and Valladolid, in 1542 and 1543. Smaller, more isolated Indian towns resisted by destroying their own maize fields and polluting their wells and sink holes. After their defeat in several formal battles, the Maya resorted to guerrilla warfare, small attacks here, there and everywhere against small parties and settlements of Spaniards. The Spanish responded with a campaign of terror and atrocities. By the late 1540s war, famine and disease had reduced Yucatán's population from approximately 800,000 at the beginning of the century to about 250,000.

Although the Spanish declared victory in 1547 the fighting never really stopped. The eastern and southeastern regions continued to resist into the nineteenth century. Here existed another contested frontier not remarkably different from those in Chile and northern Mexico. The Itzá of the Petén lakes region, in what is today the rain forest of northern Guatemala, successfully resisted conquest for another 150 years. In 1697 Canek, the lord of Itzá city Noh Petén, negotiated a peaceful surrender in a bid to maintain power under Spanish rule. A rival clan, however, seized the city and resisted the Spanish and leading the conquistadores to destroy this last independent Maya kingdom.

Although the Spanish found little to loot and no precious metals in Yucatán, the conquest still produced wealth. Conquered peoples were enslaved and sold to the mines of the Caribbean. Encomiendas were distributed to the leading conquistadores here as everywhere else the Spanish conquered. Value was found in the labor of the Mayas who produced semi-valuable exports like cotton, honey, indigo and cacao. The Maya conquistadores were generally exempt from tribute payments and were able to consolidate their local power and territorial control. Over the decades to come the Maya nobility assimilated into the Spanish population, and the ethnic divide between Spaniard and Indian became the most significant division in colonial society.

With the opening of the Atlantic in the fifteenth century, the Portuguese and the Spanish came into direct contact with "new" and "alien" peoples in Africa and the Americas. At this point begins the construction of the new Atlantic world, which was at first simply archipelagos of Iberian trading bases and small settlements joined with and often dependent upon local peoples and linked to their European homes by intermittent seaborne reinforcements and commerce. In the beginning the Iberians came to Africa and the Americas in tiny numbers, ignorant of just about everything of importance regarding these new lands and peoples. As a result, their very survival in the beginning required that they seek and obtain local cooperation and assistance. They found it. Africans and Native Americans supported, traded with, and made alliances with the Portuguese and the Spanish based on their understanding of their own self interest. Africans and Native Americans did not and could not perceive what seems so clear today, that the Iberians were invaders intent on staying in their countries and exploiting their peoples and resources. In the late fifteenth and early sixteenth centuries, "Africa" and "Africans," "America" and "Indians" did not exist in the perceptions of these peoples. Accustomed to centuries of differentiation, divided by language or custom, and often at war with one another, the most meaningful distinctions were those between local peoples, between, for example, the Mexica and Tlaxcalteca. African and Indian alliances with Europeans against local enemies made perfect sense. Why not use the powers of these newcomers against one's mortal enemies? Why not trade with the Europeans in order to obtain goods that would enhance and strengthen one's own society?

It is clear that European footholds in these new lands would have been either impossible or much more difficult and tenuous without local help. Alliances with Africans and Native Americans made the origin and success of the Atlantic world possible in the first place. The next step, conquest, seems to have been dependent upon the nature of local societies and the intention and long-term objectives of the European newcomers. In Africa the Portuguese generally adopted a policy of peaceful coexistence. The Portuguese intruded into well-formed systems of trade and slavery, which permitted them to tap into and profit from existing networks and institutions without great difficulty. Over time the Portuguese presence, particularly the ever increasing slave trade, damaged African societies. A few states would seek to regulate or abolish the trade, but for the most part the great political fragmentation of Africa's regions facilitated the policy of cooperation and trade. Conquest, which would have been quite difficult if not impossible in some places, was generally unnecessary and counterproductive.

The one exception, of course, was the Portuguese conquest of the Ndongo kingdom of Angola. The motive for a policy of war is unclear.

In 1571 crown approval of a private campaign of conquest appears to have been, in part, a result of disappointment regarding the results of the experiment in Kongo to Christianize and Europeanize an African kingdom. Perhaps envy of the Spanish in America and the mistaken Portuguese belief that rich mines existed in the interior of Angola also motivated this departure from usual policy. (And yet the gold mines of West Africa prompted no attempt at conquest.) The conquest of Angola proved to be both difficult, lengthy and partial as well as disappointing. There were no mines, and war often injured the slave trade even if it enriched individual governors who pursued war. Even with conquest, Angola remained little more than the slave trading center of Luanda.

In America, beginning in the Caribbean, the Spanish discovered that trade could not continually produce gold and the fruits of the land. Indians would not work full time for the Spanish for trade goods (or anything else) and rebelled when forced to labor. To the Spanish way of thinking, conquest became necessary and inevitable. The Portuguese on the coast of Brazil were faced with similar conditions and acted in the same way. In the Caribbean native societies were nearly defenseless; on the mainland the Spanish found powerful states organized for war. Here the Spanish could have attained considerable wealth through trade yet they choose conquest in every case. One of the reasons for this most likely is inertia. Conquest in the Caribbean began patterns of conquest: a pattern of thought, that Indians were conquerable, and a pattern of action, that the Spanish were natural conquistadores. When Cortés discovered the divisions within the Aztec empire he found the method by which he could conquer a powerful state. Plunder as a result of conquest would attain more wealth more quickly than trade. The success of Cortés in Mexico assured the continuation and expansion of the conquest pattern. Any and every Indian state, it was demonstrated, could be conquered and might possibly produce a windfall of great wealth.

Ramón A. Gutiérrez

Franciscan Evangelization in New Mexico

The Franciscans who came to New Mexico during the seventeenth century were a legion of highly disciplined ascetic virtuosi who had forsaken the world to bear witness to Christ. Heirs to the purificatory spirit of the Spanish Counter-Reformation, many of these mendicants were radicals who believed that Christianity could only be reinvigorated through the strictest interpretation of Franciscanism, with its emphasis on severity of discipline, mystical retreat, and abject poverty. As men who sought personal sanctity by emulating the life of St. Francis, vowing themselves as Francis had to a literal imitation of Christ, the Franciscans saw themselves as polemicists for spiritual life. By rejecting the male cult of sexual aggressiveness associated with warfare, by shedding the material trappings of wealth in a Spain that had grown fat on the spoils of the New World, and by forsaking the ties of kinship for a spiritual father in heaven, the friars hoped to critique the vainglories of the world, and thereby turn society to repentance. . . .

Franciscan Evangelism

. . . If the Indians were to reach God, they too would have to be led through purgation, illumination, and union. This clearly emerges when the friars outlined their mission in New Mexico as that of leading the Indians "out from the darkness of paganism and the somberness of death" and into the "Father of Light."

The purgation of the Indian's soul began with a systematic repudiation of Pueblo religion. The Indians had to renounce Satan, banish his earthly assistants (native chiefs), and forsake their superstitious beliefs and idols. To assure that the Indians did not cling to their idolatry the friars raided homes, confiscating katsina dolls, ceremonial masks, prayer sticks, and fetishes. Fray Alonso de Benavides boasted in the 1620s that on one day alone he had seized "more than a thousand idols of wood," which he incinerated before the assembled community with the derisive laughter of an iconoclast. The padres entered the kivas, profaned them, and built crosses on them to delimit a new sacred topography. Indians complained that such defilements put their gods to flight. The friars were delighted to hear this and boasted that they had driven the devil from his house.

Once the visible forms of idolatry had been destroyed, the friars turned their attention to the wretched sins of the flesh. Sex in Pueblo society was a positively valued activity that assured social and cosmic reproduction. Few restrictions were placed on sexual pleasures, and certainly guilt and remorse were not associated with such activities. Ginés de Herrera Horta marveled in 1601 at the naturalness with which the Pueblos regarded their bodies, noting how they walked about "stark naked without any . . . indication of self-consciousness." The Old Testament book of Genesis explained that Adam and Eve had experienced shame because of the Fall. Yet, here was people who went about naked without shame. Why was this? Pedro de Castañeda posed and then answered his own question in 1540, concluding that the Indians were born naked and thus "go about as they were born."

But for Franciscans who had vowed themselves to celibacy out of a deep sexual guilt, the nexus between sexuality and the sacred in the Indian world was extremely repugnant. Descriptions of Pueblo sexual practices written by the friars must be read with this bias in mind. The Pueblos certainly were sexually spirited; of this there is no doubt. The ribaldry of their dances, which ended in intercourse, the sexual toponyms that demarcated their landscape, and the "lewd" behavior that transpired at incorporation rituals, be they with humans, scalps, or game, are all too well documented from various points of view to be dismissed as clerical anxiety. Pueblo songs, myths, and tales recount with great gusto the feats, liberties, and license of "night-prowlers" and "creeping-lovers" who routinely sought the affections of women. The Puebloans practiced serial monogamy and polygamy, and seemed undisturbed by sexual variance. The main distinctions the Christian lexicon had to describe Indian sexual practices were those of sin. Thus the Pueblo *berdaches*, those half-men–half-women who symbolized cosmic harmony, were simply *putos* (male whores) and *sodomitas* (sodomites) to the Spanish. Even the position in which the Indians copulated was "bestial," said the friars, because "like animals, the female plac[ed] herself publicly on all fours." Intercourse in this *retro* (from behind) position dishonored humans, lowered them to the level of animals, and violated natural law. What appropriately became known as the missionary position was the "natural manner of intercourse," advised the seventeenth-century Spanish theologian, Tomás Sánchez, "because this manner is more appropriate for the effusion of the male seed, for its reception into the female vessel."

Should we be led by these descriptions to the conclusion the Franciscans wanted the readers of their letters, reports, and denunciations to reach, namely, that the Pueblos led lives of unbridled lust? I think not. Their comments were thick with clerical anxieties over the sinfulness of the flesh and served as a political justification for the regime of sexual repression they felt was necessary to lead the Pueblos to God. Anthropologists attest that every society has rules governing sexual comportment, especially about such things as incest. Thus when we read the 1660 Inquisitorial denunciation of Fray Nicolas de Chávez, which states that when the Pueblos staged the katsina dances they frolicked in sexual intercourse—"fathers with daughters, brothers with sisters, and mothers with sons"—we must ask: What rhetorical end did such a statement play in the contestation between Indians and Spaniards over the place and meaning of sexuality in a well ordered society? The friars clearly had an answer and thundered it wherever they preached.

The laws of God commanded chastity before marriage, fidelity within the nuptial state, life-long indissoluble monogamy, and modesty and shame in all bodily matters. Men and women who practiced "bestial" activities, who wallowed in their pagan promiscuity, violating Christian laws of sexual morality, had to be publicly whipped, placed in stocks, and sheared of their locks. Only thus would the flesh be purged of its sinfulness.

Excruciating as these punishments were, people were not so easily cowed into abandoning those practices—sexual or otherwise—that gave order to their cosmos. In all honesty the Franciscans had to admit as much. Try as they might to bridle Indian concupiscence, their successes were rather superficial. Reflecting in 1627 on his life's work among the Pueblos, Fray Tomás Carrasco concluded that it had been extremely "difficult to extirpate this evil [polygamy and promiscuity] from among them." He recounted how one day while imploring the

Indians to live monogamously, a woman confused them by preaching against it. "A bolt of lightning flashed from a clear untroubled sky, killing that infernal agent of the demon right in the midst of those good Christian women who were resisting her evil teachings." Carrasco was elated that God had struck "the witch" dead. The Indians interpreted the event differently. For them, persons struck by the germinative force of lightning immediately became cloud spirits, thus confirming that what the woman said was morally true.

Once purified, the Indians were ready to receive the illuminating light of the gospel. This stage on the road toward God required the total reorganization of Indian life through intensive religious, political, and economic education at a *doctrina* (Indian parish). Christianity was an urban religion that flourished best in towns and cities. Thus the first task of the Franciscans was to concentrate widely dispersed Indian villages. Three mission types (of occupation, penetration, and liaison), which corresponded roughly to levels of urbanization, were established. The first *doctrinas* in New Mexico were missions of occupation established among the Tewa (San Juan de los Caballeros, Santa Clara, San Ildefonso) and the Keres Indians (Santo Domingo), whose densely populated villages dotted the Rio Grande Valley. Once these groups were nominally subdued, itinerant preachers pushed into pagan areas, forming missions of penetration by concentrating small dispersed pueblos into larger towns. The missions of the Jémez area—San José Guisewa and San Diego de la Congregación—were formed in this way, gathering twelve hamlets into two towns. The entire Pueblo region underwent a similar transformation during the seventeenth century; 150 or so villages were reduced into 43. From the missions of penetration, missions of liaison were launched on the frontier. If their work was successful, they would eventually become missions of penetration, and finally missions of occupation.

The transformation of the Indians into model Christians at the missions required radical alterations of the native social structure. So hand in hand with the friars' assault on the political structure of the Indian community was their effort to drive a wedge into the main relationship that structured inequality, the relationship between juniors and seniors and between children and their parents. The model of generational conflict that the Franciscans employed for this task was that offered by their founder, whose youthful conversion had led to a renunciation of his natural father for a spiritual Father in heaven. Men who embraced a religious vocation as Franciscans underwent a similar transformation and thus logically hoped that the Indian children to whom they ministered would likewise convert to Christianity and renounce their parents for the love and benefits the padres offered them.

Through baptism "God makes Himself known to souls," affirmed Fray Estevan de Perea. Through baptism the friars became spiritual fathers to the Indians, offering them a paternity that rivaled the act of physical conception. Like the biological parenthood created through the mingling of an ovum and sperm, so through baptism—a spiritual regeneration—a person was "born again a son of God as Father, and of the Church as Mother," asserted Aquinas in the *Summa Theologica.* "He who confers the sacrament stands in the place of God, whose instrument and minister he is, he who raises a baptized person from the sacred font . . . stands in the place of the Church." Cognizant of the paternal responsibilities the sacrament of baptism engendered, New Mexico's padres strove to "make the Indians understand that the friar [was] their spiritual father and love[d] them very much." Fray Roque de Figueredo frequently proclaimed his "fatherly love" to the Indians, as did Fray Salvador de Guerra, who rationalized some of the most barbaric excesses as "fatherly love."

A century of proselytizing among New Spain's Indians had taught the Franciscans that Christianity could not be constructed easily atop pagan foundations. Certainly some Indian adults would become pillars of the church; the majority would not. If Christianity was to be planted firmly, it would be in the Pueblo youth. New Spain's Indian children were "the smartest and purest" found in the entire world, vaunted Fray Gerónimo de Mendieta. Once they matured and began to know women, "they lost their vigor" and became like the children of any other nation. The Pueblo youth were the image of godly innocence to the Franciscans. Snatched from the devil through baptism, their sexual purity still intact, these juveniles, they hoped, would become the saviors of society. The friars knew that if they could turn sons against their fathers and simultaneously win the youths' loyalties by convincing them that the paternity the padres offered was of greater value, a formidable cadre with which to extirpate idolatry and propagate the faith would have been forged. In Mexico City, in the Yucatán, and in New Mexico as well, the Franciscans tried to fashion a force to disrupt generational lines of authority in the native world. Fray Gerónimo de Mendieta stated the strategy well when he explained that the children became "the preachers, and the children were the ministers for the destruction of idolatry."

Historians of Mexico's Christianization recognized the importance the Franciscans placed on the conversion of Indian youth, but failed to place their discussions of this process in the context of kinship politics. To Friars Toribio Motolinía, Bernardino de Sahagún, Gerónimo de Mendieta, and their missionary colleagues, the politics of kinship was what most occupied them at Indian *doctrinas*. By exorcising Satan through baptism and snatching babes still warm from their mothers' wombs, the Franciscans were engaging in a war for the hearts and minds of Indian children that they had no intention of losing.

The time-tested strategy the Franciscans used to win the loyalty and obedience of the Pueblo children required first the humiliation of their parents, followed by gifts to the children calculated to endebt them to the friars. From the start of New Mexico's Christianization, the warriors of Christ were determined to show the young through naked displays of power just how impotent their fathers and native gods were before the padres.

The humiliation of fathers before their own children was most demeaning when the friars emasculated the men, thereby symbolically transforming them into women. A clerical technique occasionally used to render an obdurate and cocksure Indian submissive was to grab him by the testicles and to twist them until the man collapsed in pain. Pedro Acomilla of Taos complained in 1638 that Fray Nicholas Hidalgo "twisted [his penis] so much that it broke in half," leaving Pedro without "what is called the head of the member." Francisco Quaelone and an Indian called "El Mulato" escaped Fray Nicholas' hand, but were buggered for their insubordination, a posture that the Spanish regarded as a sign of submission.

Changes in the sexual division of labor wrought by the conquest were equally demeaning. Traditionally, men spun, wove, hunted, and protected the community. Women cared for hearth and home and undertook all building construction. The Spaniards established new work categories. Men were to toil in building arts, women were to weave, and hunting, warfare, and all native religious works were to cease. The sight of men performing women's work often provoked giggles. "If we compel any man to work on building a house," said Fray Alonso de Benavides, "the women laugh at him . . . and he runs away." Such men often took refuge among the Apaches and rarely returned to mission life.

Equally humiliating were the religious dramas the friars staged at the missions. Whatever the text of these didactic plays and dances, the subtext ensconced in the generational casting (Indian children playing angels or Christians, the Indian adults playing devils, infidels, or enemies) was the defeat of Indian culture and the subordination of adults to Christianized youths.

If for the adults the friars had only the stick and the whip, for the children there were abundant carrots. We saw in Chapter 1 that parents extracted labor and obedience from their children by controlling the gifts children needed to present to other seniors if they were to obtain the symbols of adulthood—wives, esoteric knowledge, and allies. Whenever a person accepted a gift without offering one in return, a dyadic status relationship was established, obliging the accepting party to reciprocate with perpetual obedience and respect. The Pueblo theory of gifts helps us to understand why the Indians flocked to the missions and freely gave their labor to the friars. As men vowed to evangelical poverty the Franciscans offered seeds, livestock, manufactured goods, and an immense ritual arsenal to the Indians for which they wanted nothing in return. When Fray Francisco de Porras gave gifts to the Indians he always emphasized "that the friars came to give rather than to ask of them." Fray Roque de Figueredo told the Zuñi the same thing in 1628. He had come "not for the purpose of taking away their property, because he and the members of his order wished to be the poorest on earth, but rather he was bringing them help and . . . knowledge of the one true God."

At the missions the friars offered young men livestock, meat, and education in animal husbandry in return for baptism and obedience of God's laws, just as the hunt chiefs before them had taught young men hunting techniques and hunt magic in return for corn and meat payments. Since animals disliked the smell of women and would not allow themselves to be captured by men who had recently copulated, effective native hunt magic was always dependent on temporary sexual abstinence. This fact was not lost on the friars, who distributed livestock to men who promised to live monogamously. In precolonial times seniors had enjoyed the most meat because juniors were always indebted until they reached adulthood. Now obedient and pious junior men were most favored by the friars. Thus in a few years, the introduction of European livestock eroded the hunt chiefs' authority, diminished the importance of hunting in Pueblo society, and totally transformed the age hierarchy on which meat distribution and consumption were based.

In the preconquest period, Pueblo seniors had given juniors wives by providing them with the marriage-validating gifts they had to present their senior in-laws before their marriage and the adult status it symbolized were acknowledged socially. The friars injected themselves into the control of marriage, too. Since the sacrament of matrimony was in their hands, it was only by accepting the gifts the padres offered and by reciprocating, accepting the laws of God and promising monogamy and marital fidelity, that juniors obtained wives. We will see in Chapter 3 that the friars' control of marriage and their imposition of monogamy were the tyrannies that most angered Pueblo men and became the most persuasive reasons for revolt.

The Franciscans' appeal to the Indians as powerful fathers was coupled with an appeal to the Indian women. The friars wanted the women to think of them as feminine nurturing mothers. Fray Juan de Talaban often called his followers to the mission in warm compassionate terms, telling them of God's love and how he would suckle them with the mother's "milk of the Gospel." Fray Juan de Prada spoke of nursing the Indians at "the bosom of the Church." The maternal metaphors the Franciscans used to describe their apostolate among the Pueblos had been employed in Christianity since at least the twelfth century, relying on the symbolism of female breasts, the mouth, and menstrual blood to depict the instruction the Church gave as a maternal outpouring of love.

The allure of the missions for Indian women is difficult to chronicle, because the friars, as men, focused their attention on the people they deemed all-powerful in Pueblo society, the men. As men, too, the friars were excluded from female rituals—rituals they surmised amounted to nothing more than domestic chores. In the documented cases that do exist, the padres won female allies by protecting women's rights, by respecting some of the spatial loci of their power, by instructing them that men and women were equal before God, and by allowing them to continue their worship of the Corn Mother, albeit transmogrified as the Blessed Virgin Mary. Throughout the colonial period, when men—Indian or Spanish—engaged in extramarital sex with native women and failed to reciprocate with gifts, it was the friars who protected women's rights, demanding redress from the culprits. Pueblo women, much like their European counterparts, retained control of the household and over the rearing of children, particularly of the girls who were of little import to the friars. Pueblo women were barred from active participation in male rites. So it was also under Christian rule: women served the priests as auxiliaries, cleaned the church and its altar linens, baked the communion bread, prepared food for feasting, and witnessed men's power to communicate with the gods.

The friars posed not only as fathers to their Indian parishioners, but also as mothers, offering them all the religious, social, and economic benefits of maternity. Among the matrilineal Puebloans, the mother provided one's clan name, totemically named household fetishes, care and sustenance through adolescence, and the use of seeds and land on which to cultivate them. The friar as *mater* offered the young very similar gifts, thereby indebting the children to him. At baptism they were given Christian names by the priest. He was the keeper of the Christian fetishes (religious statuary, devotional pictures, relics, and so on). Daily he called them for instruction in the Gospel and the mores of civilization. At the mission boys received wheat and vegetable seeds, fruit trees, plows and hoes to work the land more efficiently, beasts of burden to expand their cultivation, and most important of all, the recognition of land rights vested in men. Pueblo boys had little contact with their fathers before their adolescent katsina initiation into a kiva. The missions presented the children a radically different model of adult male behavior. Here were grown men caring for children. In church the youths saw images of St. Anthony of Padua fondling the infant Christ, of St. Christopher carrying the Christ child on his shoulders, and of St. Joseph holding his foster son in his arms. That the Franciscans poured so much energy into the care and rearing of juveniles must have reinforced the perception that the friars were also mothers, much as Pueblo town chiefs were regarded as the father and mother of all people.

The gifts Indian children obtained from their Franciscan "mothers" were experienced as losses by their natal mothers. Assessing the erosion of power Pueblo women experienced as a result of the Spanish conquest, we see the contours of what Friedrich Engels described in *The Origins of Family, Private Property and the State,* as the "historic overthrow of Mother Right." Conquest by a patriarchal society meant that Pueblo women lost to men their exclusive rights to land, to child labor, to seeds, and even to children. A thorough discussion of this process is beyond our scope. Here, suffice it to say that all of the Puebloans were matrilineal at the time of the conquest, and that those Puebloans who were in closest contact with Spanish towns became patrilineal or bilateral. Those Puebloans who most resisted Christianization—the Hopi, the Zuñi, and the Keres at Acoma—remained matrilineal. Among these people we still find a vibrant array of women's fertility societies, spirited ceremonials to vivify the earth, and a host of descendant earth-bound symbols that celebrate femininity. Among the Puebloans who became most acculturated to European ways—the Tewa and the Keres (except Acoma)—women's fertility societies were suppressed, their dances to awaken men's germinative powers were outlawed as too sinful, and, given the explicit phallic symbolism of the Snake Dance and the "demonic" character of the katsina dances, these elements of Pueblo ceremonialism largely disappeared. The native symbolism that remained was almost totally ascendant and masculine (sun, fire, arrows, and eagles)—symbols that meshed well with those of European patriarchal religion.

Given the many gifts the friars dispensed and their enormous magical powers, one can only surmise what contradictory emotions the children must have felt on seeing their fathers humiliated and their native gods blasphemed. One vivid example comes to us from a 1626 confrontation between Fray Martín de Arvide and a Zuñi medicine man. Angry that his son was succumbing to the friar's enticements, the Zuñi tried to win back his son. When Arvide heard of this, he angrily accosted the medicine man saying: "Is it not sufficient that you yourself want to go to hell without desiring to take your son also?" Then, turning to the boy the friar said: "Son, I am more your father and I love you more than he, for he wants to take you with him to the suffering of hell, while I wish you to enjoy the blessings of being a Christian." Father Arvide won that round, and the medicine man retreated. But Arvide's previous bouts with other men had not ended quite as well. In 1621 he publicly scolded a Picuris Pueblo elder for opposing his son's baptism. For meddling in familial government the Indians pummeled and dragged the friar around the plaza, leaving him for dead.

The protracted struggle the Sons of St. Francis waged to become father and mother to the Indian children and to turn juveniles against their parents eventually bore fruit. By injecting themselves and their gifts into a system of calculated exchanges by which seniors gained the labor, respect, and obedience of juniors, the padres forged a cadre of youths who stood ready to denounce the sins of their parents. Blas, a young Isleta boy, behaved just as the Franciscans wanted. On a January night in 1661, Blas entered Isleta's main kiva where he found the elders "invoking the devil" in indigenous ceremonial garb. "You better be careful," Blas told them, "that is what the padres abhor and have forbidden." The men admonished Blas not to tell the friars, but the boy broke his vow as soon as he left the kiva. When the fathers heard of these clandestine incantations, they had the men rounded up and publicly flogged for planting the pernicious seeds of idolatry. The sting of those whips was not soon forgotten by Isleta's men. In 1680 they would have their revenge.

The disruption of Pueblo social life at the missions, be it through the infusion of European gifts into the native economy, the relocation and reaggregation of villages, or the imposition of sexual repression, was coupled with a reorganization of Pueblo notions of time. In fact, Fray Alonso de Benavides in 1634 likened the work of the missions to a clock. "All the wheels of this clock must be kept in good order . . . without neglecting any detail, otherwise all would be lost." Imbuing the Indians with a Christian sense of time required the disruption of their daily routines and their cyclic ritual calendar. The focal point for both of these processes was the mission church.

Every morning at dawn a bell summoned Indian children to church. A lesson in tidiness began the day. The edifice was swept and cleaned, and when it passed inspection, the children took up the "ways of civilization . . . reading, writing, and singing, as well as playing all kinds of musical instruments." Men like Fray Roque de Figueredo who "was proficient in the ecclesiastical chant, harmony, and plain music as well, expert in the playing of instruments for the choir, such as the organ, bassoon, and cornet" led his children in song, hoping thus to lift their spirits. The morning was punctuated by another bell calling all the villagers to Mass. After Mass, the parish census was reviewed to insure that all except those with valid excuses attended instruction. When the day's lesson was complete the Indians went home and returned at dusk for vespers. The neophytes' day ended with singing the praises of God.

The formal education the Indians received at the missions was based largely on Fray Alonso de Molina's *Doctrina Christana*, a 1546 catechism. The pedagogy elaborated therein relied heavily on rote memorization, repeating numerous times the sign of the cross, the *Credo*, the *Pater Noster*, the *Ave Regina*, and the *Salve Regina*. Converts had to commit to memory the fourteen articles of the faith, the commandments of God and of the Church, the mortal and venial sins, the cardinal virtues, the works of mercy, and the powers of the soul and its enemies—the world, the Devil, and the flesh.

Indispensable for the missions' educational goals were the *policia espiritual*, native assistants who served the friars as "spiritual police." Each parish had several *fiscales* (church wardens), disciplinarians who maintained order during services, punished the morally lax, and supervised ecclesiastical building projects. *Fiscales* freely administered half a dozen lashes to anyone found negligent in their Christian duties, prompting many Indians to regard the whip as the Christian symbol of authority. Equally important were the *temastianos* (Indian catechists), who led converts in prayer and memorization of the catechism. After them, a coterie of cantors, sacristans, and bell-ringers were at the friars' service.

"Since not one religious knows any of the languages," said Ginés Herrera de Horta in 1601, by necessity the friars were forced to employ paraliturgies such as dances and edifying plays as their pedagogical tools to indoctrinate the Indians. The friars believed that if the Puebloans were to embrace Christianity and be kept from reverting to idolatry, magnificent ceremonies rivaling native rituals would have to be staged for them. Incense, candles, vestments, and music were essential to "uplift the souls of the Indians and move them toward the things of God," advised Fray Alonso de Molina, "because they are by nature lukewarm and forgetful of internal matters and must be helped by means of external displays."

The Franciscans' focus on paraliturgies rather than on sacramentalism as an evangelization strategy was due not only to their linguistic shortcomings, which many eventually overcame, but also to the Church's fear of inadvertently nurturing heretical beliefs. In the wake of Spanish intolerance toward Islam, Judaism, and Protestantism, the post-Tridentine fathers were hesitant to develop devotions around the sacraments that might be misinterpreted by the natives. Given the Franciscan Order's emphasis on externality (the Christ St. Francis carried in his heart was available to others through the Christ he wore on his body in the form of the stigmata) New Mexico's friars chose to celebrate among the Pueblos rituals that paralleled, or at least on the surface appeared to mimic native dances and rites of passage, regardless of their deeper meanings. For example, the katsina cult was conflated with the Christian cult of the saints. Christian sanctuaries were built atop Indian shrines. Dances for seed life and game were sanitized and allowed to occur in conjunction with devotions to saints associated with horticultural activities. How this process of superimposition and replacement developed is well illustrated in the confabulation of Pueblo prayer-sticks with the cross.

The cross, perhaps more than any other symbol, dominated Christian ritual in seventeenth-century New Mexico. In the daily lives of the Spanish, the cross was a powerful talisman against evil. One crossed oneself before a church, before and after prayers, and in moments of utter terror. Many a pious Christian, heeding St. Francis' injunction that one wear the crucified Christ on one's body, had a cruciform tattoo or cicatrix placed on their forehead. Men and women of every class wore pectoral crosses similar to those they placed over the windows and doors of their homes to mark the sacred from the profane. Helmets, armor, and parade banners bore the cross as a national symbol. Territorial acquisitions were marked with a cross, the symbol of Spanish sovereignty and emblem of the European God's power.

The Indians apparently believed that the cross was a prayer-stick, and the Spaniards thought prayer-sticks were crosses. Whenever the Puebloans called the katsina they offered them prayer-sticks—prayer-sticks that the gods always reciprocated, announcing that they would arrive in a short time. Pedro de Castañeda saw some prayer-sticks near Acoma in 1540 and concluded that the Indians worshiped "a cross . . . [which had at its base] many small sticks adorned with plumes and many withered flowers." Whenever the Spaniards approached an unknown village, they dispatched a cross-bearing emissary to announce their impending arrival. Understandably, the Indians interpreted this act as an announcement that katsina would shortly visit. The Indians greeted Espejo's 1582 expedition "with crosses painted on their heads" and "crosses of colored sticks." The Indians of Pecos Pueblo similarly welcomed Gaspar Gastaño de Sosa's 1590 expedition, "making the [sign of the] cross with their hands, saying 'amigos, amigos, amigos.' "

Once the Indians recognized the power of the men who brandished crosses, it took little to convince them to worship the cross. Fray Francisco López began converting the Mansos by constructing a cross in their settlement, explaining that if they worshiped it "they would find aid for all their needs." Teaching through example, López fell to his knees, kissed the cross, and ordered the neophytes do likewise. Then "there came an Indian woman with a toothache; with much devotion she held open her mouth with her hands and put her teeth close to the holy cross. Another, in the pains of childbirth, touched the holy tree with her body." Both women felt great "comfort and joy," the fathers tell us, and presented cornmeal offerings to the cross. One will never really know how deeply the Indians understood the meaning of the cross, considering that from the very start of the conquest they defined it in native terms. According to Barbara Tedlock, the Puebloans today believe that prayer-sticks symbolize human sacrifice. If such a meaning existed in the seventeenth century, then the idea that the cross represented Christ's sacrifice for humanity's sins must have resonated at least partially in their imaginations.

The reorganization of Puebloan temporal rhythms was also undertaken by establishing a rival ritual calendar that was incarnational and Christocentric—focused on Christ's birth and death rather than on cosmological events. For this the friars depended primarily on the *autos sacramentales*, didactic religious plays based on New and Old Testament narratives, popular Christian traditions, and episodes from the history of Mexico and New Mexico's conquest. Historians and literary critics for some time have regarded these plays as quaint folkloric curiosities, ignoring their powerful political content and the values their rhetorical gestures were intended to communicate. The text of every *auto* had a subtext concealed in the costumes, generational casting, and dramatic actions. Every text had its context. Drama was not pure entertainment but a moving, pedagogical instrument. The explicit purpose of the *auto* was to inculcate the Indians with a highly ideological view of the conquest, simultaneously forging in their minds a historical consciousness of their own vanquishment and subordination as the Spaniards wanted it remembered.

Memory of the Spanish conquest was kept vivid in the Indian mind through a tripartite ritual formula—greeting, battle, and submission—articulated by Fray Estevan de Perea in 1633. First the Indians greeted their Spanish overlords with varying degrees of pomp and pageantry as they had in 1598—if a priest, by kissing his feet; if a civilian, by kissing his hand. Next came a battle. In 1599 the Spanish unleashed their fury against Acoma Pueblo, but to teach the Indians the ideal social order under Christian rule, plays such as "The Christians and the Moors" were often enacted. Seventeenth-century performances of "The Christians and the Moors" were marked by "loud acclamations from the soldiers, with a salvo of harquebuses, and by skirmishes and horse races." The *farolitos* and *luminarias* used today as decorative lanterns announcing a major feast were then fires evocative of warfare. One Taos Indian woman recently explained that the gunfire still heard during Pueblo fiestas symbolized "the brute force the Spanish used." The didactic *autos*, whatever their themes, always ended on a common note: the Indians' defeat and their acceptance of Christian rule. Greeting, battle, and submission marked the founding of Our Lady of Guadalupe Mission near El Paso in 1668. After the friars had been welcomed, "twelve dozen firecrackers, a beautiful castle, two mounted horsemen, rockets, bombs and bombards were fired." Then the Manso Indians bowed their heads in submission to receive the waters of baptism.

Christianity's early fusions with European cosmological religions prepared it for its contact with the Indians. The preconquest Puebloan ritual year consisted of two six-month halves. A winter cycle devoted to the celebration of animal life began with the solstice on December 21 and ended with the summer solstice on June 21, initiating a summer cycle devoted to plant life. In Pueblo thought, winter was male because life was sustained during those months primarily through men's hunting. Summer was female because seeds, plant life, and the earth on which they grew belonged to women.

The Franciscans fused the calendric rhythms of Pueblo ceremonialism with Christ's life-cycle. Under Christian rule, the preparations to commemorate Christ's birth began on December 16, coinciding exactly with those four preparatory days the Indians observed before celebrating the winter solstice. During the winter solstice each town's clans and esoteric societies celebrated their unity by performing prescribed dances. Now, during roughly the same period, the friars staged a sequence of *autos* and European dance dramas. First there was a performance of *El Coloquio de San José*, telling of St. Joseph's selection as Mary's husband. *Las Posadas*, Mary and Joseph's search for hospice, was also staged on that night and on the eight that followed. Christmas eve began with the *auto* of *Los Pastores*, a play about the shepherds who traveled to Bethlehem to honor and gift the newborn Christ child. The *Misa del Gallo* (Cockcrow Mass) followed, and the night ended with a kissing of Christ's feet at the Nativity crèche. On Christmas day *Los Matachines*, a pantomime dance drama recounting the defeat of the Aztez Emperor Montezuma, his acceptance of Christianity, and obeisance before the mendicants was performed. And finally, on January 6, the feast of the Epiphany, the Christmas cycle ended with the *Auto de los Reyes Magos*, or Christ's adoration by the Three Magi.

It is probably safe to say that the Pueblo audiences did not understand many of the words they heard and had to rely on what they saw—dramatic actions, staging props, and generational casting in which Christianized junior men mocked and subordinated senior men—to make sense of the Christmas plays. So seen, the nativity cycle was a war epic that announced the epiphany of a new warlord, Christ, before whom even mighty kings humbled themselves and offered gifts. The parallels between the mythology surrounding Christ's birth and that of the Twin War Boys, the sons of Father Sun conceived miraculously when a virgin ate two pine nuts, are striking. The War Twins were rowdy and troublesome boys, equated with the forces of nature (lightning and thunder) and always depicted astronomically as comets or the Morning Star. Christ too was the son of God the Father, miraculously conceived by a virgin. The Star of Bethlehem announced his birth. His warriors possessed lightning (gunpowder) and monsters (horses) ready to kill those who did not submit to Christ as their new lord. This undoubtedly explains why at Santo Domingo Pueblo the Ahyana War Dance and at Jémez Pueblo the Bow War Dance are still performed on Christmas morning to honor the newly born war god, Jesus Christ.

The timing of the Christmas liturgies and the winter solstice celebrations were so close that the two became conflated in the Indian mind. Winter was a masculine period when Pueblo hunters and warriors sustained their villages through hunting magic and knowledge of the animal world. The portrayal of Christ as a war god (recall the conceptual relation in Pueblo culture between warfare and hunting) and the prominence of farm animals in the Nativity plays, particularly around the manger, reinforced these links.

Christ's incarnation and birth was but a necessary prelude to the fugue of his crucifixion and death. Joyful as the *glorias* of Christmas Mass were, paradoxically they had a sad, eerie tone to them. Foreshadowing events to come, many pictorial representations of Christ in the manger had on the remote horizon a cross, spikes, and a crown of thorns. Christ's death was the highest drama of the Christian year. And for the Franciscans who carried the crucified Christ in their hearts,

Holy Week was the time they imprinted the crucified Christ on their bodies.

The ritual surrounding Christ's crucifixion and death was, like the Nativity, organized around a sequence of didactic plays staged between Palm and Easter Sundays, the last week of Lent. The Stations of the Cross, fourteen episodes in Christ's final days—his condemnation to death, his carrying of the cross (John 19: 17), his assistance by Simon of Cyrene (Mark 15: 21), his meetings with the holy women of Jerusalem (Luke 23: 27–31), with his mother (John 19: 25), and with Veronica, his three falls en route to Calvary, the stripping and nailing to the cross, his death, deposition, and burial—these were the basic themes of these Holy Week *autos*.

The formal initiation of the ritual of Christ's passion began with the celebration of Mass on Holy Thursday night, commemorating Christ's last supper with his apostles. Like Christ, stripped by his accusers, when Mass ended that night, the mission's main altar was stripped of its linens and ornaments. That night, the night Christ reflected on his own death in the Garden of Gethsemane, was a night of great solemnity. The mission bells were silent that night and only the raucous noise of *matracas* (hand clackers), the doleful laments of *pitos* (flutes), and the swish of whips beating on human flesh pierced the silence of the night. Gaspar Pérez de Villagrá wrote that Holy Thursday night, 1598, "was one of prayer and penance for all." The kingdom's colonists meditated on Christ's passion

> with tears in their eyes, and begged forgiveness for their sins. . . . The women and children came barefoot to pray at the holy shrine. The soldiers, with cruel scourges, beat their backs unmercifully until the camp ran crimson with their blood. The humble Franciscan friars, barefoot and clothed in cruel thorny girdles, devoutly chanted their doleful hymns, praying forgiveness for their sins.

At noon on Good Friday the congregation gathered at church and in procession carried statues of the crucified Christ and his mother through a village circuit that led to a symbolic Mount Calvary. The way was agonizingly long for those who staggered under the weight of enormous crosses. Imagine the spectacle of 600 Curac and Tajique Indians carrying "large and small crosses on their shoulders" during their 1655 Good Friday procession. Or the Hopi who that year for their procession dressed "like penitent hermits walking about praying in penitence, carrying crosses, large beads, and wearing haircloth shirts."

Periodically the procession stopped to view tableaux of the Stations of the Cross. When each station ended, active penitents resumed their self-flagellation with *disciplinas* (sisal scourges), which sent bolts of pain through their bodies. Some penitents beat themselves to a pulp with wire-studded whips, which tore tiny morsels of flesh from their backs. Others bound themselves in buckhorn cholla and prickly pear cacti and focused the long, piecing spines on their genitals. Self-inflicted blows with nail-encrusted boards helped others expiate their sins.

When the procession reached Golgotha, St. John's passion was read before a statue of the Crucified. The crowd retired for a few hours, and at day's end, reassembled for the *Santo Entierro*, the deposition and burial of Christ. Christ was taken off the cross, his crown of thorns and the nails were removed, his hinged arms were lowered to his sides, and the image was laid in an open coffin. In a torchlight procession the coffin was carried back to the village church and placed in the niche where it rested throughout the year. With this, the commemoration of Christ's death ended.

How much of the mystery of Christ's crucifixion the Indians understood is open to speculation. As noted earlier, those chiefs and household heads who allied themselves with the Warriors of Christ also must have tried to understand the central tenets of their faith. The esoteric religious knowledge that kept the Pueblo cosmos properly balanced was secret, controlled by seniors, and only slowly and sparingly divulged to young aspirants for gifts. The friars freely preached the word of God for everyone to hear, but the relative ease with which that word was dispensed to men and women regardless of age must have made it banal. Perhaps the caciques and medicine men listened some, eager to learn what gave Christians their power. For only by admitting a superficial understanding of Christianity by the medicine men can we make sense of the calculated profanations of Christian icons that occurred during the 1680 Pueblo Revolt. Whatever their understanding of the sacrifice of Christ, the God-made-man, what was readily apparent from the pomp and solemnity of Good Friday ritual was Jesus's power and the might and sanctity of his earthly representatives, the Franciscans.

On the other hand, quite early in New Mexico's colonization the Spaniards observed the extensive flagellation and bloodletting that accompanied Pueblo male war and rain rituals, and equated them with Christian piety and penitential practice. Hernán Gallegos noted in 1582 that the rain chief look "like a flagellant." Juan de Ortega in 1601 observed that when the Indians called their gods, they flayed a robust man with reeds. This "penitent," Ortega wrote, "neither groans nor flinches in the least; on the contrary, he undergoes the penance gladly." But it was Fray Alonso de Benavides, who in the 1620s witnessed the ritual of accession for a Pueblo war chief, who most understood the ritual parallel between the war chief's ordeal floggings, which legitimated his use of force as son of Father Sun, and Christ's scourging at the pillar. Benavides writes:

> They tied the naked candidate to a pillar, and all flogged him with some cruel thistles; afterward they entertained him with farces and other games, making a thousand gestures to induce him to laugh. If with all this he remained serene and did not cry out or make any movement at the one or laugh at the other, they confirmed him as a vary valiant captain and performed great dances in his honor.

Benavides and his brothers, ever so eager to appropriate for their own ends ideas from the Indians' ritual repertoires, made every attempt to present Christ's flaying and death as a ritual that legitimated Christian political authority.

Call it piety or purely political ploy, but on Good Friday eve in 1598, the man who commanded the instruments of force in the colony, Governor Juan de Oñate, "cruelly scourged himself, mingling bitter tears with the blood flowing from his many wounds." The padres did likewise, called themselves "sons of the Sun," insinuated rain gods, and mobilized deadly force. The friars did all of this for Christ the King, the War God of war gods, and to establish their charismatic domination over the native community.

The ritualization of Christ's crucifixion and the penitential flagellation, especially the bloodletting associated with it, seems to have been interpreted by the Indians just as the friars meant it to be, as a rite of political authority. How else can one interpret the following confrontation that took place at Isleta Pueblo in 1660? Fray Salvador de Guerra emerged from his convent one day to find the Indians performing the katsina dance, which he had strictly prohibited. When his repeated exhortations to cease dancing were ignored, the friar stripped himself naked before them, began violently beating himself with a whip, placed a rope around his neck, a crown of thorns on his head, and then crisscrossed the pueblo carrying an enormous cross. When the Indians saw this they immediately stopped their dance, and some, moved to tears by the sight, asked the friar's forgiveness. The others retreated to the safety of their homes, fearing that the Christian soldiers might soon arrive.

Admittedly, there is very little evidence with which to chart the slow symbiosis between the native rituals of authority and the Christian rituals around Christ's crucifixion. Mission inventories repeatedly list paintings of Christ's scourging at the pillar. The fusion of native and Christian symbols seems complete when we hear in a nineteenth-century New Mexican penitential song:

> Upon a column bound
> Thou'lt find the King of Heaven,
> Wounded and red with blood
> And dragged along the ground.

Here a bloody Christ is not scourged at the pillar but bound to a column, just as a native war chief would have been in order to prove his majesty over the cosmic forces of the sky.

The liturgy of Christ's crucifixion became an intense rhetorical contest between the friars and native chiefs for the obedience and respect of the Indians. If the Franciscans proselytized like "madmen to the world," flogged their bodies to a crimson pulp, and dragged enormous crosses through the streets, it was to impress their opponents and to overwhelmingly convince their audiences that the extreme physical ordeals they were capable of enduring were signs of their immense sanctity and superior magical powers. The 1630 shouting match between Fray Alonso de Benavides and a Chililí medicine man illustrates both how familiar and appealing the Good Friday ritual was to the Pueblo Indians, and how the native priests saw in it a competing rite that was eroding their own religious (political) authority. The medicine man jeered at the friar saying: "You Christians are crazy; you desire and pretend that this pueblo shall also be crazy." He was apparently disquieted by how attentively the Indians observed Benavides, and by the fact that bloodletting was being practiced by Christianized Indians where formerly only chiefs had engaged in such communion with the gods.

Benavides asked the man to tell him how the Christians were crazy. He responded: "You go through the streets in groups, flagellating yourselves, and it is not well that the people of this pueblo should commit such madness as spilling their own blood by scourging themselves." Benavides tried to explain the meaning of Good Friday to the medicine man, but he refused to listen and retreated muttering that he did not want to be afflicted by Christian madness.

It is only by viewing the confrontation between the Franciscans and the Pueblo chiefs as an intense contest between two theologies for the hearts and minds of the Indian masses that we can begin to understand colonial New Mexican crucifixes with blood streaming from beneath Christ's loincloth, a symbolic wound that has no place in Catholic dogma. We saw earlier how members of Indian war, curing, and rain societies flagellated themselves with cacti to purify their bodies for contact with the holy. We saw the importance of the rain chiefs to Pueblo life and the fact that when the katsina were called or when the Snake Dance was performed, these rites began with purificatory ordeals such as flagellation and bloodletting (including penis laceration) to summon and feed the gods. If we view the flagellations and mortifications the friars routinely practiced as the other side of a polemic in which they were engaged with the rain chiefs over who had the most powerful rain magic and over which religion and which priesthood and magic was superior, we can begin to understand why the Franciscans mutilated their genitals, as the crucifixes seem to indicate. The blood that falls from beneath Christ's loincloth resembles rain drops falling from a cloud.

The Indians may have interpreted Christ's loin blood as rain fructifying the earth because blood had always been seen by them as a male nutrient of extraordinary fertilizing power. There was an equally long tradition in Christian worship of viewing Christ's blood as a nutrient (for example, the devotion to the Precious Blood of Jesus and to the Sacred Heart). The friars often said that the blood of New Mexico's Franciscan martyrs had been spilt to nurture Christian souls so that a bountiful harvest might be reaped.

Sexuality and the sacred were closely linked in Pueblo thought but antithetical to Christianity. Many saints had won their places in heaven by denying the flesh, dying as virgins. Thus it would appear that crucifixes with bleeding genitals were vivid artifacts of tormented states of mind. Of the misogyny in Franciscan culture we amply know.

"Naked," "promiscuous," and "lascivious" Pueblo women provoked deep sexual guilt in some friars, as did the sight of ritual fellatio performed by the rain chief during the Snake Dance. If, as the talion principle holds, one takes an eye for an eye and punishes the organ that causes sin, crucifixes with bleeding genitals tell us much about what the friars thought was the source of sinfulness. Understandably, the friars displaced their sexual desires by singing the praises of the Blessed Virgin Mary, a woman unblemished by her sexuality, and berating those heinous females, those wells of the devil, who celebrated the pleasures of the flesh.

Reviewing the impact of Christianization on the Pueblo ceremonial calendar we see the conflation of Christmas and the winter solstice. Such a fusion did not occur between Holy Week and the summer solstice, which were separated by several months and clashed in terms of seasonal gender concepts. Seeds, germination, and plant growth were the themes of summer Indian ceremonials. Certainly one finds parallel ideas in the liturgy of the resurrection, but for the Franciscans it was Christ's crucifixion, not his resurrection, that was the focus of Holy Week ritual. The crucifixion was a celebration of male power. The summer solstice celebrated Mother Earth's fecundity and the secret of life the Corn Mothers had given humanity. The prominence of the Mater Dolorosa in the passion plays and the Way of the Cross was certainly one attempt to gloss this seasonal gender disparity, for throughout the Old World and the New, the Blessed Virgin Mary was frequently presented to neophytes as a metamorphosed grain goddess. To accommodate the Indians' summer fertility rituals, Holy Week was followed closely by a time dedicated to Mary, the month of May. By the eighteenth century, Mary and the Corn Mothers had been merged in religious iconography and myth. The Virgin now appeared cloaked in garb decorated with corn ears and stalks with the moon at her feet, surrounded by flowers and butterflies, Indian symbols of fertility.

The feast of Corpus Christi, devoted to the living presence of Christ in the Eucharist, was another focal point of the Christian liturgical year. Corpus Christi was a moveable feast that fell anywhere from May 21 to June 24. The Catholic Church established this feast in 1264 primarily to rival pagan summer solstice rites. The main symbol of the feast of Corpus Christi was the Eucharist displayed in a solar-shaped monstrance. Little evidence exists on how Corpus Christi was celebrated in seventeenth-century New Mexico, but that it was observed is attested by the existence of Blessed Sacrament confraternities and of church inventories that list ritual paraphernalia used specifically for this feast. Moreover, Governor Bernardo López de Mendizábal in 1660 demanded that he be greeted by New Mexico's Indians with the same pomp with which they greeted the Blessed Sacrament on the feast of Corpus Christi (a desire that resulted in his prosecution before the Inquisition). If the feast was observed in New Mexico as it was elsewhere in Spain and New Spain, a solemn High Mass and a procession through the town's streets with a consecrated host were the major events of the day. The ritual function of the Mass was to create communal peace. When the Eucharist was carried in a procession through the streets, the town was integrated as one, temporarily obliterating the ranks and statuses that differentiated its various parts.

Corpus Christi ended the liturgical celebrations commemorating the major events of Christ's life, nicely rounding out the six-month period between the winter and summer solstices. No major Christian feasts were celebrated between June and December, and this relatively dead period in the liturgical calendar may have been fashioned by the early Christian fathers to accommodate pagan first-fruits, harvest, and winter hunting rituals. The anthropologist Alfonzo Ortiz noted some years ago that among the present-day Tewa a clear division exists between Catholic and ancestral rites, a religious compartmentalization that developed after the conquest. If one recalls that the Puebloans conceived of the year as two gendered six-month cycles, then the period from June to December would have left the Puebloans one cycle, the feminine cycle, intact and uncontaminated by contact with Christian ritual. One suspects that the friars may have had gender symbolism in mind here. Christian rites celebrated masculine power; the Pueblo feminine cycle was devoted to seed life and germination. Thus the Christian liturgical calendar would have reflected the gender representation of the conquest: virile Spanish victors had vanquished effeminate Puebloans.

Assessing the progress of Christianization among the Puebloans, we are left with clerical words that diverge from Indian actions. Dismissing, as the friars did, those Franciscan martyrs whose blood had been shed to nurture the Christian vine, and those "stupid" apostates ensnared by the devil into revolt, the picture the friars painted of their labor in New Mexico was always in rosy colors. Fray Alonso de Benavides, in a moment of exuberance, claimed that his brothers had encountered 500,000 souls in New Mexico in 1598. He later revised the figure downward to 80,000—the number generally accepted today as a fair approximation of the size of the Pueblo population at conquest. The first decade of colonization produced few Indian conversions, but in 1607, 7,000 Indians were quickly baptized in order to assure the continuation of New Mexico as a mission field. Christianization apparently progressed rapidly between 1607 and 1640. In 1620 the mission population was 17,000. With the arrival of additional Franciscans (66 by 1631) the neophyte population tripled by 1631 to about 60,000, growing at an annual rate of 11.1 percent.

How genuine were these conversions? Conversion is here defined as a fundamental change in beliefs whereby a person accepted the reality and omnipotence of the Spanish God and vowed to obey Him and his ministers. By this standard the number of true Christian souls was vastly inflated—an inflation born of clerical misinterpretation. There can be no doubt that there were some true conversions. There were the Christianized boys painstakingly educated by the friars who, on their instruction, ransacked pueblos extirpating idolatry. The friars tell us, too, that preconquest fissures in the organization of pueblos were further exacerbated by newborn distinctions between Christianized Indians and "pagans," between Hispanicized converts and traditionalists who clung tenaciously, if clandestinely, to ancestral ways.

The problem remaining is to assess how deeply or shallowly, how warmly or lukewarmly, "wet-heads" (baptized Indians) understood the belief they had embraced. And this is fundamentally a problem of translation. Leaving aside the fact that few of the friars spoke or understood the Indian languages, we must ask whether Catholicism, with its monotheistic emphasis on one God and its moral vision of good and evil, heaven and hell, could have been translated into terms the Puebloans fully understood, given their animistic beliefs and monistic cosmological mental universe lacking either sin or hell. I think it could not have been done too effectively, no matter how great the effort. The simple reason is that the Franciscan model of personal re-formation and evangelism, with its pronounced emphasis on externality—transforming the "outer person" (behavior) to change the "inner person" (the soul)—predisposed the friars to believe that Pueblo dissimulations were true conversions. An evangelization strategy of eradicating native rites and substituting Christian ones that mimicked indigenous gestures and paraphernalia, no matter how divergent their respective meanings, also led the friars to misinterpret the apparent piety with which the Indians worshipped God. Thus whether the Puebloans offered feathers and corn meal to the cross as they had to their prayersticks, honored the Christ child on Christmas as they had the Twin War Gods during the winter solstice, or flogged themselves on Good Friday as they had called the rain gods, the meanings attached to these acts were fundamentally rooted in Pueblo concepts. Those Puebloans who nominally pledged allegiance to Christianity and at least superficially forsook their native ways did so in part out of fear and in part to reap the technological and cultural innovations offered by the friars. For Indian residents of small New Mexican pueblos constantly under attack, despoiled of their food, and forced to abandon well-watered spots, the mission fathers offered the semblance of protection. In numbers there was strength, and behind the massive wall of the mission compound there was security. Christianization to these persons meant a reliable meat supply, iron implements of various sorts, and European foods: wheat, legumes, green vegetables, melons, grapes, and a variety of orchard fruits. It does not strain the imagination to envision why such persons, understandably nervous and ambivalent at the arrival of the "Children of the Sun," might have allied themselves as Christians with the new social order.

Jennifer L. Morgan

Male Travelers, Female Bodies

June 1647, the Englishman Richard Ligon left London on the ship *Achilles* to establish himself as a planter in the newly settled colony of Barbados. En route, Ligon's ship stopped in the Cape Verde Islands for

Jennifer L. Morgan, "'Some Could Suckle over Their Shoulder': Male Travelers, Female Bodies, and the Gendering of Racial Ideology, 1500–1770." Copyright © 1997 by the Omohundro Institute of Early American History and Culture.

provisions and trade. There Ligon saw a black woman for the first time; as he recorded the encounter in his *True and Exact History of . . . Barbadoes*, she was a "Negro of the greatest beauty and majesty together: that ever I saw in one woman. Her stature large, and excellently shap'd, well favour'd, full eye'd, and admirably grac'd. . . . [I] awaited her comming out, which was with far greater Majesty and gracefulness, than I have seen Queen Anne, descend from the Chaire of State." Ligon's rhetoric may have surprised his English readers, for seventeenth-century images of black women did not usually evoke the ultimate marker of civility—the monarchy—as the referent.

Early modern English writers conventionally set the black female figure against one that was white—and thus beautiful. In *Pseudodoxia Epidemica* (1646), Sir Thomas Browne argued that blackness and beauty were mutually dependent, each relying on the other as antithetical proof of each one's existence. Recently, depictions of black women in early modern England have attracted scholarly attention. Peter Erickson calls the image of the black woman a trope for disrupted harmony. Lynda Boose sees black women in early modern English writing as symbolically "unrepresentable," embodying a deep threat to patriarchy. Kim Hall finds early modern English literature and material culture fully involved with a gendered racial discourse committed to constructing stable categories of whiteness and blackness. As these and other scholars have shown, male travelers to Africa and the Americas contributed to a European discourse on black womanhood. Femaleness evoked a certain element of desire, but travelers depicted black women as simultaneously un-womanly and marked by a reproductive value dependent on their sex. Writers' recognition of black femaleness and their inability to allow black women to embody "proper" female space composed a focus for representations of racial difference. During the course of his journey, Ligon came to another view of black women. As he saw it, their breasts "hang down below their Navels, so that when they stoop at their common work of weeding, they hang almost to the ground, that at a distance you would think they had six legs." For Ligon, their monstrous bodies symbolized their sole utility—their ability to produce both crops and other laborers.

Ligon's narrative is a microcosm of a much larger ideological maneuver that juxtaposed the familiar with the unfamiliar—the beautiful woman who is also the monstrous laboring beast. As the tenacious and historically deep roots of racialist ideology become more evident, it becomes clear also that, through the rubric of monstrously "raced" Amerindian and African women, Europeans found a means to articulate shifting perceptions of themselves as religiously, culturally, and phenotypically superior to those black or brown persons they sought to define. In the discourse used to justify the slave trade, Ligon's beautiful Negro woman was as important as her six-legged counterpart. Both imaginary women marked a gendered whiteness that accompanied European expansionism. Well before the publication of Ligon's work, New World and African narratives that relied on gender to convey an emergent notion of racialized difference had been published in England and Europe. Although this article is primarily concerned with England and its imperial expansion, by the time English colonists arrived in the Americas they already possessed the trans-European ethnohistoriographical tradition of depicting the imagined native in which Ligon's account is firmly situated.

Ligon's attitude toward the enslaved has been characterized by modern historians as "more liberal and humane than [that] of the generality of planters." Nevertheless, his text indicates the kind of negative symbolic work required of black women in early modern English discourse. As Ligon penned his manuscript while in debtors' prison in 1653, he constructed a layered narrative in which the discovery of African women's monstrosity helped to assure the work's success. Taking the female body as a symbol of the deceptive beauty and ultimate savagery of blackness, Ligon allowed his readers to dally with him among beautiful black women, only seductively to disclose their monstrosity over the course of the narrative. Travel accounts, which had proved their popularity by the time Ligon's *History . . . of Barbadoes* appeared, relied on gendered notions of European social order to project African cultural disorder. I do not argue here that gender operated as a more profound category of difference than race. Rather, this article focuses on the way in which racialist discourse was deeply imbued with ideas about gender and sexual difference that, indeed, became manifest only in contact with each other. White men who laid the discursive groundwork on which the "theft of bodies" could be justified relied on mutually constitutive ideologies of race and gender to affirm Europe's legitimate access to African labor.

Travel accounts produced in Europe and available in England provided a corpus from which subsequent writers borrowed freely, reproducing images of Native American and African women that resonated with readers. These travelers learned to dismiss the idea that women in the Americas and Africa might be innocuous, unremarkable, or even beautiful. Rather, indigenous women bore an enormous symbolic burden as writers from Walter Ralegh to Edward Long employed them to mark metaphorically the symbiotic boundaries of European national identities and white supremacy. The struggle with perceptions of beauty and assertions of monstrosity such as Ligon's exemplified a much larger process through which the familiar became unfamiliar as beauty became beastliness and mothers became monstrous, all ultimately in the service of racial distinctions. Writers who articulated religious and moral justifications for the slave trade simultaneously grappled with the character of the female African body—a body both desirable and repulsive, available and untouchable, productive and reproductive, beautiful and black. This article argues that these meanings were inscribed well before the establishment of England's colonial American plantations and that the intellectual work necessary to naturalize African enslavement—that is, the development of racialist discourse—was deeply implicated by gendered notions of difference and human hierarchy.

Europe had a long tradition of identifying Others through the monstrous physiognomy or sexual behavior of women. Pliny the Elder's ancient collection of monstrous races, *Historia Naturalis*, catalogued the long-breasted wild woman alongside the oddity of Indian and Ethiopian tribal women who bore only one child in their lifetime. Medieval images of female devils included sagging breasts as part of the iconography of danger and monstrosity. The medieval wild woman, whose breasts dragged on the ground when she walked and could be thrown over her shoulder, was believed to disguise herself with youth and beauty in order to enact seductions that would satisfy her "obsessed . . . craving for the love of mortal men." The shape of her body marked her deviant sexuality; both shape and sexuality evidenced her savagery.

Thus, writers commonly looked to sociosexual deviance to indicate savagery in Africa and the Americas and to mark difference from Europe. According to *The Trends of Sir John Mandeville*, "in Ethiopia and in many other countries [in Africa] the folk lie all naked . . . and the women have no shame of the men." Further, "they wed there no wives, for all the women there be common . . . and when [women] have children they may give them to what man they will that hath companied with them." Deviant sexual behavior reflected the breakdown of natural laws—the absence of shame, the inability to identify lines of heredity and descent. This concern with deviant sexuality, articulated almost always through descriptions of women, is a constant theme in the travel writings of early modern Europe. Explorers and travelers to the New World and Africa brought expectations of distended breasts and dangerous sexuality with them. Indeed, Columbus exemplified his reliance on the female body to articulate the colonial venture at the very outset of his voyage when he wrote that the earth was shaped like a breast with the Indies composing the nipple.

Richard Eden's 1553 English translation of Sebastian Münster's *A Treatyse of the Newe India* presented Amerigo Vespucci's voyage to English readers for the first time. Vespucci did not mobilize color to mark the difference of the people he encountered; rather, he described them in terms of their lack of social institutions ("they fight not for the enlargeing of theyre dominion for asmuch as they have no Magistrates") and social niceties ("at they're meate they use rude and barberous fashions, lying on the ground without any table clothe or coverlet"). Nonetheless, his descriptions are not without positive attributes, and when he turned his attention to women, his language bristles with illuminating contradiction:

> *Theyr bodies are verye smothe and clene by reason of theyre often washinge. They are in other thinges fylthy and withoute shame. Thei use no lawful coniunccion of mariage, and but every one hath as many women as him liketh, and leaveth them agayn at his pleasure. The women are very fruiteful, and refuse no laboure al the whyle they are with childe. They travayle in maner withoute payne, so that the nexte day they are cherefull and able to walke. Neyther have they theyr bellies wimpeled or loose, and hanginge pappes, by reason of bearing manye chyldren.*

The passage conveys admiration for indigenous women's strength in pregnancy and their ability to maintain aesthetically pleasing bodies, and it also represents the conflict at the heart of European discourse on gender and difference. Vespucci's familiarity with icons of difference led him to expect American women with hanging breasts; thus he registers surprise that women's breasts and bodies were neither "wimpeled" nor "hanginge." That surprise is inextricable from his description of childbearing. His admiration hinges on both a veiled critique of European female weakness and a dismissal of Amerindian women's pain. The question of pain in childbirth became a central component of descriptions of Africa and Africans. Vespucci presented a preliminary, still ambiguously laudatory account of Amerindian women. Nonetheless, he mobilized the place of women in society as a cultural referent that evoked the "fylth" and shamelessness of all indigenous people. Thus the passage exposes early modern English readers' sometimes ambivalent encounters with narratives that utilized women's behavior and physiognomy to mark European national identities and inscribe racial hierarchy.

In the narration of Columbus's voyage that appears in A *Treatyse*, Münster situated women both as intermediaries between the intrusive and indigenous peoples and as animal-like reproductive units. On arriving at Hispaniola, Columbus's men "pursewinge [the women and men who had come down to the shore] toke a womanne whom they brought to theyre shyppe . . fyllinge her with delicate meates and wyne, and clothing her in fayre apparel, & so let her depart . . . to her companie." As Stephen Greenblatt has illustrated, the female "go-between" was crucial in encounter narratives. This woman figured as a pliable emissary who could be returned to her people as a sign of Spanish generosity (in the form of food and wine) and civility (in the form of clothes). She could be improved by the experience. Indeed, her ability to receive European goods—to be made familiar through European intervention—served as evidence of her own people's savagery, disorder, and distance from civility.

In a passage that closely follows, Münster considered another role for indigenous women and children, a role whose proximate contradiction evokes the complicated nature of European assessment of women and their bodies. Describing the behavior of so-called cannibals, Münster avowed that "such children as they take, they geld to make them fat as we doo cocke chikyns and younge hogges. . . . Suche younge women as they take, they keepe for increase, as we doo hennes to laye egges." The metaphor of domesticated livestock introduced a notion that became an *ideé fixe* concerning indigenous and enslaved women's twofold value to the European project of expansion and extraction. This metaphor, however, did not fully encompass the complexity of dangers indigenous women presented for Europe. Despite his respect for female reproductive hardiness, at the end of the volume Vespucci fixed the indigenous woman as a dangerous cannibal:

> *there came sodeynly a woman downe from a mountayne, bringing with her secretly a great stake with which she [killed a Spaniard.] The other wommene foorthwith toke him by the legges, and drewe him to the mountayne. . . . The women also which had slayne the yong man, cut him in pieces even in the sight of the Spaniardes, shewinge them the pieces, and rosting them at a greate fyre.*

Vespucci made manifest the latent sexualized danger embedded by the man-slaying woman in a letter in which he wrote of women biting off the penises of their sexual partners, thus linking cannibalism—an absolute indicator of savagery and distance from European norms—to female sexual insatiability.

The label savage was not uniformly applied to Amerindian people. Indeed, in the context of European national rivalries, the indigenous woman became somewhat less savage. In the mid- to late sixteenth century, the bodies of women figured at the borders of national identities more often than at the edges of a larger European identity. The Italian traveler Girolamo Benzoni, in his *History of the New World* (a 1572 narrative that appeared in multiple translations), utilized sexualized indigenous women both as markers of difference and indicators of Spanish immorality. His first description of a person in the Americas (in Venezuela in 1541) occurs at the very beginning of his story:

> *Then came an Indian woman . . . such a woman as I have never before nor since seen the like of; so that my eyes could not be satisfied with looking at her for wonder. . . . She was quite naked, except where modisty forbids, such being the custom throughout all this country; she was old, and painted black, with long hair down to her waist, and her ear-rings had so weighed her ears down, as to make them reach her shoulders, a thing wonderful to see. . . . her teeth were black, her mouth large, and she had a ring in her nostrils . . . so that she appeared like a monster to us, rather than a human being.*

Benzoni's description invokes a sizable catalogue of cultural distance packed with meaning made visible by early modern conventions of gendered difference. His inability to satisfy his gaze speaks to an obfuscation Ligon enacted one hundred years later and Greenblatt argues is the defining metaphor of the colonial encounter. His "wonder" situated her distance. In the context of a society concerned with the dissemblance of cosmetics, as Hall argues, her black-faced body was both cause for alarm and evidence of a dangerous inversion of norms. Her nakedness, her ears, and her nose—all oddities accentuated by willful adornment—irrevocably placed her outside the realm of the familiar. Her blackened teeth and large mouth evoked a sexualized danger that, as Benzoni himself explicitly states, linked her and, by implication, her people to an inhuman monstrosity.

In evoking this singular woman—the like of whom he had never seen—Benzoni departed from his contemporaries. He used his description of her to open his narrative and, through her, placed his reader in the realm of the exotic. This "wonderful" woman alerted readers to the distance Benzoni traveled, but he deployed another, more familiar set of female images to level a sustained critique of Spanish colonial expansion and thereby to insist on the indigenous woman's connection, or nearness, to a familiar European femininity. . . .

Benzoni utilized the pathetic figure of the fecund mother and the sexually violated young girl against the Spaniards. Such a move was common in the aftermath of Las Casas's *In Defense of the Indians* (circa 1550) and amid the intensified resentment over access to the Americas directed toward Spain by other European nations. In "Discoverie of the . . . Empire of Guiana" (1598) Ralegh stated that he "suffered not any man to . . . touch any of [the natives'] wives or daughters: which course so contrary to the Spaniards (who tyrannize over them in all things) drewe them to admire her [English] majestie." While permitting himself and his men to gaze upon naked Indian women, Ralegh accentuated their restraint. In doing so, he used the untouched bodies of Native American women to mark national boundaries and signal the civility and superiority of English colonizers — in contrast to the sexually violent Spaniards. Moreover, in linking the eroticism of indigenous women to the sexual attention of Spanish men, Ralegh signaled the Spaniards' "lapse into savagery." Benzoni, too, inscribed the negative consequences of too-close associations with indigenous women. For him, sexual proximity to local women depleted Spanish strength. As he prepared to abandon the topic of Indian slavery for a lengthy discussion of Columbus's travels, he again invoked motherhood to prove Spanish depravity: "All the slaves that the Spaniards catch in these provinces are sent [to the Caribbean] . . . and even when *some of the Indian women are pregnant by these same Spaniards,* they sell them without any consciences."

This rhetorical flourish, through female bodies, highlighted the contradictions of the familiar and unfamiliar in the Americas. The woman who opened Benzoni's narrative, in her nakedness and her monstrous adornments, could not be familiar to conquistadors and colonizers, yet in her role as mother, sexual victim, or even sexually arousing female, she evoked the familiar. Benzoni sidestepped the tension inherent in the savage-violated-mother by mobilizing her in the service of publicizing Spanish atrocity. In effect, the Black Legend created (among other things) this confusing figure of pathos—the savage mother whose nurturing quality is both recorded and praised. In order to facilitate the ultimate roles of extractors and extracted, the indigenous woman's familiarity had to be neutralized. Thus the pathos of raped mothers ultimately reverberated back onto Europe, signifying disdain for the Spanish and disregard for monstrous women.

The monstrosity of the native mother had an important visual corollary. A mid-sixteenth-century Portuguese artist, for example, depicted the Devil wearing a Brazilian headdress and rendered his demonic female companions with long, sagging breasts. Toward the end of the century, a multivolume collection of travel accounts, published in Latin and German, augmented the evolving discourse of European civility with visual signs of overseas encounters. As Bernadette Bucher has shown, the early volumes of Theodor de Bry's *Grand Voyage* (1590) depicted the Algonkians of Virginia and the Timucuas of Florida as classical Europeans: Amerindian bodies mirrored ancient Greek and Roman statuary, modest virgins covered their breasts, and infants suckled at the high, small breasts of young attractive women. These images were always in flux. In the third de Bry volume, *Voyages to Brazil,* published in 1592, the Indian was portrayed as aggressive and savage, and the representation of women's bodies changed. The new woman was a cannibal with breasts that fell below her waist. She licks the juices of grilled human flesh from her fingers and adorns the frontispiece of the map of Tierra del Fuego. Bucher argues that the absence of a suckling child in these depictions is essential to the image's symbolic weight. Their childlessness signified their cannibalism—consumption rather than production. Although cannibalism was not exemplified by women only, women with long breasts marked such savagery among Native

Americans for English readers. Other images of monstrous races, such as the headless Euaipanonoma, the one-footed Sciopods, and the Astomi who lived on the aroma of apples, slowly vanished from Europe's imagined America and Africa. Once in Africa, however, the place of motherhood in the complex of savagery and race became central to the figure of the black woman. Unlike other monstrosities, the long-breasted woman—who, when depicted with her child, carried the full weight of productive savagery—maintained her place in the lexicon of conquest and exploration. . . .

When Ligon arrived in Barbados and settled on a 500-acre sugar plantation with one hundred slaves, African beauty—if it ever really existed—dissolved in the face of racial slavery. He saw African men and women carrying bunches of plantains: " 'Tis a lovely sight to see a hundred handsom Negroes, men and women, with every one a grasse-green bunch of these fruits on their heads . . . the black and green so well becoming one another." African people became comparable to vegetation and only passively and abstractly beautiful as blocks of color. Ligon attested to their passivity with their servitude: they made "very good servants, if they be not spoyled by the English." But if Ligon found interest in beauty, as Jobson did in shame, he ultimately equated black people with animals. He declared that planters bought slaves so that the "sexes may be equall . . . [because] they cannot live without Wives," although the enslaved choose their partners much "as Cows do . . . for, the most of them are as near beasts as may be." When Ligon reinforced African women's animality with descriptions of breasts "hang[ing] down below their Navels," he tethered his narrative to familiar images of black women that—for readers nourished on Hakluyt and de Bry—effectively naturalized the enslavement of Africans. Like his predecessors, Ligon offered further proof of Africans' capacity for physical labor—their aptitude for slavery—through ease of childbearing. "In a fortnight [after giving birth] this woman is at worke with her Pickaninny at her back, as merry a soule as any is there." In the Americas, African women's pain-free childbearing thus continued to be central in the gendering of racism.

By the time the English made their way to the West Indies, decades of ideas and information about brown and black women predated the actual encounter. In many ways, the encounter had already taken place in parlors and reading rooms on English soil, assuring that colonists would arrive with a battery of assumptions and predispositions about race, femininity, sexuality, and civilization. Confronted with an Africa they needed to exploit, European writers turned to black women as evidence of a cultural inferiority that ultimately became encoded as racial difference. Monstrous bodies became enmeshed with savage behavior as the icon of women's breasts became evidence of tangible barbarism. African women's "unwomanly" behavior evoked an immutable distance between Europe and Africa on which the development of racial slavery depended. By the mid-seventeenth century, that which had initially marked African women as unfamiliar—their sexually and reproductively bound savagery—had become familiar. To invoke it was to conjure up a gendered and racialized figure who marked the boundaries of English civility even as she naturalized the subjugation of Africans and their descendants in the Americas.

Sylvia R. Frey and Betty Wood

The Survival of African Religions in the Americas

Jon Butler has recently argued that the transatlantic slave trade shattered African systems of religion, describing it as "a holocaust that destroyed collective religious practice in colonial America." It would not have been altogether surprising had those who experienced the trauma of separation and sale in West and West Central Africa, who were herded like cattle on to the slave ships, completely lost their faith in gods who seemed to have abandoned them and in deities who appeared unwilling or unable to protect them. Some, believing perhaps that their gods had indeed forsaken them or that the superior "magic"

From *Come Shouting to Zion: African American Protestantism in the American South and British Caribbean to 1830* by Sylvia R. Frey and Betty Wood. Copyright © 1998 by the University of North Carolina Press. Used by permission of the publisher.

of their European oppressors had prevailed, might have lost their faith, either permanently or temporarily; the majority did not.

Enslaved Africans turned to their gods and deployed their religious convictions in ways that gave structure and meaning to the present and challenged the total authority over their persons being claimed by Europeans. By remembering and recreating the past, they produced hope for the future, whatever that future might hold. That those taken on board the slave ships had been torn from the institutional frameworks of their traditional religious cultures is patently obvious. However, those who survived the Middle Passage showed enormous courage, resilience, and ingenuity in devising new religious structures to cope with the demands that enslavement in the British plantation colonies made on them.

Millions of Africans were forcibly removed from cultural, social, economic, and political contexts that were not precisely identical and fed into the international slave trade. Indeed, the trade thrived on often violent antagonisms among different ethnic groups and African nations, which sometimes resurfaced in the New World. But there were also some highly significant similarities in the religious cultures and languages of many of those shipped to British America. Profits dictated that slave ships be filled and dispatched as quickly as possible, and this usually involved loading at a single port rather than "coasting." That did not necessarily mean that all those taken on board a particular vessel came from the immediate vicinity of the port, but they had probably been obtained "from a restricted and culturally quite homogeneous zone." The "comparative cohesiveness" of the religious and linguistic traditions that crossed the Atlantic would be critically important in the reformulation of traditional West and West Central African religious cultures in the New World. Those cultures would retain some "explicitly West African . . . forms."

Most Africans transported from their homeland before the closing of the slave trade in the early nineteenth century subscribed to traditional religious cultures, and they would encounter Christianity for the first time in the Americas. However, the slave ships also included a smattering of people who adhered to their own versions of Islam and Christianity. These religious convictions would also survive the Middle Passage and take their place alongside traditional beliefs and practices in the very different contexts of the New World.

Capture and sale of slaves in Africa usually destroyed the ties of family and kinship that were of such significance to African peoples, and the personal and communal cost of that destruction to those who remained as well as to those who were taken should be neither forgotten nor underestimated. But the physical, psychological, and emotional brutality of the Middle Passage did not destroy memory, beliefs, experience, and expertise. Although stripped of much of their material culture, every African who survived the Middle Passage retained cultural attributes that could be put to creative use in the Americas.

The captains and crews of British slave ships felt no burning sense of mission to proselytize, but they were neither ignorant of nor indifferent to the often religiously inspired behavior of their human cargoes. Most were acutely conscious of the fact that those on board their vessels were not totally demoralized but at any moment might seek what was their common objective: their return to Africa. The arrangements on the slave ships made organized resistance difficult but not totally impossible once the vessels had left African waters. There is no record of the number of uprisings that occurred on the Middle Passage, but during the eighteenth century they averaged two a year on British slavers. Many involved women as well as men, and some depended upon traditional religious beliefs and practices for their inspiration and execution. . . .

For captive Africans, in one sense the arrival of a slave ship in the New World marked the end of one stage in their journey and the beginning of another. On another level, however, surviving the Middle Passage proved to be but one point, albeit a critically significant one, in a continuum of religious beliefs and practices. Once they were in the New World, the convictions that had so fortified these men and women while they were en route to the Americas were neither casually forgotten nor discarded as unnecessary or irrelevant. The ritualistic expressions of these convictions would be broadly similar to West and West Central African ones, but the local circumstances in which enslaved Africans found themselves dictated that they could never be identical. Nowhere in the Americas would Africans be able to duplicate their traditional religious systems. What they were able to do, and often very successfully, was to piece together new systems from the remnants of the old.

There were significant variations in the plantation economies that evolved in British America through the middle years of the eighteenth century. Thousands upon thousands of Africans entered against their wills public worlds that increasingly they helped to shape and define and private worlds that they struggled to create for themselves. The precise ethnic mix on particular estates and in particular neighborhoods was of obvious importance, as was the size and proximity of those estates. Sex ratios and age structures played a critical role in the formation of sexual partnerships, in the definition of family and kinship networks, and in the reconstitution of spiritual community. Mortality rates, together with the attitude of slave owners toward the disposal of their human property, profoundly influenced the duration of partnerships, the integrity of family and kinship networks, and the precise composition of spiritual communities. All of these factors interacted in an infinitely complex, ever-changing fashion with traditional African beliefs and practices to shape the domestic and communal lives of bondpeople. The private worlds that evolved in the slave quarters of the British Caribbean and Southern mainland between the mid-seventeenth and mid-eighteenth centuries differed not so much in kind as in the degree to which it proved possible for enslaved people to draw upon their African pasts to deal with present realities and future possibilities. . . .

Just as significant in the definition of slave culture as the total number of Africans imported and the ebb and flow of imports over time were the ethnic origins of those taken to the plantation colonies. Africans, wrote Richard Ligon in the mid-seventeenth century, were "fetched [to Barbados] from . . . Guinny and Binny, some from Cutchew, some from Angola, and some from the River of Gambia." They spoke "several languages, and by that means, one of them understands not another." Toward the end of the century an anonymous British author explained that "the safety of the Plantations depends upon having Negroes from all parts of Guiny, who not understanding each others languages and Customs, do not, and cannot agree to Rebel, as they would do . . . when there are too many Negroes from one Country." These two commentators were right about the diverse backgrounds of the Africans being shipped to Barbados, but they failed to record the often highly significant similarities between their "languages and Customs." These similarities reflected a combination of factors operating in West and West Central Africa together with evolving planter preferences for Africans from particular regions and ethnic groups.

The ethnic origins of the Africans shipped to the British plantation colonies varied regionally and over time. However, the ultimately reconcilable ethnic identities of many newly enslaved Africans are readily apparent. Before the mid-eighteenth century three regions of Africa, the Windward Coast, the Gold Coast, and the Bight of Benin, supplied roughly two-thirds of the Africans transported to the Americas by British slavers. By 1807, however, "approximately two-thirds of the African-born populations" of the British Caribbean had been drawn from the Bight of Biafra and central Africa. However, there were important variations in the African origins of the enslaved peoples of the British sugar islands. Thus, "the Bight of Biafra was the most important source of slaves [for] the southern Caribbean, but in the Leeward Islands Central Africa and Senegambia dominated." Just under half of all the Africans landed in Jamaica before 1807 were Ibos from the Bight of Biafra or BaKongo people from Central Africa.

In the Southern mainland, around 60 percent of the Africans imported into Virginia between 1718 and 1726 were from the Bight of Benin; during the 1730s roughly 85 percent came from the Bight of Biafra or Angola. Under 70 percent of the 8,045 Africans shipped to Charleston during the late 1730s had been brought from Angola, and another 6 percent are known to have originated in the Gambia region. Around 40 percent of the 2,500 Africans landed in Savannah between 1766 and 1771 came from Gambia, 16 percent came from Sierra Leone, and 10 percent came from Angola. Another 6 percent were said to be from "Gambia and Sierra Leone," while 3 percent had been brought from Senegal. Of the remainder, 14 percent were identified as having come from the "Rice Coast," 5 percent from the "Grain Coast," and the others simply from "Africa."

The African regions that predominated in the slave trade to the British plantation colonies were not ethnically monolithic, but "a single ethnic group often accounted for a large proportion of the slaves from a particular region." The extent to which particular groups were able to preserve their "cultural habits" once in the New World depended upon many factors, one of the most important of which was their concentration on any given estate or in any given neighborhood.

The precise local mix of ethnic origins in particular colonies varied, as did the size and the proximity of the estates upon which enslaved Africans found themselves. Slaveholdings in the Southern mainland were much smaller and far more dispersed than they were in the

British Caribbean. Local ratios of Europeans to Africans also varied, but everywhere in the Southern mainland they were much higher than in any of the sugar islands. In the early eighteenth century, for example, the South Carolina parish of Goose Creek contained around 500 enslaved Africans but about twice that number of Europeans; in Barbados and Jamaica, on the other hand, a single sugar plantation was likely to be worked by two or three hundred slaves under the direction of one white overseer. Colonial Georgia's largest slaveholder, Governor James Wright, held 523 bondpeople, thereby putting himself on a par with premier sugar planters. His slaves, however, were employed not on one but on eleven different plantations, indicative of the belief that the optimum number of workers per unit of rice production was between thirty and forty. Eminent rice and sugar planters may have had similar numbers of slaves, but they organized their operations very differently and in ways that were to be highly significant in the definition of the private lives constructed by their workforces.

Sex ratios and age structures were important in shaping many aspects of life in the slave quarters. As we have seen, most slave ships carried at least two men for every woman, and this imbalance persisted for varying lengths of time in the New World. For instance, during the 1730s, a decade of particularly heavy slave imports in Prince George's County, Virginia, the sex ratio was in the order of 187 men to every 100 women. On estates with more than ten slaves it soared to 249 to 100. Between 1755 and 1775 the ratio of men to women on Georgia estates was around 146 to 100, but on plantations with more than forty slaves it rose to 152 to 100. Depending upon the slaves' ethnic mix, the preservation of "cultural habits" might have been more viable on larger plantations, but it is also possible that their imbalanced sex ratios may have generated intense rivalries among men who were in search of sexual partners.

Richard Ligon and the anonymous pamphleteer of 1694 believed that varied African "language and customs" could be used by Europeans as a highly effective means of securing racial control. Their arrogant assumption was that Africans were intellectually incapable of transcending the linguistic and cultural differences that existed among them. In fact, these linguistic differences were not always as severe, or as insurmountable, as these contemporary commentators imagined them to be. Some Africans could find themselves in the unenviable position of Olaudah Equiano, who upon his arrival in Virginia discovered that he "had no person to speak to that I could understand," but many more, and perhaps the majority of those arriving in the plantation colonies through the middle years of the eighteenth century, did not.

The practice of loading slave ships at a single West African port meant that planters were often making their choices from among Africans who, if not "culturally homogeneous," were in all probability culturally compatible. These choices, especially in the case of eminent planters, usually involved the purchase of more than one person from any given shipment. Such purchases often resulted in the separation of couples, families, and friends, but they could also mean that "on large estates . . . slaves would typically have no trouble finding members of their own nation with whom to communicate." Subsequent purchases from slave ships that had set sail from a different African port could introduce to the plantation representatives from other ethnic groups. The resulting linguistic and cultural variations may have reflected a deliberate policy of ethnic mixing, but they could also have reflected nothing more than pragmatic decisions to satisfy labor requirements as and when the opportunities to do so arose.

The manner in which the transatlantic slave trade was organized and the purchasing habits of planters meant that enslaved Africans could be both united and divided by language. The reconciliation of linguistic differences was achieved in each of Britain's plantation colonies with a speed and a facility that often astounded Europeans. The spread of Islam in West and West Central Africa was a particularly important part of this process, providing as it did the fragments of a common vocabulary, if not of a common language. Within a comparatively short time, each of the plantation colonies had developed its own lingua franca. . . .

Writing in 1750, Hughes, the Anglican rector of the Barbadian parish of St. Lucy, noted that the "Mirth and Diversions" of the island's enslaved population "differ according to the Customs of so many Nations intermixed." He added that "the Negroes in general are very tenaciously addicted to the Rites, Ceremonies and Superstitions of their *own Countries*," but he did not suggest that these strongly held religious convictions were a source of overt physical conflict. Nor did he conclude, as have some recent scholars, that the communal performance of "Rites" and "Ceremonies," which he did not describe in detail, "may well have been occasions to recall national religions." Instead, Hughes chose to emphasize a different aspect of these religious celebrations that surely must have been as obvious to those in the ethnically commingled slave quarters of Barbados as it was to him: the essential compatibility of many of these "Rites, Ceremonies and Superstitions." . . .

In the early 1680s Morgan Godwyn, a churchman who was instrumental in persuading the Anglican hierarchy in London of the necessity and the desirability of proselytizing enslaved Africans, had claimed that bondpeople in Barbados and Virginia clung tenaciously to their "*Heathen Rites,*" to their "barbarous . . . behaviour and practice in *Worship* and *Ceremonies* of *Religion* . . . their *Polygamy* . . . their *Idolatrous Dances,* and *Revels.*" They had "brought out of Africa," Godwyn continued, various "*Recreations* and *Customs*" that demonstrated beyond any shadow of a doubt their "*Impiety*" and their "*Barbarity.*" Among the three "*Recreations* and *Customs*" specifically mentioned by Godwyn, probably because they were the best known to him, were the "*Idolatrous Dances,* and *Revels;* in which they usually spend their *Sunday* after the necessity of labour for their Provisions . . . has been complied with."

Godwyn acknowledged that "the *Gentiles* anciently did esteem and practice *Dancing,* as a part of *Divine Worship;* and no less also did the *Jews,*" but he claimed that the dances performed by Africans in Barbados and Virginia were but one of the more obvious manifestations of their "Idolatry." He based his "Conjecture" on the fact "that they use their Dances as a *means to procure Rain,*" presumably for their provision grounds rather than for their owners' cane and tobacco fields. Godwyn did not describe these ritual dances, but Ligon did. He emphasized that, in Barbados at any rate, there was "no mixt dancing" but that men and women performed their dances separately and "may dance a whole day [to] their Musick." As for "Their motions," Ligon recorded that "their hands [have] more of motion than their feet, and their heads more than their hands."

Writing a quarter of a century after Godwyn, Sir Hans Sloane made no mention of men and women dancing separately, but he did comment that their ritual dances entailed "great activity and strength of Body, and keeping time if it can be." The dancers had "Rattles ty'd to their Legs and Wrists, and in their Hands, with which they make a noise, keeping in time with one who makes a sound answering it on the mouth of an empty Gourd or Jar with his hands." In addition, it was "very often" the case that "they . . . tie Cow Tails to their Rumps, and add such other things to their Bodies in several places, as to give them a very extraordinary appearance." European commentators would continue to be both fascinated and repelled by what they regarded as the eroticism of the ritual dances performed by enslaved Africans. Unfortunately, their descriptions of these dances were usually so generalized as to preclude any possibility of linking them to specific African antecedents.

Just as distasteful to Morgan Godwyn as ritual dancing was the "confidence" placed by enslaved Africans "in certain Figures and ugly Representations, of none knows what besides themselves." In the absence of "more *Magnificent Temples*," these "Deities" were "usually enshrin[ed] in some *Earthern Potsherds*." Such was the power attributed to these "Deities," continued Godwyn, that "Fugitives and Runaways" were utterly convinced that they were "able to protect them in their Flight, and from Discovery." Godwyn failed to mention who had made and supplied these "Representations," but almost certainly they had been sanctified, if not made, by sacred specialists in the slave quarters.

The third of the "Customs" that Godwyn correctly surmised had been "brought out of Africa" was what he mistakenly referred to as "*Polygamy*." The main point at issue here was not the absence of sexual morality but the absence of a particular sexual morality: that predicated upon Anglican beliefs and assumptions concerning sexuality and marriage. In Barbados, Godwyn maintained, neither planters nor Anglican churchmen took much interest in the sexual partnerships formed by slaves. Bondpeople entered into such partnerships "by mutual agreement amongst themselves" and with a "frequent *repudiating* and changing of . . . Wives, usual amongst most *Heathens*." Godwyn concluded that it was principally because of the "*Connivance* and Toleration" of their owners that enslaved Africans continued to practice "Polygamie." Most planters, he charged, "esteeming them but as Cattle, and desirous of their *Encrease*, are apter to encourage, than to restrain them from it." . . .

Most European commentators, including the clergy, had little to say about the formation of family and kinship ties by slaves, including the patterns of courtship that preceded the taking of a marriage partner, whether the widespread African convention of dowries persisted, or the circumstances that might result in the voluntary dissolution of a marriage. However, from the few clues left by contemporary Europeans, it is clear that traditional African assumptions and practices were adapted to meet the requirements of the slave quarters. As John Woolman commented of the Chesapeake colonies in the 1740s, "Negroes marry after their own way."

One of the earliest descriptions of a marriage ceremony devised by slaves in the Southern mainland dates from 1731. The ritual took place in North Carolina and, in its fundamentals, would have been instantly recognizable in many parts of West and West Central Africa. According to John Brickell's account, "Their *Marriages* are generally performed amongst themselves, there being very little ceremony used upon that Head; for the Man makes the Woman a Present, such as a *Brass Ring* or some other Toy, which if she accepts of becomes his Wife; but if ever they part from each other, which frequently happens, upon any little Disgust, she returns his Present: These kind of Contracts no longer binding them, than the woman keeps the pledge give her." . . .

. . . [M]arriage was also a cause for public celebration, which affirmed and reaffirmed, at the same time it created, ties of family, kinship, and friendship that often extended beyond the boundaries of the plantation or plantations upon which the couple resided. In the 1740s, for example, Thomas Bacon wrote of the "small congregations . . . brought together" by slave marriages on Maryland's Eastern Shore. Almost forty years later, James Barclay remarked of the custom in the Carolina Low Country that if the couple to be married were "well acquainted in the place, multitudes of men, women and children, to the amount of several hundreds," would "flock together from the neighbouring plantations" to participate in the festivities. He added that marriages were usually "kept in the night," not for any specifically religious reason but "because in the day-time [slaves] must work for their masters." . . .

By the mid-eighteenth century sacred specialists figured prominently in virtually every European account of Africans in the British Caribbean. Europeans frequently confused the activities and precise significance of different sacred specialists, more often than not employing the generic term Obeah, or Obi, abbreviated forms of the Ashanti word *Obaye*. However, they were accurate on several points: It was generally held that "the Professors of *Obi* are, and always were, Natives of Africa, and none other" and that they had "brought the Science with them." This "Science," claimed Europeans, was "universally practiced" in the British Caribbean.

In describing Obeah, Europeans wrongly applied the term to witchcraft or sorcery and often confused witches with Myalmen and women. In fact, Obeah was the result of a fusion of religious offices, several of which originally had overlapping powers and functions, and shared common beliefs and practices of different African peoples. The fusion of functions is apparent in the powers that were ascribed to them by European observers. They included diagnosing and treating diseases—in Africa usually the work of a medicine man or a herbalist and sometimes a diviner; obtaining revenge for injuries or insults, or curing the bewitched—in Africa the responsibility of the witch doctor; the discovery and punishment of theft or adultery—in Africa the work of the diviner; and the prediction of future events—in Africa the work of highly trained mediums or diviners.

The cultural traditions of the various religious specialists were preserved directly through the slave trade, the vehicle by which they were transported to the New World. Under the disintegrating effects of bondage, most of the regalia of the sacred specialists and the paraphernalia of their practices was lost. However, many, if not most, of the ancient remedies, magical potions and ornaments, rattling gourds, and feathers and animal parts used in the conduct of religious offices, survived. The sacred offices themselves also survived, but they too began to change. By the eighteenth century they reappeared in a different form known in all the plantation colonies as Obeah.

PART

III Trades: The Atlantic Economy

To a considerable extent, it was trade that made the kingdoms, colonies, and ports of the North and South Atlantic into a mosaic of human experience, an "Atlantic world." Networks of trade crossed the Atlantic in all directions creating the famous triangular trade routes but also bilateral trade, quadrilateral trade, and additional combinations and interconnections of commerce. Trade not only connected different regions; it also linked various peoples. Mutual interests as well as force brought peoples together under the aegis of merchant capitalism.

The Portuguese and the Spanish were the first Europeans to create Atlantic trading networks. Carla Rahn Phillips examines the *Carrera de Indias,* the famous "Indies Run" of the treasure fleets to Seville from Panama and New Spain. The treasure of gold and silver, of course, was mined by Amerindian workers in Mexico and Peru. This labor force was largely coerced by means of tribute demands and systems of forced labor. Phillips also reveals the diversity of Spanish American trade with the metropolis: hides and dyes had an important place in Atlantic trade. In the northern reaches of North America, the "treasure" was beaver pelts and other animal skins, which were harvested by the fur trade. As Denys Delâge shows, this commercial relationship was voluntary and based on mutual self-interest, and strictly followed Indian procedures and customs.

In the tropical zones of the Atlantic, rich plantations with complex processing factories or mills were developed by the Portuguese, Spanish, Dutch, English, and French. From the fifteenth through the eighteenth century, this plantation complex produced some of the few Atlantic products—sugar and tobacco—that were as valuable as Asian spices. These agricultural and industrial enterprises were among the most capital-intensive businesses in the early modern world. Labor was scarce, however, in Madeira, the Canary Islands, Fernando Po, and São Tomé off the African coast and in Brazil, the "wild coast" of Guiana, and Barbados and other islands of the Caribbean. The plantations became dependent upon constantly renewed supplies of African slave labor. Hugh Thomas explains the interrelationship between the plantation complex and the Atlantic slave trade and reveals how Africans themselves were profoundly involved in this trade.

All of the threads of the Atlantic economy are woven together in the concluding essay by Charles Bergquist. He describes the "Atlantic system" of trade and production and traces the roots of modern development and underdevelopment to the use of free and coerced labor in the diverse American colonies. Why did the richest colonies become some of the poorest nations? Why did some of the poorest colonies become the core of the nation that became the richest in the world? An explanation of this paradox requires a broad, comparative—Atlantic—perspective.

Carla Rahn Phillips

The Spanish Treasure Fleets

Within the first fifty years after the first voyage of Columbus, the Spanish crown licensed expeditions all over South America and as far north as the southern quarter of North America. Local and regional governments were staffed by bureaucrats from the peninsula and integrated with the central government in Madrid. A system of taxes and tribute payments was established on the model of the Aztec and Inca systems. In addition to sustaining the local economies, production in the Indies supplied large quantities of gold, silver, precious gems, and industrial raw materials for Europe. Following the common mercantilist approach, the Spanish government sought to ensure that its colonies would support the home economy rather than compete with it. The colonies were organized to supply what Spain did not produce and to purchase manufactured goods and some agricultural products from Spain. Foreigners were legally excluded from direct trade with what the Spanish called the Indies; instead they had to deal through the port of Seville in the sixteenth and seventeenth centuries and through the port of Cádiz for much of the eighteenth century. Although monopoly trades rarely find favor with modern analysts, contemporary observers more often complained about being excluded than about the notion of monopoly itself.

The system regulating trade to the Spanish Empire was set up in 1503, under the so-called House of Trade (Casa de Contratación). From Seville, it supervised and regulated private trade and the vessels that carried it, and saw that tribute and the taxes on trade were collected and turned over to the crown. The merchants themselves had primary jurisdiction over commercial disputes, working through their

Carla Rahn Phillips, "The Growth and Composition of Trade in the Iberian Empires, 1450–1750," in *The Rise of Merchant Empires: Long-Distance Trade in the Early Modern World, 1350–1750,* James D. Tracy, ed. (Cambridge: Cambridge University Press, 1990), pp. 76–79, 100–101. Reprinted with the permission of Cambridge University Press.

Consulado in Seville. Although merchants generally preferred to arrange their own transport, it soon became clear that an organized system of convoys was the best way to protect shipping across the Atlantic. By the 1540s one fleet each year sailed for the Indies, dividing into two parts in the Caribbean. One part sailed on to New Spain (Mexico) and the other to Tierra Firme (northern South America) and then to Panamá. Later, two separate fleets served the two destinations. . . .

For the early years of imperial trade, figures on volume are very hard to come by. In their monumental study of the Indies trade, Pierre Chaunu and Huguette Chaunu relied on the number of ships and their recorded or calculated tonnage. By the 1520s nearly a hundred ships each year carried merchandise across the Atlantic between Spain and its American colonies. Together, the ships represented about 9,000 *toneladas* of carrying capacity, each tonelada being equivalent to about 1.42 cubic meters. By the late sixteenth century, a yearly average of 150–200 ships was involved in the Indies trade each year, with a total tonnage of about 30,000–40,000 toneladas (an average of 200 toneladas per ship). The number of ships had doubled since the 1520s, and their average size had also doubled, leading to a fourfold increase in carrying capacity. For comparison, Fernand Braudel has estimated that there were about 350,000 tons of shipping capacity in the Mediterranean in the late sixteenth century and 600,000–700,000 tons in the Atlantic for all maritime activities, including fishing.

In the late sixteenth and early seventeenth centuries, a regular guard squadron of six to eight galleons usually accompanied the Tierra Firme fleet; the New Spain fleet had a smaller escort of two galleons. The Tierra Firme squadron collected the year's treasure at Portobelo and returned to Spain as the escort of the previous year's merchant fleet. Although the convoy system was not as all-inclusive as its planners intended, it still accounted for about 85 percent of the trade. Even when convoys were abolished in the late eighteenth century, 85–90 percent of the trade still used the same timing and routes, which had proved ideal for sailing conditions in the Atlantic.

The system of imperial trade was fed by production in the Indies, reorganized from traditional patterns to suit the needs of international commerce. Livestock introduced from Europe multiplied easily in the New World, which had few domestic animals and no cattle, horses, or pigs before Spaniards brought them across the Atlantic. Soon hides and

tallow became major exports for the transatlantic trade. Other important exports were sugar, indigo (a blue vegetable dye), cochineal (or
grana, a red dye derived from small insects), exotic woods for construction and dye making, and a wide range of aromatic and medicinal
plants, either native to the Americas or introduced there for export production. A Dutch writer in the early seventeenth century noted that
combined plant and animal products from the Indies exceeded the
more famous gold and silver in value.

Figures for the exchange of individual products become available
from about 1550 on. By the early 1560s, about 27,000 hides a year were
exported from the Caribbean islands and New Spain. By the early
1570s, the number had risen to about 83,000, and by the early 1580s to
over 134,000. One recent study estimates the value of hides shipped in
the late sixteenth century at an average of 78,000,000 *maravedís* a year.
Exports of sugar from Spanish America were estimated at just over half
that, about 40,000,000 maravedís per year. The yearly export of sugar
could fluctuate widely. Fairly reliable figures show a yearly average of
about 32,000 arrobas in 1581–5 and only about 10,000 in 1586–90, at a
time when the Spanish colonies were under attack from pirates. Indigo, estimated to have been worth about 30,000,000 maravedís a year
in the late sixteenth century, also experienced wide yearly fluctuations.
Figures for indigo do not become available until the late 1570s, averag-
ing between 1,000 and 2,000 arrobas each year from then until the end
of the century. One of the most valuable single items was cochineal, estimated at about 125,000,000 maravedís a year in the late sixteenth
century, or nearly 42 percent of all products from the Indies. Its price
showed considerable fluctuation from year to year, but its quantity rose
fairly steadily, from about 1,800 arrobas in the late 1550s, to about
8,000 in the late 1580s. . . .

There is no question that the volume of long-distance trade from
southern Europe increased enormously during the early modern period, most of the increase coming from the overseas trading empires
first developed by the Portuguese and the Spanish. During the same
period trade within Europe, by land and sea, seems to have increased
as well, along with population and agricultural and industrial output.
Because much of the increase in trade within Europe was related to
overseas colonies and markets, it is difficult to separate long-distance

and intra-European trade. Nonetheless, it seems likely that the total volume of trade was substantially higher in 1750 than it had been in 1350.

The relationships between trade flows and other parts of the economy are infinitely complex. Although the discovery of silver in Spanish America (ca. 1545) and the discovery of gold in Brazil (ca. 1695) undoubtedly influenced the expansive phases of trade that followed them, it would be unwise to neglect other factors, such as changes in population size and in agricultural and industrial production, to explain that expansion. In other words, trade was not necessarily the driving force in the early modern economy, although it was often more visible and measurable than other activities. The role of trade can be fully understood only in relation to the economy as a whole. Trade to and from the Iberian empires served as a conduit for European agricultural and manufactured goods and American treasure, both inside and outside official channels. As precious metals from the Spanish and Portuguese empires flowed around the world, they supported the growth in global trade that characterized the early modern period.

The long-term expansion in trade carried within it several short-term fluctuations. Between about 1350 and 1450, the volume of trade in the Mediterranean seems to have declined, although some merchants in Italy and the Levant were able to profit despite the depression. Their success has often tended to mask the general contraction that followed the Black Death. From about 1450 to about 1610 or 1620, the global volume of trade expanded greatly, most visibly in the Asian trade of the Portuguese and the transatlantic trade of the Spanish. Then, from about 1620 to about 1680, a major slump occurred in the volume of trade across the Atlantic, across the Pacific, and within Europe, if the available figures can be trusted. By about 1680, most of the available figures had turned upward again. The eighteenth century experienced a generally upward trend, although with at least one setback. This pattern for long-distance trade is strikingly similar to the timetable now established for the European population and economy as a whole. It seems clear that a global system had emerged during the early modern centuries, linked by trade but not determined by it.

Denys Delâge

The Fur Trade
of New France

The French were the first to find themselves in a position to trade for furs in the Saint Lawrence. In terms of the weather, however, the choice of the shores of the Saint Lawrence for a European colony in North America had many drawbacks compared to other sites along the Atlantic coast. In general, the land around Quebec was free of frost for only about 130 days per year, and for only about 100 days downriver, northeast of Baie-Saint-Paul. The river froze over for four months of the year. This factor complicated trade with the West Indies. Furthermore, navigation on the Saint Lawrence was difficult. However, the French did not take these factors into account, as they merely intended to trade, not to colonize or farm the land. In 1608, a fort at Quebec offered distinct advantages for trade. Quebec had a commanding view of the river, and ships venturing into the narrows would come within range of French cannon. The Saint Lawrence and its tributaries covered an immense watershed, draining half the continent and providing access, especially northward, to the best furs. Also, because the French had arrived first and were well situated, they had established commercial alliances with the Algonkians and the Hurons, tribes that since pre-Columbian times had exchanged merchandise over a territory stretching from the Great Lakes to Hudson Bay. The French were the first Europeans to graft their activities onto this exchange network. At Quebec itself, trade took place with the Montagnais, using a sort of pidgin language that was half Montagnais, half French.

We may ask why, when intensive trading already took place at Tadoussac, the French wanted to establish themselves at Quebec and run the risk of the dangerous navigation involved in sailing upriver. It was

Reprinted with permission from Denys Delâge, "Trade and Merchant Capital in New France," in *Bitter Feast: Amerindians and Europeans in Northeastern North America, 1600–64* (Vancouver: UBC Press, 1993), pp. 93–98, 102–103.

precisely because trading was so intensive that the French sought another site. At Tadoussac, trading had been going on for almost a century, attracting numerous French and Basque ships as well as Dutch vessels. Competition had brought prices and profits down all over the Gulf, from the Acadian coast to Tadoussac.

In the seventeenth century, profits dropped drastically in North America, just as in Europe. The solution was to penetrate the interior in order to make contact with other Amerindians who were less familiar with trade, and to exclude European rivals by effectively establishing a monopoly. When Champlain came to Quebec in 1608, he did so in the name of the monopoly of Sieur de Monts and proceeded to build the first fort to block passage upriver, thereby excluding commercial rivals. The Basque merchants from Tadoussac tried to foil this plan by attempting to kill Champlain and gain entry to the fort, using the locksmith Jean Duval as a would-be assassin.

The French merchants who had been excluded—traders from La Rochelle, Saint-Malo, Saint-Jean-de-Luz, and Dieppe—applied pressure at home, and the monopoly was revoked in 1609. Free trade was restored between 1610 and 1612, and competition increased, as would be expected. The Montagnais, who were already seasoned traders, took advantage of the situation. At Tadoussac in 1611, these Amerindians, who had become "clever and crafty," refused to trade until "several ships had come together, in order to have better terms." This attitude, which ran counter to the rules of contractual commerce, can only be accounted for by the fact that a century of trade had been practised in a context of dog-eat-dog competition among fishing boats—transactions in which no one side could get the upper hand. The Montagnais had been forced to alter their traditional mode of exchange, as they had been unable to form a long-term alliance with a stable European partner, and probably because, in addition, they had been unable to obtain gifts that corresponded to their own generous presents.

The merchants then moved upriver to Montreal, where the Europeans' rapacious habits angered the Algonkins and Hurons, who were still unaccustomed to direct dealings with the newcomers. The large number of traders resulted in a surplus production of furs in France, followed by a drop in prices. However, the Amerindians were also competitive. For some years European products had been arriving via the Gulf, from where they were distributed through the ancient trade networks. The Montagnais and Micmacs were the initial middlemen, and at the turn of the century they were joined by the Algonkins and Hurons. The Iroquois (mainly the Mohawks), who were far from trading sites or boxed into their territory, managed to get trade goods by raiding and pillaging the Algonkin and Huron canoes. The latter tribes asked Champlain for military aid in driving off their rivals. Champlain and his men made two armed incursions against the Mohawks, one in 1609 and the other in 1610, reaching Mohawk territory via the Richelieu River. The surprise effect of French muskets made victory easy.

In the meantime, rival merchants from Rouen and Saint-Malo agreed to launch a new monopoly called the Société des Marchands. This new monopoly made the price of European products rise, much to the displeasure of the Montagnais, who now sought every opportunity to trade with smugglers downriver from Tadoussac. The Hurons and Algonkins, unfamiliar with the rules of international trade, were not yet aware of the connection between a monopoly and prices. For them, exchanges were carried out in an almost ritual fashion, in a context of celebration with speeches and dancing. There was no question of driving a bargain. The French profited from this ignorance. Around 1610, the Mohawks stopped raiding the Saint Lawrence valley. Champlain's victories notwithstanding, this was mainly because European goods could now penetrate the interior via the Hudson River, where the Dutch had begun to trade. However, the Oneidas and the Onondagas, Iroquois tribes that were still without easy access to European goods, continued to raid the Algonkins and the Hurons, who had to gather a thousand warriors to repel the attackers. These raids forced the Algonkins to ally themselves with the Hurons, who assumed leadership of the alliance. The Algonkins had a smaller, more dispersed population and were dependent on Huron corn for their survival; they were therefore obliged to give up their role as middlemen to the Hurons. In 1615, during a journey to Huron country, Champlain undertook a third military offensive against the Iroquois, and this sealed the alliance between the French and the Hurons—the most powerful Amerindian confederacy. From this moment on, soldiers armed with muskets lived among the Hurons to guarantee effective military defence against the Iroquois. A few missionaries and company agents joined them. In all, there were some thirty Europeans living with the Hurons.

In this way, the French assumed a position of strength in the fur trade. They had an excellent geographical position with access to the best source of furs in terms of quality and quantity, they had conducted a successful military campaign against the rivals of their Amerindian allies, they were associated with the most powerful Amerindian confederacy in the northeast, and finally, they held a monopoly with no immediate challengers in their trade with relatively naive Amerindian commercial partners.

Champlain, more than anyone, understood that simply being a trader was not enough when engaging in the fur trade. Amerindian mores must be taken into account. This was the secret of his success — not just the force of his personality, but his ability to organize the fur trade in ways that were compatible to the two economies. It was not a question of prices. For example, at the request of the Hurons, who met the French for the first time in 1609, an alliance was formed, then a common military expedition undertaken. There was an exchange of people who became both hostages and interpreters. An exclusive relationship was established between the two trading partners. In this respect, the French monopoly of the fur trade, although objectively disadvantageous to the Hurons in terms of the world market, was exactly what the latter sought. If trading also meant making peace, practising diplomacy, and creating friendships, then it was impossible to conclude treaties with a large number of competing sellers. The Hurons had no desire to trade with Champlain's competitors who went up the Saint Lawrence as far as Lac Saint-Louis just above Montreal. The Hurons refused to trade with merchants on whom they could not count for military support, and they formed an alliance with Champlain because he agreed to accompany them on military expeditions against the Iroquois. In more general terms, European powers gained a substantial foothold in North America because Amerindian societies insisted that the Europeans participate in their wars as a condition of trade.

When the French and Hurons met, whether at Sault Saint Louis, the mouth of the Richelieu, Trois-Rivières, or Quebec, their encounters were always accompanied by festivities that lasted several days. The merrymaking included shooting contests (with muskets), the exchange of presents, feasts, speeches, the actual trading, farewell presents, and so on. Quite apart from the ritual of exchange, Champlain had comprehended a more fundamental aspect of Amerindian society—the spirit of giving. To get a picture of this, we must look at two passages, one describing the beginning of a trading session in 1611, and another describing the end of one in 1633.

The 1611 trading session opened thus: "After they had spun and danced enough, the others [Hurons], who were in their canoes also began to dance by several movements of their bodies. When the song was over, they came on land with a few furs and gave gifts similar to those offered by the others. We reciprocated with presents of equal value. The next day, they traded what little furs they had, & again gave me a special present of thirty beavers, for which I recompensed them."

The closing of the 1633 session was described thus: "Sieur de Champlain made his presents, which corresponded in value to those that the Hurons had made him. To accept presents from the Savages is to bind oneself to return an equivalent."

What is striking about these two citations is the insistence on exchanges of equal value, on reciprocity. Merchants were usually looking for surplus value and often boasted of having bartered shoddy goods for the furs received. In both the operations described above, Champlain made no profit—a circumstance that seems amazing at first glance. In the first round of giving, Champlain gave generous gifts, which obliged the Hurons to be more generous in the second round. However, the real trading took place in this second round—that is, the bartering of furs for French merchandise. With the exchange finished, Champlain showed renewed generosity on the last day by offering gifts that encouraged the Hurons to come back the next year. Thus, "without breaking with the custom of the country," Champlain turned the Huron rules of exchange to his advantage. . . .

Each year the Hurons would come down from their country to meet the French. On the day of arrival, they settled in and built longhouses. On the second day, they held council and made gifts to the French to reaffirm their friendship. Speeches and presents were always symbolically linked. A gift was one's word, and one's word was a gift. To refuse a gift was to refuse the word that accompanied it. The French accommodated themselves to this and to other customs of the country, and learned the language of gifts and metaphors. They in turn gave presents that spoke of friendship and hospitality and offered a great feast to their trading partners: "sagamité, composed of peas, of breadcrumbs or powdered sea biscuit, and of prunes; all this was boiled together in a great kettle which is used for making beer, with water and no salt." During the third and fourth days, the Hurons exchanged their pelts and tobacco for blankets, axes, kettles, cloaks, iron arrowheads, little glass cannons, shirts, and similar articles. A council was again held on the fifth day, to the accompaniment of dancing and singing. The French gave a farewell feast and displayed their gifts in the middle of the meeting place. The governor usually took the opportunity of insisting that the Hurons convert to Christianity, giving more presents to new converts, and finally wished them a good journey. "Monsieur le chevalier had these people [the Hurons] told that he presented them a barrel of hatchets and of iron arrow-heads. Part of this was to waft their canoes gently homewards, part to draw them to us next year."

At last, the Hurons left, or as the *Jesuit Relations* described it, "The next morning they disappear like a flock of birds." There was little of the European marketplace in all this. Trading was carried out largely according to the forms of primitive commerce: an alliance that joined the partners in a pact of generosity, carried out in a highly symbolic ceremony; the absence of competitive bargaining on either side; trading sessions lasting several days, and so on. Despite appearances, however, trading was dominated by the market economy. The French offered lavish hospitality, and the Hurons were obliged to do the same. At precisely the moment when the Hurons were the debtors according to their system of giving, they entered the company trading post for the exchange of goods. The French had been generous in diplomacy; now the Hurons must be generous in "business." Champlain's strategy continued to prevail—no profit in the public arena, all the profit during trading in the company store. The company was obliged to maintain fairly fixed prices, nevertheless, because the Hurons would have interpreted any fluctuation in relation to the market as trickery and treason.

The French had decoded the Amerindian system of exchange. They had understood that gifts circulated and were sure to bring a return, but that by definition time was needed to produce any reciprocal benefit. Since the idea of a term (in the sense of a payment at a later date) was current in primitive commerce, the French were able to link this with extending credit, which they did following the destruction of Huronia. Merchants made increasingly large advances of merchandise to resident Amerindians. What was a financial transaction for one party was a transaction of honour for the other.

Hugh Thomas

The Transatlantic Slave Trade

The Atlantic slave trade took the shape that it did in consequence of the survival of slavery in the Mediterranean world during the Middle Ages. Black slaves had been carried to all the principalities in North Africa and the eastern Mediterranean for hundreds of years, beginning in ancient Egypt. Those slaves in antiquity derived principally from Ethiopia, with the consequence that, as late as the fifteenth century, black slaves were often known as "Ethiops," whencesoever they really derived. The expansion of Muslim power in West Africa during the Middle Ages made possible an expansion of a trade in black slaves northwards across the Sahara from West Africa: the traveler Ibn Battutah recorded meeting them at almost every stage of his journey there in the fourteenth century; and he left with six hundred women slaves. Black Africans worked as servants, soldiers, and in fields in the Arab Mediterranean. Throughout modern history, blacks were especially sought after as eunuchs in the Muslim world, for use both as civil servants and in harems: the well-known picture by the painter Levnî in Istanbul entitled *The Chief Black Eunuch Conducts the Young Prince to the Circumcision Ceremony* is dated c. 1720–32; but it could have represented a scene at any time between 1000 A.D. and 1900.

Some black slaves reached Muslim Spain and Portugal from Africa in the late Middle Ages, and some went to the Christian territories: indeed, the religious brotherhood still known as "Los Negritos" was founded in Seville in the late fourteenth century by a benign archbishop.* Not long afterwards, the Portuguese began first to kidnap, and then to barter for, slaves as they made their way down the west coast of Africa in the second half of the fifteenth century. They were looking for

---

*The brotherhood seems now to be entirely white, but it was black until the eighteenth century.

Reprinted with the permission of Simon & Schuster from "The Slave Trade: A Reflection," in *The Slave Trade: The Story of the Atlantic Slave Trade: 1440–1870,* by Hugh Thomas (New York: 1998), pp. 792–98. Copyright © 1997 by Hugh Thomas.

gold but, finding little of it, made do with men and women. These slaves were brought back to Lisbon and sold either there or in Spain or Italy; the Lisbon Florentine Bartolommeo Marchionni, a renaissance man in every sense of the word, became the first modern European slave merchant on the grand scale.

King Ferdinand the Catholic of Aragon and the King-Emperor Charles V did not realize that they were initiating a great change when, in the early sixteenth century, they gave permission, first for two hundred, then for four thousand, slaves to be carried to the New World. Yet they were nonetheless the pioneers of the slave trade as we know it: when the admirable North American novelist Louis Auchincloss caused his character Winthrop Ward, in the story "The Beauty of the Lilies," to ask himself, walking down to his office in Wall Street in 1857, why had "the first blithering idiot to bring a black man in irons to the New World not been hanged?" he was unwittingly referring to those monarchs.

The reason why the Atlantic slave trade lasted so long is that, in the Americas, the Africans proved to be admirable workers, strong enough to survive the heat and hard work on sugar, coffee, or cotton plantations or in mines, in building fortresses or merely acting as servants; and, at the same time, they were good-natured and usually docile. Many black slaves had experience of agriculture and cattle. Both indigenous Indians and Europeans seemed feeble compared with them. That was why European slaves, of whom there had been some in Spain, especially from Greece or the Balkans, in the fifteenth century, were never tried out in the Americas. African Muslim slaves were more difficult to control for, as the Brazilians found in the 1830s in particular, some of them were at least as cultivated as their masters, and were capable of mounting formidable rebellions.

This large labor force would not have been available to the Europeans in the Americas without the cooperation of African kings, merchants, and noblemen. Those African leaders were, as a rule, neither bullied nor threatened into making these sales (for sales they were, even if the bills were settled in textiles, guns, brandy, cowrie shells, beads, horses, and so on). When, in 1842, the sultan of Morocco told the British consul that he thought that "the traffic in slaves is a matter on which all sects and nations have agreed from the time of the sons of Adam," he could have been speaking for all African rulers; or indeed all European ones fifty years before. There were few instances of Africans' opposing the nature of the traffic desired by the Europeans.

Some slaves were stolen by Europeans—"panyared," as the English word was—and some, as occurred often in Angola, were the victims of military campaigns mounted specifically by Portuguese proconsuls in order to capture slaves. But most slaves carried from Africa between 1440 and 1870 were procured as a result of the Africans' interest in selling their neighbors, usually distant but sometimes close, and, more rarely, their own people. "Man-stealing" accounted for the majority of slaves taken to the New World, and it was usually the responsibility of Africans. Voltaire's sharp comment that, while it was difficult to defend the conduct of Europeans in the slave trade, that of Africans in bartering each other was even more reprehensible, deserves to be better remembered. But then there was no sense of Africa: a Dahomeyan did not feel that he had anything in common even with an Oyo.

The slave trade was a disgraceful business even if considered in relation to the other brutalities of the time: the ill-treatment of workers generally in Europe (as well as of sailors and of soldiers), and the harsh way in which indentured English laborers, for example, or their French (the *engagés*) and other European equivalents were looked after. The traveler William Baikie was right when he pointed out, after a journey to Africa in the 1850s, "There is no captain who has carried slaves who has not been, either directly or indirectly, guilty of murder, [for] a certain number of deaths are always allowed for." For captains, read also merchants; for, though some of those traders were quite insulated from knowing what the slave trade was, and looked upon it as just one more business, a high proportion of them had once been captains or mates in the traffic and, in their calm houses in Liverpool or Nantes, could easily imagine the crowding, the smell, the savagery, and the fears normal on every voyage which they financed.

The consequence for the Americas was remarkable. In the first three and a quarter centuries of European activity in the Americas, between 1492 and 1820, five times as many Africans went to the New World as did white Europeans; and, even in the next fifty years, until 1870, probably as many blacks were taken to Brazil and Cuba as there were white men arriving in the continent. Most of the great enterprises of the first four hundred years of colonization owed much to African slaves: sugar in Brazil and later the Caribbean; rice and indigo in

South Carolina and Virginia; gold in Brazil and, to a lesser extent, silver in Mexico; cotton in the Guianas and later in North America; cocoa in what is now Venezuela; and, above all, in clearing of land ready for agriculture. The only great American enterprise which did not use black labor extensively was the silver mining at Potosí in Peru, and that was only because they were at too high an altitude for Africans to be able to work there with their usual energy. The servants of the Americas between Buenos Aires and Maryland were for four centuries usually black slaves.

Henri Wallon, the moralistic French nineteenth-century historian of slavery in antiquity, argued that the discovery of the Americas was an accidental development which led to retrogression in Europe: the settlement of America offered, he said, to a small group of selfish merchants and planters the chance to upset, through the development of large-scale slavery, the course of progress. But slavery had continued throughout the Middle Ages in Europe, and it was not only merchants, but kings and noblemen who inspired much of the early slave trading. Yet there is a sense in which Wallon was right: most of northern Europe had said good-bye to slavery by the early twelfth century. Most countries there which allowed themselves to become implicated in the slave trade to the Americas had some hesitations first. Richard Jobson in England, Bredero in the Netherlands, Mercado and Albornoz in Spain, Fernão de Oliveira in Portugal, not to speak of King Louis XIII in France were exponents of a different attitude at the end of the sixteenth century or at the beginning of the seventeenth. The reason why these humane doubts or even open hostility had no effect is surely to be accounted for by the memory of antiquity which dominated culture and education for the next three centuries. If Athens had slaves with which to build the Parthenon, and Rome to maintain the aqueducts, why should modern Europe hesitate to have slaves to build its new world in America? Busbecq's regret should be remembered.

The effect of this traffic on Europe and on the Americas was considerable. The slave trade should not be seen as the main, much less the sole, inspiration of any particular development in industry or manufacture in Europe or North America. The memory of Dr. Eric Williams may haunt the modern study of the Atlantic slave trade, but his shocking argument that the capital which the trade made possible financed the industrial revolution now appears no more than a brilliant *jeu d'esprit.* After all, the slave-trading entrepreneurs of Lisbon and Rio, or Seville and Cádiz, did not finance innovations in manufacture. Yet those who became rich as a result of trading slaves often did put their profits to interesting uses: Marchionni, for instance, invested in Portuguese journeys of discovery, as did Prince Henry the Navigator; John Ashton of Liverpool, helped to finance the Sankey Brook Canal, between his own city and Manchester; René Montaudoin was a pioneer of cotton manufacture in Nantes, and so was James de Wolf in Bristol, Rhode Island. Such investments aside, the slave trade had a great effect on shipbuilding, on marine insurance, on the rope industry, on ships' carpenters in all interested ports, as also on textile manufacture (such as linen in Rouen), the production of guns in Birmingham and Amsterdam, and iron bars in Sweden, of brandy in France and rum in Newport, not to speak of beads from Venice and Holland, and on the sugar refineries near important European and North American ports.

The effect of this emigration on Africa is extraordinarily difficult to estimate, for it is unclear what the population of Africa was at any stage before 1850. Still, most of the millions of slaves shipped from Africa were not members of an established slave population, but ordinary farmers or members of their families, suddenly deprived of their liberty by fellow Africans in response to what a modern economist might call "growing external demand." Professor W. M. Macmillan, in *Africa Emergent*, argued that Africa was, for many centuries, underpopulated. He attributed the continent's backwardness to the "lack of human resources" adequate to tame an inhospitable environment. Then Dr. Dike, most eminent of a new generation of African historians in the 1960s, insisted that, whatever might be the position in Central Africa, that could not be true of Iboland, in what is now southeastern Nigeria, where land hunger has been the most important "conditioning factor" in history.

The truth is that, though a drop in population may have been caused by the sustained trade in slaves, a fertile population would have added as many as, or more than, it lost in the slave trade as a result of normal reproduction. Most statistics suggest that females, after all, constituted only a third of the slaves transported, even if most of them probably were of childbearing age. A fast-growing population might even have found relief from the inevitable pressure on resources through the export of some of its members. If, as seems possible, the population of West Africa in the early eighteenth century was about twenty-five million, enjoying a rate of growth of, say, seventeen per thousand, the effect of the export slave trade (say, 0.2 percent of the population a year) would merely have been to check the growth in population, since the rate of slave exports and that of natural increase would have been more or less the same. The introduction of those two wonderful crops, maize and manioc, also did something to compensate Africa for whatever loss it suffered in population by being implicated in the Atlantic slave trade.

There were some obvious political effects. One was to strengthen those monarchies or other entities which collaborated with the Europeans, above all, naturally, the coastal kings; and the riches obtained from the sale of slaves enabled some rulers to extend their political, as well as their commercial, activities into the interior. The growth of the slave trade clearly helped some states, such as Dahomey, to expand and consolidate themselves. But Benin avoided the trade and also matured as a state. The slave trade must have encouraged African monarchies not just to go to war (they had always done that) but to capture more prisoners than before, and to substitute capture for killing in battle. Dispersed coastal communities often experienced, as a result of the slave trade, territorial growth, political centralization, and commercial specialization. That may have been a consequence of European traders' desire to gather an entire cargo from a single port. Thus the city of New Calabar vigorously developed its own version of monarchy. By 1750, the Efik had excluded all other Africans from contacts with the Europeans, and their political leader (Duke Ephraim, of Duke Town, in the nineteenth century) had political control over all the local slave trade, dominating his city without being formally a ruler, much as the Medici had done in Florence. But Calabar was a tiny city-state considered against the powerful internal empires, even if it was important in the coastal slave trade; and those empires, from the Songhai to the Oyo, not forgetting the Vili in Loango or the Congo and the various monarchies in what is now Angola, seem to have risen and declined without being decisively affected by the Atlantic commerce.

The effects on the African economy, apart from the matter of population, were also diverse. One was to stimulate the idea of a currency: thus cowries became a general trading currency in the Niger Delta, displacing old iron currencies there, while European-made iron bars, copper rods, and brass manillas also played a part. Yet cowries were increasing in circulation in "Guinea" before the doom-laden Portuguese caravels first drew inshore.

One effect on coastal African agriculture was to stimulate the growth of rice, yams, and later manioc and maize, and even the development of cattle, to provide the slave ships or the slave prisons—the *"captiveries,"* as the French customarily described them—with at least a modicum of food while the captives were awaiting embarkment. The success of slaving as a commercial proposition also implied that many older businesses—such as the trade in palm oil, gum, cattle, kola nuts, even ivory—diminished. Only gold remained an effective competitor to the slave trade. But all those other things survived, especially the first, to be revived in the nineteenth century.

The entrepreneurial spirit of Africa must have been stimulated by the Atlantic slave trade. Most European captains came to realize that their negotiating partners knew as much about European practices as the Europeans knew of them. The era of the trade also saw a great expansion of fairs, and an expansion too of the overall level of trade, in which the traffic in slaves formed only a part. Africans involved in the trade, however, benefited greatly. Some of that wealth was creatively used locally. The prosperity of the entrepôts stimulated employment; and the trade necessitated large numbers of porters, canoemen, and guards at every port along the West African coast.

It is also interesting to speculate on the effects of the imports deriving from the sale of slaves. The slave-trading peoples chose carefully the goods which they exchanged for slaves, and so slave ships had often to be floating general stores, for a European trader would look foolish if he arrived off Loango, say, with a supply of brandy when a previous ship had sold all that the ruler or the merchants concerned needed at that time.

As has been repeatedly noticed, the item most commonly exchanged for slaves was cloth. The import of woolens and cottons did not inspire a tailoring industry, because most Africans liked to wear those European goods untailored, wrapping the cloths round them. But local spinning, weaving, and dyeing did not as a rule suffer. The production of African woolen cloth even appears to have expanded in many places. Despite the apparent abundance of imports, foreign cloth remained rare enough in the hinterland of, say, southeastern Nigeria not to compete with traditional local products either in price or quality.

The most interesting aspect of the slave trade is that, during the five hundred years of constant contact between the Africans and the Europeans, the former did not develop further in imitation of the latter. The reluctance of Africans to Europeanize themselves is often presented as a weakness. But it is more likely to be explained by some innate strength of the African personality which, however close the political or commercial relation with the foreigner, remains impervious to external influence. . . .

Any historian of the slave trade is conscious of a large gap in his information. The slave himself is a silent participant in the account. One may pick the slave out of a seventeenth-century engraving of Benin, let us say, in one of the many handsome illustrations to the famous travelogue of Jean Barbot. One learns a little of a few slaves in the reports of Eustache de Fosse in the fifteenth century or de Marees in the sixteenth; the sieur de la Courbe Barbot, or Bosman in the seventeenth, or, let us say, Alexander Falconbridge or Captain Landolphe, among innumerable memoirs, in the eighteenth. Pío Baroja, a great Spanish writer, has vividly depicted the life of nineteenth-century slave captains in fiction. In the nineteenth century, there are the splendid designs of Rugendas, some of them reproduced in the book. He may find a few direct testimonies of slaves from the late eighteenth or the nineteenth century. . . . The best of these is probably the memorable work of Equiano, several times cited. But how pitifully small is the material! Nor has the historian any means of knowing whether those few spokesmen speak for the captives whose fate he has followed as best he can over five centuries. For the slave remains an unknown warrior invoked by moralists on both sides of the Atlantic, recalled now in museums in one-time slave ports from Liverpool to Elmina, but all the same unspeaking, and therefore remote and elusive. Like slaves in antiquity, African slaves suffered but the character of their distress may be more easily conveyed by novelists such as Mérimée than chronicled by a historian. Perhaps, though, the dignity, patience, and gaiety of the African in the New World is the best of all memorials.

Charles Bergquist

The Paradox of American Development

Climate, race, and culture are fundamental to understanding the divergent development of the societies of the Americas. But each was mediated historically by the economic roles the colonies came to play in the wider Atlantic trading system. The nature of those roles, in turn, structured the evolution of the labor systems that defined the developmental potential of each colony. Although a variety of labor systems existed in all of the American colonies, and all of them experienced free labor as well as forms of coerced labor, over time one type of labor system or the other, free or coerced, came to typify each of them. Around these systems of free or coerced labor developed characteristic patterns of social stratification, income and land distribution, political institutions, and cultural attitudes. Together, these factors structured the developmental potential of the colonies, and that of the independent states they became.

The divergent development of the American colonies is sharply framed by the paradox signaled in the title of this chapter. How did the wealthiest American colonies become the poorest nations of the hemisphere, and the poorest colonies become the core of the nation that became the richest in the world? Answering that question reveals the fallacies in explanations of United States and Latin American development that make culture, race, and climate the determining factors. The extreme examples of divergent development sketched below point instead to the centrality of colonial labor systems in the development of the United States and Latin America.

Charles Bergquist, "The Paradox of American Development," in *Labor and the Course of American Democracy: U.S. History in Latin American Perspective* (London: Verso, 1996), pp. 14–25. Copyright © 1996 by Verso.

Saint Domingue/Haiti. By the end of the eighteenth century, the French colony of Saint Domingue, situated on the western third of the Caribbean island of Hispaniola, was the largest sugar producer in the world. Measured in terms of the wealth it generated, it was also the richest colony in the Americas. In 1791 its 480,000 black slaves (in a total population that included a mere 40,000 whites and some 25,000 mulattos) were producing more than 78,000 tons of sugar a year, which accounted for more than half of the value of France's colonial trade. Today independent Haiti is the poorest nation (measured in income per person) in the Western Hemisphere.

Upper Peru/Bolivia. During the sixteenth and seventeenth centuries, silver made Upper Peru the most lucrative Spanish colony in South America. Most of the silver was extracted by Indians forced by Spanish authorities to labor in the mines. In 1570, the population of Potosí, located at the richest mine, numbered some 160,000, making it the largest city in the Americas. Silver was by far the most important export of colonial Spanish America, and, along with Mexico, Upper Peru produced almost all of it. Yet today independent Bolivia has the lowest per capita income of Spain's ex-colonies in South America.

New England. In contrast, the British colonies of New England were initially the poorest of the Americas. Having neither precious metals, nor the warm climate to produce agricultural staples in demand in Europe, they met their subsistence and local needs largely through small-scale diversified farming and craft production based on family and free wage labor. By the end of the colonial period, however, these societies were among the most prosperous and dynamic in the Americas. Following independence, and the victory of the North over the South in the Civil War, their institutions shaped the nation that became the richest and most industrialized in the hemisphere.

South Carolina. Quite different was the experience of the British colonies of southern North America. The rice-exporting region of eastern South Carolina, for example, an economy based on slave labor, had the highest white per capita wealth of any part of British North America in the late eighteenth century. Yet by 1900 this region was the poorest part of the poorest census zone in the United States.

These are extreme examples, but they highlight broader patterns of colonial development in the Americas. They show how climate, natural resources (particularly precious metals), and labor supplies deeply influenced the economic possibilities of the American colonies, and the role each would play within the wider Atlantic system.

The European powers created the Atlantic system as a consequence of their chronic trade deficit with Asia. Except for precious metals, which they mined in limited quantities, Europeans produced little that they were able to exchange for the spices and luxury items they imported from the East. Mercantilism, the theory that guided the economic policies of the European states in the sixteenth and seventeenth centuries, was a direct response to these balance-of-trade problems. Acting on mercantilist principles, governments sought to maximize the nation's exports, minimize its imports, and accumulate bullion (gold or silver) in the hands of the state. Colonies outside Europe came to play a central role in mercantilist strategy. They served as sources of the bullion and raw materials European nations could not produce for themselves. Colonies also consumed exports, preferably high-value manufactures, of the metropolis. Each European power sought to acquire an empire, and, by monopolizing trade within it, pursued maximum advantage against its European rivals. War between the powers was often the result. The colonies were the spoils.

The European explorers of the fifteenth and sixteenth centuries sought new sources of gold more than anything else. Exploration also aimed at reducing the cost of Asian imports by seeking a way around the Near-Eastern middlemen who controlled the trade between Europe and Asia. Beginning in the fifteenth century, the Portuguese located supplies of gold in Africa, and by the end of that century they had discovered the way around Africa to Asia. It was the Spaniards, however, searching for a shorter, more direct western route to Asia, who discovered America and appropriated its most valuable parts.

Once in the New World, Spaniards' quest for gold quickly led them to the great highland agrarian civilizations of Mexico and Peru. There they discovered the most numerous and most tractable labor force in the Americas. In Mexico, as was to happen all over the Americas, European contact led to rapid population decline among the native Americans. Indians died resisting European conquest and settlement. They lived shorter lives as a result of labor exploitation and reorganization of patterns of land use and settlement. Most of all they died from European diseases, from which they had no immunity. The result was a demographic disaster of a magnitude unequalled in recorded human history. In central Mexico alone an indigenous population estimated at 25 million on the eve of conquest in 1519 fell to little more than a million a century later. The Spaniards extracted tribute and labor service from this rapidly declining Indian population. Slowly they consolidated the large rural agricultural estates worked by dependent labor that came to characterize Spanish colonial society throughout the Americas.

But mining, not agriculture, was to be Spanish America's primary role in the Atlantic system during the colonial period. By the mid-sixteenth century the Spanish had discovered great silver mines in Mexico and Upper Peru, and silver became the main export of Spanish America to Europe during the next two and a half centuries. American silver had a major impact on European development, contributing to the economic decline of Spain and the rise of Spain's Western European rivals, especially Britain. Silver-driven price inflation undercut the competitiveness of Spanish manufactures and financed Spain's costly and ultimately fruitless military pretensions in Europe. Manufactures from Britain, funnelled legally through Spanish merchant monopolies, or illegally through the contraband trade, eventually supplied the bulk of the import needs of Spanish America, and those of Portuguese Brazil as well.

The Portuguese in Brazil encountered Indian peoples much smaller in numbers than those the Spaniards found in Peru and Mexico. These lowland peoples were also more egalitarian in social structure and less sedentary and dependent on agriculture than the Indian societies of the highlands. For all these reasons the Indians of Brazil—like their counterparts in the rest of lowland South America, the Caribbean, and North America north of central Mexico—proved much more resistant to European encroachment and labor demands. They fought a running battle to maintain their way of life along the advancing frontier of European settlement. Eventually, all these peoples—in Brazil and in the rest of the Americas outside the South and Central American highlands—were virtually exterminated.

The Portuguese then turned to African slaves for labor. They already controlled the West African coast and had developed a trade with Europe in African slaves. Slaves provided the labor for the large sugar estates the Portuguese established in northeast Brazil in the sixteenth century. Slaves produced all the major exports of Brazil during the next three centuries. They mined the fabulous gold and diamond reserves discovered in central Brazil in the eighteenth century. They produced the coffee, grown in the south-central region, which by the time of abolition in 1888 supplied roughly two-thirds of world demand. Brazil alone consumed almost half of the estimated ten million African slaves shipped to America.

On the Caribbean islands, many of which, like Saint Domingue, were originally claimed by Spain but fell to other Western European powers in the seventeenth and eighteenth centuries, the pattern was much the same. The indigenous people were rapidly exterminated and eventually huge numbers of African slaves (almost half those sent to America before the nineteenth century) were brought in to produce staples, primarily sugar, for export to Europe.

Table 1, drawn from Ralph Davis, *The Rise of the Atlantic Economies*, reveals the timing and magnitude of reliance on slave labor in the European colonies of the Americas. Readers should be aware that these figures are estimates. The precise numbers of slaves imported into the Americas remain in doubt.

TABLE 1	Imports of Slaves to America (in thousands), 1600–1781			
	Before 1600	*1600–1700*	*1700–1781*	*Total*
British North America	–	–	256	256
Spanish America	75	293	393	761
Brazil	50	560	1,285	1,895
Caribbean				
British	–	261	961	1,222
French	–	157	990	1,147
Dutch and Danish	–	44	401	445
Total	125	1,315	4,286	5,726

While the Spanish and Portuguese were the first to rely on slave labor, by the seventeenth century and, especially, the eighteenth the other

European powers, the British primary among them, were importing massive numbers of slaves into their colonies in the Americas.

Before they turned to slave labor, however, the non-Spanish European colonies of the Caribbean — as well as those of the North American mainland — depended on another form of coerced labor, indentured servitude. Under this system workers (primarily young males) contracted in Europe to come to America on the condition that they work for three to five or more years. Following their service they were to be granted land, a wage (often paid in kind as a quantity of sugar or tobacco), or tools and clothing. They could then aspire to become independent farmers or artisans, or at least free wage workers. Indentured servants, like slaves, had no political rights and were often subjected to brutal exploitation. Like slaves they could be punished for insubordination or attempted flight with whippings or even mutilation.

Reliance on the labor of indentured servants differentiated the American colonies of the other European powers, especially those of Britain, from the colonies of Spain and Portugal. During the seventeenth and eighteenth centuries population growth and the rapid commercialization of the British and Western European economies created a large pool of uprooted poor, many of whom seized the opportunity to improve their situation by binding themselves in temporary servitude in the New World. Spain and Portugal, in contrast, experienced no such fundamental internal transformation. The modest number of immigrants they sent to the New World were usually free and often of considerable means. Unable to take advantage of coerced white labor drawn from the mother country, the Spanish and Portuguese depended from the beginning on coerced Indian labor and African slaves in their American colonies.

But while the other European colonies in America initially depended heavily on the labor of white indentured servants, only some of them eventually came to rely on African slaves to meet their labor needs. Why did some of these colonies come to depend on slave labor, while others did not? The answer to this question holds the key to understanding the paradox of American development. It is revealed most clearly in the experience of the British American colonies, especially those that eventually formed the United States.

From virtually the beginnings of settlement, all of the American British colonies depended on indentured servants to meet part of their labor needs. Most of these colonies — from New England to the West

Indies—developed initially as diversified agricultural economies, in which patterns of landholding and income distribution were, certainly by European standards of the day, relatively egalitarian.

Wherever there was a shift in these colonies to large-scale production of agricultural staples for export, however, African slaves, not white indentured servants, came to supply the bulk of the labor force. Scholars estimate that during the whole period up to the time of the declaration of US independence in 1776, a million and a half slaves were imported into the British colonies in America. Roughly a million and a quarter of these slaves went to the sugar colonies of the West Indies, most of the rest to the southern colonies of the North American mainland. The best estimate of the number of indentured servants who came to British America during the same period is 350,000, more than a quarter of the slaves imported.

The decision by planters in the British colonies to rely increasingly on African slave labor was a complex one, and the relative weights of the numerous considerations involved are still debated by historians. Contrary to modern myth, white servants proved capable of hard agricultural labor in the tropics. Yet Europeans never considered enslaving their own kind. Racial and cultural attitudes reserved the brutality of outright slavery for black, initially non-Christian, aliens. The temporary bondage of Europeans from the laboring classes did, however, prove an attractive alternative to African slavery, at least at the beginning. As noted above, in Britain during the seventeenth and eighteenth centuries there was an abundant supply of unemployed or poor farmers, artisans, and laborers who were willing to indenture themselves in America in the hope of eventually improving their condition. Indeed, indentured servants continued to stream into the southern as well as the northern mainland British colonies until the end of the colonial period.

Initially, at least, the cost to planters of a servant's passage to America was similar to the cost of an African slave. And unlike owners of slaves, masters of servants had special reasons for working their servants to death, which many seem to have done. During the seventeenth century most indentured servants in North America died before their service was up, eliminating any need to compensate them. Toward the end of that century, however, in places like Virginia, mortality rates declined and the option of buying a slave for life, rather than contracting with a servant for a few years, became more attractive.

The decision by planters to shift away from reliance on white indentured servants toward African slave labor seems to have been decisively affected by their judgments of the relative capacity of their laborers to resist. Unlike slaves, servants could appeal to the courts. And because they were white, and shared the culture and spoke the language of the free people in these societies, they had special reasons to insist on their rights and even to believe they might escape. Indentured servants were also armed psychologically by the fact that they had voluntarily submitted themselves to temporary bondage in order to improve their situation in life. When those expectations were frustrated they could become an explosive social force.

This dynamic has been documented most clearly in the shift toward slave labor in Virginia. The shift began in earnest in the tobacco-producing region of the colony in the 1680s, following a major revolt known as Bacon's Rebellion. That rebellion began as an assault on Indian lands by land-hungry whites. It ended in a movement that challenged royal authority and the planter elite itself. The rebels included some slaves promised freedom by the insurgents, but the majority were whites, primarily debt-ridden small farmers and indentured servants.

Plantation export agriculture dependent on slave labor eventually transformed all the British American colonies with warm enough climates to grow commodities that Western Europe wanted but could not produce efficiently itself. Beginning in the West Indies in the early seventeenth century, export agriculture enveloped the British colonies all the way to Maryland by the end of that century. Between 1700 and 1781 these colonies alone consumed well in excess of a million African slaves (see Table 1). As export agriculture transformed these colonies, African slaves replaced white indentured servants as the primary labor force, and land became highly concentrated. White small farmers were forced to sell out to big planters and migrate to areas where opportunities were greater. As sugar transformed the British Caribbean colony of Barbados in the early seventeenth century, for example, thousands of small farmers sold out and migrated to British North America. As tobacco transformed the tidewater area of Virginia a century later, smallholders were forced to migrate inland.

These trends were especially pronounced in sugar production, the most important American agricultural export to Europe during the colonial period. Sugar production for export required heavy investment in expensive milling machinery, which in turn encouraged extreme concentration of landholding and extreme reliance on slave labor. The same pattern of large-scale production, land concentration, and dependence on slave labor occurred in rice cultivation in eastern South Carolina, which involved large investments in irrigation.

Tobacco, the major export from the British mainland colonies, had more limited capital requirements and could be grown competitively for export by both large and small producers. Large-scale production developed where planters had sufficient capital to purchase prime land and a labor force that could be permanently denied access to it. Planters in tide-water Virginia, many of them European investors, provide the clearest example. In contrast, small-scale white tobacco producers using relatively few slaves were able to survive in the interiors of Virginia and the Carolinas.

Wherever this transition to export agriculture and slavery occurred within British America, the relatively egalitarian distribution of land and wealth, products in part of the indentured labor system, began to break down, and society became polarized into a small wealthy elite of white planters and a large class of impoverished black slaves. Land, wealth, education, literacy, and political power were monopolized by the few and denied to the vast majority. This polarization went furthest in the small sugar-producing islands of the Caribbean like Barbados and Jamaica. But it is readily discernible in the larger, geographically and economically more diverse colonies of the North American mainland such as tobacco-producing Virginia. On the mainland, however, it was rice-producing South Carolina that most closely resembled the Caribbean sugar colonies. There, blacks became a majority as early as 1708.

Nothing of this sort happened in the British colonies of New England and the mid-Atlantic seaboard, although slavery was present there as well. Despite important differences in the economies of these two groups of northern colonies, all of them depended throughout the colonial period on farming and craft production oriented toward domestic consumption. Fishing provided an important supplement to the economy of New England, and eventually shipbuilding became an important addition to the economies of both regions.

Production in these northern British colonies was based on family labor and an ever-growing proportion of free wage workers. Indentured servants continued to flood into the northern colonies during the eighteenth century, the vast majority going to the mid-Atlantic colonies of

TABLE 2	Population of the British Colonies in America excluding Canada (in thousands; slave population in parentheses), 1640–1775		
	1640	*1700*	*1775*
New England	20	130	676 (25)
New York, New Jersey Pennsylvania, Delaware	–	65	623 (50)
Virginia, Maryland	8	87	759 (230)
Carolinas, Georgia	–	12	449 (140)
Barbados	–	54 (42)	86 (68)
Jamaica	–	53 (45)	210 (197)
Other British West Indies	20	43 (31)	113 (97)

Pennsylvania, New York, New Jersey, and Delaware. The small numbers of slaves in the northern colonies were employed mainly as urban domestic servants and artisans. As production grew and society became more prosperous, the northern colonies experienced prodigious internal population growth and, in relative terms, relied less and less on the importation of labor from abroad. These population and labor trends, which sharply differentiate the development of the northern British colonies from those of the south, are graphically illustrated in Table 2. (The table is also adapted from Davis, and carries the same warning about the reliability of the absolute numbers.)

Comparison of the British colonies, northern and southern, helps us to understand the relationship between culture, climate, race, and labor systems in the divergent development of all the European colonies of the Americas. In the British colonies the influence of British culture was a constant, so it is easier to assess the independent action of climate, race, and labor. All the British colonies were products of the same colonizing power, all were peopled initially by immigrants from British society, all were subject, more or less, to the same imperial institutions.

It is true that significant differences existed in the manner in which the British colonies were initially organized and settled. Some began as collective efforts by people of some means to establish societies based on religious tenets, others were granted to a single proprietor, who proceeded to distribute land to others at a price, and others were run for profit by companies of investors. But by the start of the eighteenth century, the two distinct economic and labor systems that would decisively affect their subsequent development were firmly set in place. The southern colonies from Virginia to the Caribbean specialized in producing export crops, especially sugar and tobacco, with slave labor for the world market. The northern colonies from New England to the mid-Atlantic produced food and manufactures largely for the domestic market using family and free labor.

The southern British colonies became the great economic success stories of Britain's mercantilist American empire. The more specialized they were in export production, the more heavily dependent on slave labor, the more concentrated and undemocratic their landholding patterns, the wealthier they became. These, not their poor northern neighbors, were the colonies that contributed handsomely to the British metropolis. They provided sugar and tobacco for the rapidly growing British internal market. They furnished commodities for industrial processing and for re-export. And they generated, through these transactions, sizeable tax revenue for the state. On the eve of the independence of the colonies that became the United States, exports per person averaged £4.75 for the British West Indies, £1.82 for the Virginia-Maryland region, £1.78 for the Carolinas and Georgia, £1.03 for the mid-Atlantic colonies, and only £0.84 for New England.* Figures on average wealth per person in the thirteen colonies at the same point in time were £54.7 for the southern colonies, £41.9 for the middle colonies, and £36.6 for New England. As these figures reveal, the northern colonies were of limited use to Britain. What exports they had generally competed with British goods. And far from producing revenue for the government, their administration and defense were an absolute drain on the imperial treasury.

Comparison of the British colonies in America helps us isolate the determining role of labor systems in the divergent development of all the European colonies in America. Slavery, and other forms of coerced labor—and the concentration of land and wealth that accompanied them—had similar effects in all the colonies where they took hold, whether they were Spanish or British, Portuguese or French. Coerced

---

*Throughout this paragraph the eighteenth-century currency is expressed in decimals for convenience.

labor took hold in the Americas everywhere the Europeans found viable indigenous labor supplies, or opportunities to produce precious metals or tropical agricultural exports. To stress this point is not to deny real differences in the culture and institutions of the European colonizing powers. It is simply to point to the overwhelming similarities that coerced labor and large-scale production of export commodities created despite these initial differences.

New England and the mid-Atlantic colonies were exceptions to the pattern of coerced labor that influenced the development of all the European colonies to their south. It was not some unique cultural or racial attribute that explains their exceptionalism. It was their fortuitous location on lands lacking precious metals and with a climate unsuited to cultivation of the agricultural commodities Europe wanted. Their inability to produce primary commodities for export to Europe, their relative isolation from the main circuits of trade within the Atlantic system, allowed them to preserve and develop their unique free-labor system.

Paradoxically, however, by the eighteenth century New England and the mid-Atlantic colonies were able to assume a function within the Atlantic economy that in some ways resembled the role of European metropolis more than it did that of American colony. Unable to produce much that Britain needed, yet dependent on imports of British manufactured goods, these northern colonies began to balance their trade with Britain by provisioning the slave-based economies of the southern North American mainland and the Caribbean. This new role set the northern colonies on a path toward industrialization and political democracy that sharply distinguished their development from the other colonies of the Americas. To understand how that happened we must look more closely at the relationship between the American colonies and the workings of the Atlantic system as a whole.

The Atlantic system, as it operated from the sixteenth through the eighteenth centuries, can be usefully described as a great triangular trade between Europe, Africa, and the Americas. Europeans traded manufactures in Africa for slaves, then sold them in America. Slaves in America produced staples, primarily sugar and tobacco, and along with other workers, free and coerced, they mined the precious minerals that were America's other major exports to Europe. European nations, especially Britain as time went on, sold America manufactures and financed the commerce of the whole triangular trade.

The role each point of the triangle played in this vast Atlantic trading network fundamentally influenced its economic and social evolution over time. Imports of European manufactures undercut African artisan industry, while the slave trade deprived African societies of many of their most productive members. With the infusion of slave labor the American plantation societies grew rapidly. Their economies, like those of the mining colonies of the American interior, came to revolve around the production of primary commodities for export. Meanwhile, imports of European manufactures and mercantilist restrictions stunted the growth of their manufacturing sectors. European commerce benefited from the influx of precious metals, and imports of agricultural commodities lessened the importance of domestic agriculture. Europe's exports to Africa and America stimulated the development of its manufacturing industry. Finally, because Europe controlled Atlantic commerce, it reaped profits and tax revenues on virtually every exchange within the triangular trade. It also furnished the ships, warehousing, and the insurance that made the trade possible. In elemental terms, if economic development is defined as the emergence of an expanding industrial economy, then the triangular trade fostered economic development in Europe, economic growth but not development in America, and economic retrogression in Africa.

IV Newcomers: The Flow of Peoples

The European discovery of the Americas set in motion the largest migration of peoples in history. During the first three centuries of conquest and colonization, indigenous populations were displaced by hundreds of thousands of Europeans intent on bettering their condition and by millions of Africans brought in chains to make ambitious planters rich from their labor. The New World's original inhabitants succumbed by the millions to epidemic diseases from Europe and Africa. Survivors responded to the invasion in a variety of ways, some remaining as tributary laborers on ancestral lands, others forging trading partnerships with the new arrivals; still others pressed inland onto territories of rival groups as European colonists occupied the coasts. The swirl of peoples from the European countryside across the Atlantic converged with a much greater flow from Africa to produce still more migratory currents that spread out across the New World landscape.

The following set of readings explores some of the most salient conditions that gave rise to this vast migratory flow and examines a few of its many currents. Alfred W. Crosby reminds us that the European and African settlement of the Americas, though often thought of as planned from the beginning, was one of history's great ironies—an unintended consequence flowing from an unwitting introduction of European epidemic diseases that decimated the conquerors' indigenous labor supply. The depopulation of the New World did far more than the subjugation and forced removal of surviving Amerindians to trigger a transatlantic flow of peoples, which has continued into the present. The acute labor shortage ensured that during the first three centuries of colonization, the overwhelming majority of migrants were not the intrepid European adventurers of older histories, but Africans who arrived on American shores in chains. In Crosby's telling, even most Europeans experienced transatlantic migration as a wrenching process.

The first newcomers to the Americas were the Spanish. Because they were first, the records of their coming are incomplete and fragmentary. Lyle N. McAlister assembles the scanty evidence to provide a picture of who emigrated, where they came from, why they left home, and how many arrived in the first, founding wave of immigration.

The most numerous newcomers to the Americas in the three centuries following 1492 were Africans, "the involuntary colonists," as the author of the next selection, Felipe Fernández-Armesto, puts it in his title. As with all immigrants, voluntary and forced, their story necessarily involves the conditions of their homelands, which "pushed" them out as well as their New World, which "pulled" them in. Despite their enforced migration and enslaved condition, Fernández-Armesto recounts that Africans nevertheless created some space of autonomy and like other immigrants made new lives in their new lands and new communities.

The concluding two selections compare the immigration patterns of two European neighbors, France and England, in their colonization of North America in the seventeenth century. Allan Greer explains why so few Frenchmen left their homeland, the most populous kingdom in western Europe, for Canada, while so many Englishmen left their less populous country. James Horn examines English immigration to the Chesapeake region, Virginia, and Maryland and shows who came and why, which makes an interesting comparison to French immigration to New France.

Alfred W. Crosby

Infectious Disease and the Demography of the Atlantic Peoples

Let me begin with what some will consider a startling premise. I believe that in 1492, population densities in the areas occupied by advanced peoples of the Old and New Worlds (Europe, Persia, India, China, Mesoamerica, Peru, etc.) were not very different. For instance, it seems likely that the density of settlement in the central valley of Mexico was not far less than that in the Yangzi Valley. Such areas were more numerous and several of them more extensive in the eastern than in the western hemisphere, but these were, I suggest, roughly similar in density of inhabitants. . . .

After 1492

If the preceding statement is true, then it leads us to a paradox. How could post-Columbian migration from the Old World to the New have been as enormous and swift as it was if the New World were as heavily populated as I claim? Transatlantic migration leaped from zero migrants and zero significance to immense numbers and immense significance in what was, by any standard but that of the recent past, a very short time indeed. The *Völkerwanderung*, the *Drang nach Osten*, the Bantu advance south into Khoisan Africa, the Chinese advance into the Yangzi Valley and beyond—these were driftings that took many centuries; they must be contrasted against rather than compared with the Atlantic since 1942.

The efficiency of the sailing vessels of Renaissance Europe, then the steamship, and finally the airplane help to explain the size and speed of transatlantic migration, but these astonishing machines only

Alfred W. Crosby, "Infectious Disease and the Demography of the Atlantic Peoples," *Journal of World History*, Volume 2, Number 2 (1991), pp. 119–133. Copyright © 1991 by University of Hawaii Press.

explain how, not why, the post-Columbian millions made the trip. After all, the machines also provided fast transportation to India and China, where fortunes and empires were to be made, but only thousands, not millions, of migrants embarked from the Atlantic world for Asia. The abruptness and magnitude of the transatlantic transfer of population to the New World were the products of a phenomenon more complicated than innovation in transportation technology.

Today North Americans of all ancestries are apt to think of colonization as the seizure of land and the elimination and displacement of the incumbent population by invaders. But that is not the way conquest has usually worked. It was not, for instance, what William the Conqueror had in mind when he and his Normans took over England in 1066. Land is worthless without laborers, who are as essential to a conquest as the land's flora and fauna. Most of the *conquistadores* and their early successors in America were not trying to propagate an ideology or a religion or their particular subspecies of *Homo sapiens* so much as they were trying to rise economically and socially in the traditional way, through the acquisition of lands with families of laborers to work them.

The first European colonists, Portuguese as well as Spanish, did not want Amerindians to die. They wanted them to be producers, customers, tribute payers, serfs, peasants, peons, and servants. Columbus's original plan for Española (modern-day Haiti and the Dominican Republic) was not that it should become a colony of settlement, but that Europeans should establish trading "factories" there, such as those his fellow Italians had in the Levant and the Portuguese had on the coast of west Africa—small colonies of merchants and their aides organized to carry on trade with and milch the indigenous people. The plans of many of the first Spanish colonists in newly discovered Española were somewhat different, but even more in line with European tradition. They did not want to trade with Amerindians on anything like an equal basis; they wanted to become their lords, supported by the native Americans with gold, food, and labor. The demand of Spanish rebels in Española in 1499, a demand to which Columbus had to acquiesce, was for *encomiendas*, which were defined not as grants of land, but as grants of rights to the labor and tribute of native communities. If Columbus and the sixteenth-century European colonists had been able to do what they had originally planned, there might have been no greater a proportion of Europeans crossing the Atlantic after 1492 than Normans crossing the English Channel after 1066. But then came the epidemics, which changed the colonists's plans, all American societies, and Europe — indeed, the entire world.

The Epidemics

The arrival of large numbers of Europeans and Africans in a given area of the Americas was always followed by a rapid, even catastrophic, decline in the aboriginal population. The invaders' gross mistreatment of the indigenes steepened the decline, but its chief cause was the pathogens the invaders inadvertently brought with them, germs that caused numerous epidemics of an extent and mortality comparable to the fourteenth-century Black Death in Eurasia and North Africa. Scholars and scientists have carefully assembled various lists of diseases that arrived in the Americas with Europeans and Africans. These lists vary somewhat in length and content, being products of what must be speculation, however well informed. Most contain the following maladies: smallpox, measles, diphtheria, trachoma, whooping cough, chicken pox, bubonic plague, malaria, typhoid fever, cholera, yellow fever, dengue fever, scarlet fever, amoebic dysentery, influenza, and certain varieties of tuberculosis. Whether a disease should be added or subtracted is relatively unimportant. What is important is that there was undeniably an avalanche of disease that decimated all native American peoples, and even obliterated many, such as the Tainos of the Greater Antilles, who were struck by the micro-invaders and the macro-invaders simultaneously.

The World's Greatest Labor Shortage

In 1493 Columbus dropped into the laps of Europeans an unprecedented opportunity for conquest, empire, and fortune. Fertile lands, mines of silver and gold, and myriads of Amerindians to work them were to be had by right of arms. Amerindians, however, did not wear well. The demographic collapse in the highlands of the Aztec and Inca empires is more fully documented than that of other Amerindians for the simple reason that in central Mesoamerica and Peru lived the populations most coveted by those Spanish monarchs and their subjects who were or aspired to become holders of the *encomiendas*. These highland populations fell by ninety percent or so in the first postconquest century, and vast, sparsely staffed *haciendas* sprawled where the *conquistadores* had anticipated manors teeming with native laborers. The decline in the number of Amerindians of the hot, wet, coastal lowlands is not so fully recorded, although it was even more extreme. In the comparatively cool highlands the chief killers were the diseases that had been circulating in Europe: pustular infections, such as smallpox and measles, and respiratory infections, such as whooping cough and pneumonia. The peoples of the lowlands were afflicted by the same diseases *plus* diseases from the Old World tropics, including malaria, yellow fever, dengue fever, and amoebic dysentery. These swept into oblivion the small number of West Indians who had survived the initial European onslaught and early epidemics of infections such as smallpox, and eliminated most of the inhabitants of the littoral of the Gulf of Mexico and the Caribbean and, in time, the occupants of lowland Brazil and the hot, humid Pacific coasts. The Maya of Yucatán were the greatest exception to the generality that lowland Amerindians melted away after the Old World peoples arrived. The reason for their survival in large numbers might be that their stony and seasonally arid peninsula was a difficult environment for the anopheles mosquito. Be that as it may, survival of Amerindians of the sultry lowlands was the exception, not the rule. Father José de Anchieta wrote from Bahia, Brazil, in the 1560s that the native population had plunged precipitously during the previous twenty years, and that "one never believed that so many people would ever be used up, let alone in such a short time." A century after Columbus, the historian of the Spanish empire, Antonio de Herrera, wrote that Spain's lowland Amerindians laborers were "so wasted and condemned, that of thirty parts of the people that inhabit it, there wants twenty-nine; and it is likely the rest of the Indians in a short time will decay."

As their lowland Amerindians subjects died off, Europeans reached out to the Bahamas, Nicaragua, and the backlands of their Brazilian settlements for slaves, but the newly enslaved died off as rapidly as those who were first subjugated. A century and more later, the English in Carolina tried to make do with Amerindian slaves as local labor and an export commodity but also failed.

European conquerors faced the greatest labor shortage of all time. With Amerindians dying so precipitously, who was to do the work of reshaping the Americas in accordance with the schemes of imperial governments and the demands of the European and the world market?

Who, for example, was going to do the brute labor of making Jamaica into a giant sugar plantation and Maryland into a giant tobacco plantation? The new masters of the American lowlands tried to persuade Europeans to volunteer for work that would make a mule balk and to live in environments with tropical diseases that killed Europeans about as fast as the diseases had Amerindians. Convicts were conscripted, and some unfortunates were simply kidnapped, but there were never enough laborers. White laborers rattled around like peas in bucket-sized vacancy.

Epidemics and Slaves

Epidemics often produce labor shortages, which strengthen the hand of the yeoman in his negotiations with the squire, and also encourage slavery as a way to refill the ranks of laborers. In the sixth century, Justinian's plague swept through the Mediterranean basin, creating a servant shortage that made it profitable to reach beyond the epidemic's farthest ravages to obtain slaves from northern and especially eastern Europe to supply the Christian and Muslim slave markets. "Slav" is the root for words meaning slave in all western European languages and also the root for *sakaliba*, which is Arabic for both slave and eunuch. The return of plague in the fourteenth century stimulated the slave trade between southern Europe and the Black Sea, and also black Africa. Mediterranean Europe wanted slaves for domestic, artisans, sexual partners, and, in Portugal, for field hands. By 1551 slaves made up 10% of the population of Lisbon; there were more slaves in the countryside.

The influx of slaves into western Europe, however, amounted to no more aliens than the resident populations could and did assimilate socially and genetically within a few generations. Population expansion in fifteenth- and sixteenth-century Europe made up for much of the plague losses and presumably would have eventually reduced to naught the Europeans' demand for slaves. Europe's African slaves would have been lost in the footnotes of history books, as were the Tartar and Circassian slaves from an earlier time. But then Europe reached out for the Americas where its touch quite literally killed.

The history of transatlantic migration divides into two periods. Until the end of the eighteenth century, most migrants were African and slave, about ten million, as compared with perhaps as few as two million European migrants in the same period. After 1800 most migrants (by an enormous margin) were European and free. The first migration was appallingly coercive and brutal; the second was less so but scarcely humane. Mass movements across the face of the earth are not accomplished without human suffering. The horror of the near extinction of native Americans was echoed in the agony of Africans enslaved to replace them, and faintly in the anxieties of the uprooted Europeans who followed.

European demand for tropical crops such as sugar was the economic force that drove the Atlantic migration in the first period. The Christian effort to seize the Holy Land from the Muslims had failed several centuries before Columbus, but the Crusades did introduce western Europeans to sugar, the cultivation of which spread throughout the Mediterranean from the Levant to Granada, and then to Madeira, the Canaries, and São Tomé in the near Atlantic. Madeira and São Tomé were uninhabited when Europeans landed, and imported disease and brutal invaders quickly destroyed the aborigines of the Canaries. From Europe the new masters of these islands brought convicts, Jewish children, and recent converts to Christianity from Islam, but there were never enough laborers to work the plantations. The solution to the labor problem lay in the Berber and later in the black African. Before depopulation in the Americas raised the question of where laborers were to be found to cut the cane, chop the cotton, and pick the coffee beans, the plantation masters of the islands of the eastern Atlantic had the answer.

Africa's Millions

The greatest transoceanic migration and probably the greatest long-distance migration by water or land before the nineteenth century was that of African slaves crossing the Atlantic to the New World. Between the first decade of the 1500s, when the Spanish monarchy authorized the shipment of slaves directly from Africa to the Antilles, and 1870, when the last American market for slaves locked its gates, ten million Africans arrived alive in American ports, most of them to work in plantations raising cash crops for the European market: sugar, tobacco, rice, indigo, cotton, and coffee. Ninety percent went to fill the vacuum left in the hot, wet tropics by the now-extinct aboriginal populations. Brazil alone took 38% of the slaves, the Caribbean Islands 40%. Saint

Domingue (the French name for Española) received twice as many African slaves as the thirteen colonies and later the United States.

The classic plantation lands from Brazil through the Guianas and around the West Indies never established self-sustaining slave populations in colonial times, and could not have maintained their exports of cash crops to Europe without continually importing workers from Africa. The birth rate of their black populations fell far short of their death rate. There are many explanations for this: overwork, inadequate diet, the preponderance of males over females (plantation masters found it more practical to replace dying workers than to encourage the birth of American-born replacements), and disease. The pathogens and parasites that had eliminated the native Americans from most of the lowlands also shortened the lives of those who came to replace them. Africans were, genetically and by childhood exposure, more resistant to malaria, yellow fever, and many of the various tropical parasites than were the whites, but Africans were by no means immune to all strains of invasive species. Although the disease environments of torrid America were more like those of west Africa than of Europe, they were not identical. In America the Africans were also subject to infections brought overseas by their European masters. In hot, wet America, disease eliminated Amerindians, kept Europeans to a small number, and killed many Africans, stimulating the need for slaves down to the time of José Martí.

Europe's Millions

The greatest century of the transatlantic slave trade in terms of absolute numbers was the eighteenth, when six million crossed from Africa. In the next century, slavery was abolished in one after another of the transatlantic empires and finally in the United States and Brazil; after the arrival of two million more Africans, the trade finally came to an end. The change was not a comfortable one for the plantation elite. Former slaves tended to avoid work on the old plantations: "They turn out to work when they like," one white Jamaican complained, "do what they choose, take what days they like — in fact, do as they think proper." To replace them in the West Indies, a few Europeans, a greater number of Chinese, and hundreds of thousands of East Indians were brought in as contract laborers. Many East Indians returned home after a few years, but the descendants of those who remained today comprise half of Guyana's population and well over a third of Trinidad's, representing the most ethnically distinctive additions to the New World's tropical population since the first waves of Europeans and Africans.

The last two million black slaves and the East Indian influx were ripples in comparison with the wave of Europeans that rolled across the Atlantic in the nineteenth and early twentieth centuries, veered away from the tropics, and broke on the shores of the American temperate zones: Canada, the United States, southern Brazil, Argentina, and Uruguay. The Europeans swept far inland, where the number and morale of Amerindians had been drastically reduced by two centuries and more of European and African-American pressure and imported disease.

Europeans, in contrast with Amerindians, had the advantage of long contact with many of the world's chief infectious diseases, which had thereby become endemic rather than epidemic, that is, something more in the nature of an incubus than a lightning bolt. In addition, public health and prophylactic techniques were at long last having some positive effects, and diet was improving in quantity and quality, enabling Europeans to survive all infections in greater numbers than ever before. Demographically, their story in the late eighteenth and nineteenth centuries was opposite that of Amerindians: Europeans were experiencing a population explosion.

In the seventeenth and early eighteenth century, western Europe's population had staggered along, its mortality rates, especially for children, always high and in some years extremely high. Births barely exceeded deaths even in the best of times. War killed soldiers and peasants indiscriminately. Hunger accompanied war and killed on its own behalf. Worse than famine and war on average and amplified by both in its effects was disease, particularly bubonic plague, the chief arbiter of demography during the *ancien régime*.

For four hundred years, from the mid-fourteenth to the first years of the eighteenth century, plague epidemics in western Europe never ceased for long, if at all. In eastern Europe they continued for another century. The plague commonly killed 60 to 80% of those it infected. There was no known cure, and no one understood its etiology. In the second half of the seventeenth century, it began to retreat. London's last plague epidemic took place during 1665 and 1666, and the disease made its last sweep through the south of France in 1720. The retreat was a truly blessed mystery. Diseases can spontaneously lose their virulence and communicability, and it is possible that subtle changes in western European architecture and general behavior and in the use of quarantine and *cordon sanitaire* might have been effective in battling the disease.

The retreat of plague left Europeans with only war, hunger, and a raft of other infections to deal with, such as smallpox, measles, tuberculosis, and various dysenteric infections. None of them were singly as deadly as the bubonic scourge, but they were quite enough in their sum to cause, with the help of chronic malnutrition, an extremely high mortality rate. Armies, bit by bit, became professional, murdered fewer civilians, and lived off their own provisions rather than what they ravaged from an impoverished peasantry. The problems of crop failures and peacetime food shortages were harder to solve, but they were solved, and healthier populations resulted. Improved transportation sped the transfer of food from areas of surplus to areas of hunger and turned epidemic diseases into endemic diseases, thus softening their impact on society. When endemic diseases kill, they usually carry off the most expendable and easily replaced members of society, that is, immunologically inexperienced children.

The improvements in agricultural techniques that historians have collectively entitled "the agricultural revolution" were also significant, although not decisive in initially sparking the population explosion. Populations were already increasing before that revolution had proceeded far enough to make much difference in the availability of food supplies. In the beginning, the key factor might have been the cultivation of Amerindian crops in Europe, especially maize and white potatoes, which produced more food per hectare than any traditional European crop. By the eighteenth century, maize was well on its way to becoming the staple of millions of the poorer peasants in a band of territory from northern Portugal to the Black Sea, and the potato was launched as the basic food of the Irish and impoverished farmers and urban lower classes of northern Europe. All of this occurred before the agricultural revolution, before the rise of the sanitationist movement, and certainly before medical science and the practices of variolation and vaccination had much influence on mortality rates.

Europe's population was about eighty million when Columbus sailed. In the period circa 1800, when the United States and the nations of Latin America won their independence and the transatlantic slave trade entered its final decline, the population of Europe was about 180 million. In the same three centuries, the inhabitants of the British Isles—the English, Welsh, Scots, and Irish—the most migratory of all Europeans, leaped from five to sixteen million. Europe and the British Isles were ready to export people. In fact, they had to. But where?

They went to Australia, New Zealand, southern Brazil, Uruguay, Argentina, Canada, and, above all, to the United States. Aboriginal populations, ravaged by unfamiliar diseases, epidemic and newly endemic, were plunging in all these areas, probably none more steeply than in North America. In 1800 there were probably no more than six hundred thousand Amerindians in the United States, down from an estimated five million in 1492; the European and African-American population of the United States was more than five million and climbing. In terms of absolute numbers, there were probably as many people in the area of the United States as there had been three hundred years before, but much had changed. Early Europeans had exposed the natives of North America to a score of new infections to which they had not had time to adapt, immunologically or through medical or public health practices. (For example, while the statistics of the 1800 census were being compiled, epidemics were devastating Amerindians in the interior of North America, reducing the Omaha by two-thirds.) Europeans had, in their many centuries of experience with these diseases, adapted to them in one way or another. They had also mastered systems of agriculture and animal husbandry that enabled them to live in North America in numbers several times over the maximum pre-Columbian population. . . .

An Interim Assessment

Columbus and his blue-water emulators initiated a transoceanic revolution of unprecedented magnitude and significance by carrying Old World microlife across the ocean. The migrant pathogens and parasites obliterated millions of Amerindians, broke the morale of the survivors, and rendered vacant large parts of the New World, or at least reduced the population of the original inhabitants to such small numbers that the invaders could claim that the land was going unused—an offense to God! As a result, some Europeans set aside their ambitions for conquest to become lords of the manor, importing millions of Africans and transforming themselves into masters of plantations.

Europeans who remained at home benefited from improvements, technological and administrative, in their transportation system. Food moved rapidly from areas of surplus to areas of want, as did infections. The former process almost eliminated absolute starvation, and the latter homogenized the disease environment, ameliorating epidemics that had dictated Europe's demography since the coming of the Black Death. In increasing numbers, Europeans turned to the immensely productive Amerindians crops for sustenance. The resulting surplus of people then diffused to areas of lesser population density on the other side of the oceans, almost as if in obedience to laws of physical chemistry.

Lyle N. McAlister

Spanish Emigration to the Indies

The Spaniards had some preconceptions about how to go about colonizing the Indies, but the changing numbers and qualities of the populators themselves conditioned the methods and instruments employed. Beginning with the European element, its formation occurred through immigration and natural increase. The gross number of immigrants to the Indies and their qualities depended on both individual initiatives and royal policies. Individuals and families went to the New World for diverse reasons: to win a fortune, to improve their status, to escape royal justice or the attentions of the Holy Office, to serve God as missionaries and the king as royal officials, or to accompany or find husbands. The crown had fairly definite ideas about who should go and who should not. In general, it encouraged the immigration of Catholic Castilians of good character and provided incentives in the form of grants of land, agricultural supplies and implements, and exemption from direct taxes for first settlers and their eldest sons. It particularly

Lyle N. McAlister, *Spain and Portugal in the New World, 1492–1700* (Minneapolis: University of Minnesota Press, 1984), pp. 109–111, 115–117. Copyright © 1984 by the University of Minnesota. All rights reserved.

encouraged the immigration of women, because it regarded the monogamous Christian family as the basis of social formation in the new lands, and of artisans and laborers, who, it hoped, would not only perform essential productive tasks but would also provide a model of thrift and industry for the indigenous peoples. It also tried to direct emigrants to less favored provinces that had shortages of settlers.

Isabella discouraged the emigration of non-Castilians but never absolutely prohibited it, and upon her death in 1504 Ferdinand formally opened the Indies to Aragonese. Emperor Charles adopted an even more liberal policy by extending the right to the subjects of his non-Hispanic kingdoms. But on one point the Catholic Kings and their successors remained adamant. They absolutely forbade Jews, crypto-Jews, Muslims, *moriscos*, and heretics to go to their American dominions. To enforce its policies, the crown required all emigrants to obtain licenses from the *Casa de Contratación* (Royal House of Trade) in Seville, excepting clerics, soldiers, sailors, and servants. It is likely, however, that individual initiatives and ingenuity had more to do with the quantity and quality of emigration to the Indies than did the wishes of kings.

The number of emigrants to the Indies during the period of discovery and conquest cannot be determined with any exactitude. The main source of information on the subject is the registers of licenses issued by the *Casa*, some of which have been gathered and published by the Archivo General de Indias as *Catálago de pasajeros a Indias durante los siglos xvi, xvii y xviii*. This source lists 15,480 persons but has several shortcomings. Despite its ambiguous title, it covers only the years 1509–59, and even within this span registers for a number of years are fragmentary or missing. The licensing system, moreover, functioned loosely. Although crown regulations required all vessels sailing for America to register with the *Casa* in Seville, many departed clandestinely from other Spanish ports and even from Portugal carrying unlicensed passengers. Not a few persons avoided controls by passing themselves off as sailors, soldiers, and servants. Licenses could be forged or purchased from legitimate holders or from venal officials. Finally, registers do not reveal how many people actually departed, how many survived the long and hazardous trans-Atlantic passage, how many perished quickly in the unhealthy American tropics or became casualties of the Conquest, and how many returned to Europe.

Because of deficiencies in passenger lists, it has generally been surmised that the number of persons who actually emigrated exceeded
substantially the number of registered passengers, and this is confirmed
by the American historical linquist Peter Boyd-Bowman in connection
with his research on the origins of New World Spanish dialects. Sup-
plementing passenger lists with information gleaned from a variety of
other published and unpublished contemporary sources, Boyd-Bowman
identified 45,374 persons of European origin known to have resided in
the Indies between 1493 and 1579. He believes that this count represents almost one-fifth of the actual number of such individuals and
that, if it is accepted and multiplied by five, then the total volume of
emigration must have approached 226,870. This is the best estimate
presently available.

Using the same sample, Boyd-Bowman calculated that almost 95.0
percent of emigrants hailed from the dominions of the Crown of
Castile, only 2.0 percent from the realms of the Crown of Aragon and
from Navarre, and 2.8 percent from outside of Spain. Andalusia provided more than a third of the total, and this province, along with
Extremadura, and the two Castiles, better than three-quarters. Over the
eighty-six-year span, no really significant change occurred in proportions furnished by the several regions of Spain. Thus, the conquest and
colonization of the Indies was accomplished mainly by individuals
from the south and west of Spain. . . .

Data on social backgrounds of passengers to the Indies have been
less systematically collected than information on regional origins, but
they reveal some rough proportions and trends. Analyses of expeditions
of conquest along with Boyd-Bowman's samples and other sources
show that during the first three decades of the century immigrants included no titled nobles and only a handful of legitimate hidalgos. Most
arrivals were of base birth. Laborers and artisans predominated, followed by men-at-arms of common estate, sailors, and a few clerics and
representatives of the urban middle classes. Although the rosters of expeditions generally listed an *oficio* (occupation) for each member, it is
likely that many were simply adventurers or became so immediately
upon arrival.

As pacification proceeded, the quality of immigrants gradually
changed. Between 1540 and 1579, the proportion of hidalgos remained
low, slightly over 4.0 percent of Boyd-Bowman's sample, but among

commoners new types appeared. Between 1560 and 1579 one of every sixteen was a merchant or business agent. Between 1540 and 1559 almost 10.0 percent were classified as servants, and during the next twenty-year period 13.6 percent were so classified. New immigrants also included sober artisans come to ply their trades, missionaries come to evangelize the indigenes, and officials come to staff expanding agencies of royal government. Lawyers arrived in increasing numbers. Colonial governors protested that their presence only fomented unnecessary litigation, and in response the crown discouraged and, on occasion, forbade their immigration, but they continued to come. One of the most significant trends was the steady increase in the percentage of women. The sample figures are: 1493–1519, 5.6 percent (308 out of 5481); 1520–39, 6.4 percent (845 out of 13,262); 1540–59, 16.4 percent (1480 out of 9044); and 1560–79, 28.5 percent (5013 out of 17,587).

One another element in Hispanic migration to the Indies must be mentioned. Despite rigorous prohibitions, *conversos* and crypto-Jews from Spain and Portugal made their way across the Atlantic to escape the attention of the Inquisition or, like Christian Spaniards, simply to improve their lot in life. As early as 1506, ecclesiastical officials on Española denounced the steady arrival of "Hebrews," and the conquerors counted New Christians among their companies. Indeed, one of Cortés's followers became the first New World martyr of his race when he was burned at the stake for relapse into Judaism. Also, American inquisitorial records provide presumptive evidence of the presence of the People of the Book in the major urban centers, where they engaged mainly in artisanry and small entrepreneurial activities. Their numbers cannot be determined. They lived in secret communities, practiced endogamous marriage, and adjusted to their environment by adopting pseudo-Catholic practices. Unless apprehended by the Holy Office, they were not officially identified and became invisible in population counts.

It is impossible to calculate the rate of natural increase among the European population because of the lack of firm data on natality, mortality, and other variables in the demographic equation. Scattered contemporary evidence points to rapid multiplication. Despite a badly unbalanced sex ratio, the efforts of crown and church to promote domesticity bore fruit. A census of Española taken as early as 1514 revealed that Spanish wives lived with their husbands in every town on the island. The Spanish, moreover, were a fecund people, their households abounded in servants, and they populated the land in true bibli-cal fashion. Royal cosmographer and geographer Juan López de Velasco, who between 1571 and 1574 prepared the first general census of the Indies, reported 300 *vecinos* in Asunción and "more than 2,900 chil-dren of Spanish parents." Such discursive observations produce no sta-tistics, but they suggest that by the 1560s natural increase had sur-passed immigration as a source of European population growth.

Although much remains to be learned about the processes that formed the European population, the quantitative results can be esti-mated using López de Velasco as a point of departure. In his day cen-suses were not head counts of men, women, and children but enumer-ations of *vecinos* in a community, that is, residents who owned houses and freeholds and whose names were inscribed in registers maintained by municipal councils. To arrive at a total population, contemporaries customarily multiplied the number of *vecinos* by five, the estimated av-erage size of a household, which included the nuclear family, depen-dents, and servants. Relying mainly on López de Velasco's census, the Argentine historian Angel Rosenblat estimates that 23,364 *vecinos* dwelt in the Spanish Indies around 1570. Applying a conversion factor of 5 produces a total population of 116,820, or 120,000 rounded out. López de Velasco himself, however, estimated in his summary of the temporal and spiritual state of the Indies that 200 *pueblos de españoles* (Spanish towns) and around 32,000 *vecinos* existed in Spanish Amer-ica, figures somewhat greater than the sums of his local counts. Per-haps he made a mistake in addition, or perhaps he allowed for towns for which he did not have specific information. In any case, multiply-ing his general estimate of *vecinos* by 5 yields a total European popula-tion of 160,000. The count of *vecinos*, moreover, does not include cler-ics who dwelt in the Indies or Spaniards living in Indian communities and on rural estates.

Modern investigation tends to support an even higher figure. Some scholars believe that a multiple of 6 rather than 5 should be used to calculate the total European population in the Indies because of "the great number of children of the Spaniards" and the large numbers of relatives and hangers-on who attached themselves to patriarchal households. Applying the larger multiple to Rosenblat's tally of 23,364 *vecinos* produces a total of 140,184 and to López de Velasco's general estimate of 32,000, a total of 192,000. Woodrow Borah, furthermore, found partial downside errors in the chronicler's count in Mexico, and, if these are corrected the number of *vecinos* increases from 6114 to 10,061. Whether comparable errors exist in López de Velasco's data for other regions is not certain. Let us, therefore, go along with the Argentine historian Nicolás Sánchez-Albornoz and guess that somewhere in the neighborhood of 220,000 Europeans dwelt in Spanish America around 1570. At first glance this figure raises an awkward problem when compared with an estimated European immigration of 226,870. Among other things, it leaves little room for natural increase, a patently absurd result. But, assuming that Boyd-Bowman's count actually constituted a 20 percent sample, the apparent discrepancy can be accommodated by supposing that many of the persons he identified had died by 1570, some had returned to Europe, and others were not registered *vecinos*.

Some qualitative changes in the European population accompanied gross quantitative trends. As conquest merged into colonization, conquerors settled down to live on the tribute and services rendered to them by their charges. The diverse occupational types who arrived too late to become conquistadors or who, perhaps, preferred more sedate life-styles, settled in towns and cities to practice their Old World skills. The growing proportion of women immigrants encouraged family formation, and the number of female children they bore accelerated the process. Taken together, these developments created a more complex but less volatile population.

Felipe Fernández-Armesto

Africans, the Involuntary Colonists

The first man to farm wheat in Mexico was Juan Garrido. This conquistator-companion of Cortés had seen Tenochtitlán submit, made an expedition to California, and was custodian for his fellow-citizens of the aqueduct of Chapultepec which supplied Mexico City with water. He was also Black.

He was not unique among people of his colour in establishing a position of responsibility in colonial society in Spanish America; he was, however, to say the least, highly exceptional in making his life there of his own accord. However strong the pioneer spirit in the metropolitan bases of early-modern empires, the home countries—except perhaps for China—were insufficiently well populated to supply the labour needs of their colonies themselves. In some areas because of the emptiness of the colonial lands; in others because of the intensive labour demands of successful cultigens; in others, because of demographic catastrophe, slaves became essential to the sustaining of colonial enterprise in the sixteenth and seventeenth centuries.

The only source which could supply them in adequate quantities was Africa. As a consequence—though Black slave labour remained important in parts of India and, in some contexts, in Europe and China, while a significant new market was created in the seventeenth century by Dutch spice-planting enterprises in the East Indies—the biggest single transference of population in the course of early-modern colonization was from Africa to the Americas.

The slaves came—in varying degrees at different times—from Atlantic-side Africa, especially the west African bulge, the Congo, and Angola. Overwhelmingly, they were obtained by their Black vendors by war and raiding, which reached many hundreds of miles into the interior. Despite the breadth of the catchment area, it is hard to believe

Reprinted with the permission of Scribner, a Division of Simon & Schuster, from *Millennium: A History of the Last Thousand Years* by Felipe Fernández-Armesto, (New York: Scribner, 1995), pp. 269–275. Copyright © 1996 by Felipe Fernández-Armesto.

that the export of manpower on the scale demanded cannot seriously have affected the victim-societies. Most slave communities in America did not reproduce naturally, for reasons which are still little understood. Constant new imports were therefore required just to maintain labour levels. To augment economic activity substantial inputs were needed. Over 1.5 million Black slaves reached the New World by the end of the seventeenth century, and nearly 6 million more in the eighteenth. The numbers shipped out of Africa were somewhat larger, for the passage across the Atlantic was fatal to many. From the best available figures, something approaching 400,000 of those exported from Africa during the eighteenth century never reached America. The demographic and economic impact is hard to assess. For a time the Angola region seems to have developed a marked excess of females over males; on the fringe of Black slave-trading societies, some areas may have been depopulated. The political effects are glaring in some instances, however, and can be followed, for example, in the history of the rise of the kingdom of Dahomey.

Two images of Dahomey were projected to eighteenth-century Europe. In one engraving which illustrated a contemporary history, King Agaja (reigned 1708–40) affects the posture of a society huntsman's portrait, as he leans on one of the long muskets that constituted the basis of Dahomey's military might. He wears a white tricorne, a richly embroidered Turkish silk shirt, and a long robe with gathered sleeves like a western university doctor's gown. With his fine-bridged nose, butterfly lips, and Mediterranean complexion, he is as far removed as may be from a White stereotype of the Black; the naked savage peeps out of his attire only below the knee, where bare legs are shod in the sandals which were a privilege of royalty. This is the Agaja who was said by a French visitor to resemble Molière and who asked European traders to bring him a suit of armour. In a rival depiction of "the king of Dahomey's Levée," published by a slave-trader in 1793, a Stepin Fetchit in a feathered straw hat lolls drunkenly among his simpering, bare-breasted women, sucking at a long pipe while he receives the comic salutations of grovelling subjects. To an extraordinary degree, for White visitors, this realm combined extremes of civility and savagery. Guests dined with silver-handled forks on the dishes of their homelands, prepared by cooks "instructed in Europe or, at least, in the different forts," but had to approach the king's chamber over a path of skulls and were obliged to witness the human sacrifices with which the

Dahomeyans celebrated royal funerals and annual commemorations of former kings.

Dahomey lived by war, and all other values were subordinated to a ferocious warrior-cult — the insatiable thirst after blood, the barbarous vanity of being considered the scourge of mankind, the savage pomp of dwelling in a house garnished with skulls and stained with human gore." The kingdom arose in the interior of the present state of Benin in the early seventeenth century, founded, according to tradition, by exiles from the dynastic conflicts of the rich city-state of Allada. By the 1640s, Allada was already a magnet for European slave-traders; its port, with its nearby rival at Whydah, gave the area the name of Slave Coast. Around the middle of the century, Dahomey began to accumulate European muskets for slaves, obtained by raiding further north. The eighteen tributary communities subject to King Wegbeja (c. 1650–80) had grown to 209 in Agaja's time. His greatest prize was the coastland between the rivers Ouémé and Mono, conquered—he told European traders—to give him access to the outlets for slaves.

With a productive home territory in an area with a long tradition of middle-range commerce, Dahomey cannot be said to have depended on slaving, which may have accounted for no more than a fortieth of the economy. Slaving apologists frequently pointed out that Dahomeyan aggression was inspired by a less discriminating lust for conquest and that war captives were prized more as potential sacrifices than as slaves. It was claimed that slave-traders performed a work of mercy by redeeming their victims from certain death. Yet the facts are clear: Dahomey rose and fell with the rhythms of the slave trade, and the cult of ferocity coincided with the market for captives of war. The economics of the trade obliged its suppliers to be warriors or bandits. The prices Europeans paid made it worth raiding but not worth raising slaves. They were a form of livestock profitable only when rustled.

From Agaja's time, Dahomey was overshadowed by an even greater kidnapper-kingdom, the Oyo state, which had its heartland around the headwaters of the Ogun, south of the now-dessicated Moshi River. Just as Dahomey relied on the slave trade for its supply of muskets, so, indirectly, Oyo sold slaves to finance its own technology of warfare, which was based on the horse. Europeans brought a few horses as gifts, but the cavalry of Oyo was mounted on purchases from the savannah lands further north, paid with the profits of slaving. Their trade was so copious—especially after they captured Porto Novo, about

100 kilometres west of Lagos, and opened a direct route to the sea—that as well as raiding slaves they imported them from Hausa country. When Oyo attacked Dahomey to safeguard its own access to European posts, the mounted lancers proved superior to Dahomeyan musketeers. This seems a curious inversion of the trend in the rest of the world but is probably accounted for by the Dahomeyans' lack of bayonets—they preferred to close with axe or cutlass—and inexperience in shooting to kill. The object of their warfare, after all, was to take prisoners for slaves or sacrifice. They could never cope with horses: on ceremonial occasions their king had to be propped up in the saddle by flanking attendants on foot.

Further west, the history of Ashanti shows that state-building on an even greater scale was possible with resources other than slaves. Gold was the basis of Ashanti's spectacular rise from the 1680s to the dimensions of a great kingdom by the mid-eighteenth century, occupying 10,000 square miles of present-day Ghana and commanding a population of 750,000. The royal chest was said to be able to hold 400,000 ounces of gold. The throne was a golden stool said to have been called down from the sky. The court sheltered under parasols as big as trees. For the annual yam ceremony, the capital at Kumasi housed 100,000 people when the king's tributaries gathered with their retinues. More adaptable than Dahomey, Ashanti was able to use firepower to defeat mounted armies from the savannah, while coping with a variety of environments and fronts. Part of the armies' success was owed to outstanding intelligence and logistics, with fast runners operating along cleared roads. Even Ashanti, however, became increasingly reliant on slaving to supplement its riches in tributary gold. To the east of the gold coast, Akwamu was another substantial slave-stealing state, of a distinct character: its ruler enslaved large numbers of subjects by arranging trumped-up denunciations for adultery—a crime punishable by servitude in many African states—and by mobilizing gangs of "smart boys" to carry out abductions.

Our traditional images of the horrors of the middle passage and the degradation of life in slave communities derive from slaves' memoirs and abolitionist tracts. Sceptics have wondered whether shippers can have been so careless of their cargo as to tolerate—and even invite—heavy losses of life en route; yet evidence such as the often-reproduced deck-plan of the slaveship *Brookes* in 1783, where the slaves were stacked "like books on a shelf," or the tell-tale case of the Liverpool captain in 1781 who had 130 slaves thrown overboard for the insurance confirm the horror stories of the slaves who survived. Some shippers had more rational policies for the protection of their investments, but the extent of both inhumanity and inefficiency in the trade are enough to shock moralists and pragmatists alike.

At their destinations the slaves were usually the great majority of the colonial population: 45,000 to 8,000, for instance, in Jamaica in 1700. In 1553—when Blacks in Mexico were doing little more than domestic labour—the Viceroy was afraid that White settlers would be swamped. In much of the hemisphere, Blacks came to outnumber the indigenous population, too: in North America from Virginia southwards, in most of the West Indies, in some coastal areas of Central America and Venezuela, where plantation economies gradually grew up, and in the sugar lands of Guyana and Brazil. These disparities gave Blacks a potential power which was seldom realized; drawn from too many places and nations they were rarely able to adopt solidarity. When they did, the results could be such as were captured in a painting by Adrián Sánchez Galque of Quito in 1599. The three Black leaders of a Cimarrón community—a republic of runaway slaves in the interior of Peru—are shown richly robed and bejewelled, with extravagant ruffs at their collars and gold nose- and ear-ornaments of Indian workmanship, each dignified with the style of Don, the prefix of nobility. The canvas commemorates the treaty by which they rejoined the Spanish monarchy, retaining local power in their area for themselves. These—and there were many like them—were the spiritual forebears of Toussaint l'Ouverture and Nat Turner.

Even in tightly controlled plantations, slave communities were able to create autonomous institutions: in Jamaica, the British were never able to eliminate the secret power of the "Obeah-men" and "Myal men" whom they denounced as sorcerers, or curb the benches of elders which were the self-regulating judiciaries of the slaves. Though the issue is much debated by the specialists, the social orders of plantation life—the family structures, the regulation of relationships, the behavioural norms—seem, where the evidence has been studied in British North America, to have been evolved by the slaves themselves. Moreover, outside the reach of Spanish religious orders, most slaves were, at best, lightly evangelized until the nineteenth century. The result wherever slaves were congregated was that in the early-modern New World colonial society was more African than European.

North and west of the plantation world, Blacks were already an ethnic minority, composed of domestic servants, concubines, freedmen in unpopular occupations (especially at sea), or—if they came from the right part of Africa—technicians in the mining industry. Paradoxically, the fewer they were in relation to other colonists and natives, the easier for them to integrate or introduce offspring into the White and mixed-race élites. Under the Spanish and Portuguese crowns, at least, the descendants of free Blacks enjoyed equality with Whites before the law: spectacular cases of the exploitation of these rights include Dom Henrique Dias and Dom Joào Fernandes Vieira, ennobled for their services in Brazil's War of Divine Liberty against Dutch invaders from 1644 to 1654. Generally, however, administrative discrimination and knee-jerk racism kept them repressed.

Depictions of the life of Black societies in their American heyday range from the idyllic through the picturesque and the satirical to the horrific. But the crack of the cat can be heard between the lines even of William Beckford's idealized account of the Jamaica in which he was a slave-owner in 1788. In South America no area had a rosier reputation than eighteenth-century Minas Gerais for the degree of "liberty" attainable within a slave's condition; yet even here, slaves were free chiefly to obtain their gold quotas by extortion or prostitution. Whites preserved order by techniques of selective terror, exploitation of enmity between rival Black nations, and copious ministrations of rum and tobacco.

Allan Greer

French Colonization
of New France

. . . In all, about 27,000 French people came to Canada over the century and a half preceding the Conquest and, of these, perhaps two-thirds (mostly soldiers, government administrators, and contract workers) returned home without leaving descendants in the colony. This suggests that today's 6 million French Canadians can all trace their ancestry to some 10,000 original immigrants. Given the fact that Canada was France's principal settlement colony and that France was by far the most populous nation of Europe at the time, this figure for total immigration seems surprisingly small, especially when we note that the British colonies that later became the United States received more than 1 million immigrants, most of them from a country with a quarter of France's population. Certainly there was no shortage of grinding poverty in *ancien régime* France, and a move across the Atlantic would have improved most people's material prospects substantially. Why, then, did so few take the plunge? The answer lies in a combination of "pull factors" (Canada's attraction to potential immigrants), "push factors" (France's tendency to generate emigrants), and government efforts to channel and regulate the movement of people.

In the mother country, the image of New France was hardly paradisical. The severity of the winter climate was well known and the horrors of war with the Iroquois had been widely publicized by Jesuit missionaries. Government efforts to boost the colony's population by bringing over men bound as indentured servants or soldiers had the effect of associating emigration and servitude in the popular mind. "Canada has always been regarded as a country at the end of the world," wrote an official, "and as an exile that might pass for a [sentence] of civil death." A party of would-be colonists passing through a

Allan Greer, *The People of New France* (Toronto: University of Toronto Press, 1999), pp. 12–17, 19, 22–23, 26. Copyright © 1999 by University of Toronto Press.

small town in Normandy once provoked a riot on the part of towns-people who, refusing to believe the travellers were leaving France voluntarily, insisted on "rescuing" them from the colonial exile awaiting them. The dangers of Canadian life were exaggerated, and the economic advantages, especially for the peasant masses, were insufficiently appreciated, but the fact remains that the basic standard of living, though higher than that of the old country, was not dramatically better.

Canada's poor image was not the only reason for the meagre flow of transatlantic migration. The fact is that French people of the seven-, teenth and eighteenth centuries tended to stay in France, not only resisting the chilly charms of New France, but showing little inclination to move to any other part of the world. The English, the Scots, even the Germans, who possessed no state, and therefore no colonies of their own, were much more apt to emigrate. These other nations do not seem to have been poorer or more overpopulated than France; why, then, did so many of their inhabitants uproot themselves while the French shunned colonial exile? This is really a question for European social historians, but my own hunch is that this stay-at-home quality stemmed primarily from the relatively powerful situation of France's peasantry. Peasants formed the majority throughout Europe at this time and, in some countries—notably the British Isles—they were quite vulnerable and liable to be thrown off the land through processes of enclosure or eviction. Swelling the ranks of the urban unemployed, these dislocated farming people helped fuel the demand for overseas emigration. In France, by way of contrast, peasants had managed to maintain a more secure hold over the land, and landlords had less ability to rid themselves of "surplus" tenants. Inheritance practices may also have acted to discourage emigration. The tendency in *ancien régime* France was for property to be divided equally among all the heirs, giving everyone a stake, no matter how small, in the family home. In other countries, the law often allowed for greater inequality among heirs, so that some children would inherit the parents' property, while others would be driven to seek their fortunes far from home.

In addition to these socio-economic "push" and "pull" factors, migration to New France was also affected by government regulation, notably the policy of excluding Huguenots (French Protestants). The Huguenots were one element of French society who did emigrate in large numbers, particularly after the revocation (1685) of the Edict of Nantes ended official toleration of their religion. Hundreds of thousands of them took refuge in other parts of Europe, as well as in Britain's North American colonies, but they were prohibited by law from settling in New France. The result was that, for a time, there were more French speakers (all of them Huguenots) in New York than in Canada. Thus religious politics played a part in blocking the flow of one major category of potential settlers, though how large a part is impossible to say, since we cannot assume that many Protestants would have wished to live in Canada, even if they were allowed. On the other hand, France's government did contribute to the movement of Catholics to the colony through a variety of shipping regulations and subsidies. Accordingly, the heaviest flow of population to New France occurred in the 1660s and 1670s, when Louis XIV's government was engaged in a lavish program of colonial development and subsidized immigration. Even so, arrivals numbered only about 250 per year during those decades of peak immigration.

Throughout the French regime, the typical French immigrant was poor, male, and unattached. Few crossed the Atlantic as couples or in family groups, though many individuals came in the footsteps of a brother or a relative of some sort. Not usually the poorest of the poor, they seem to have been worryingly close to indigence at the time of embarkation. Almost half came from cities, more from Paris than any other single locality, though many of these rootless urbanites had been born in the country and had only recently moved to the city. Even so, the colonial emigrants formed an exceptionally urban group in a country that was predominantly rural and agrarian, and if we can believe the occupational titles they claimed, most were craftsmen and few had an agricultural background. All the provinces of France contributed to the peopling of Canada, but the bulk of migrants came from the western part of the kingdom, especially the Atlantic port of La Rochelle and its hinterland, as well as Paris, Rouen, and the Perche.

Most of these male immigrants arrived at Quebec in some form of bondage. A few were convicted criminals, or victims of a "lettre de cachet," exiled to the colony by judicial order. Much more numerous — indeed, the majority of all seventeenth-century immigrants — were the "engagés" (indentured servants), workers who contracted to serve in Canada for a three-year term in return for food and lodging, a small salary, and return passage across the ocean. Their masters were commonly settlers, merchants, or religious communities, but their services could be bought, sold, or rented. *Engagés* performed much of the colony's heavy labour in the early years, unloading ships, constructing buildings, and clearing the land for farming. They could not marry, nor could they conduct trade on their own account, and, if they tried to escape, they could face severe criminal punishment: flogging, branding, or even death. Not surprisingly, many *engagés* chose to return to France at the end of their terms, but about half opted to stay in the colony, merging into the colonial peasantry or embarking for the western interior in pursuit of the fur trade.

In the eighteenth century, the colonial military garrison became the most important source of French settlers. The men (that is, those below officer rank) of the *troupes de la marine* were virtually all recruited in France, most from among the marginal and desperate elements of the cities of the kingdom. "Racolage," the use of subterfuge and coercion, up to and including kidnapping, was a common, though unacknowledged, recruitment technique, and so we have no way of knowing how many soldiers came to Canada voluntarily. The colonial authorities generally awarded a number of discharges every year to men who undertook to marry and settle in the colony permanently, and since the normal term of enlistment was essentially unlimited, men were glad to leave the service on these terms.

Whereas soldiers and *engagés* account for the bulk of male immigration, the largest number of women immigrants came as "king's daughters" (*filles du roi*), the term historians have attached to the young women who arrived between 1663 and 1673 as part of the government program of subsidized female immigration. At this time French men of marriageable age outnumbered single French women six to one in Canada, and administrators were intent on giving a boost to procreation by balancing the sex ratio. Of course, potential wives might have been found closer to hand, but they were all Native women and, although there had been talk earlier in the seventeenth century of encouraging the marriage of French men and Native women, the idea had been quietly dropped by the 1660s. Thus the "king's daughters" program represented a racial reorientation as much as a demographic developmentalist agenda. At any rate, about 770 women came, most of them aged twenty-five or under, the majority orphans ("enfants du roi"). Even more than male immigrants, the women who came to New France were of urban background: the bulk of them came from one gigantic hospital/asylum in Paris, La Salpêtrière. They crossed the sea, landed at Quebec, and then plunged straight into the life of colonial society with head-spinning rapidity: within weeks of arrival, most had chosen a mate from among the eager bachelors, had married, and were on their way to a pioneer farm. . . .

The number of French people in the St. Lawrence valley expanded rapidly and steadily. There were about 3,000 colonists in the mid-1660s, when the government began its great program of colonial development; by the early 1680s, after a major spurt of immigration, the figure had risen to some 10,000; when the British took over seven decades later, there were perhaps 75,000 French Canadians. The numbers are quite small, but the growth rate, with its doubling every generation, was phenomenal by the standards of both aboriginal North America and pre-industrial Europe. Moreover, this rate of increase was mostly the product of natural growth. Immigration played an important role only in priming the demographic pump; otherwise, it was basically a matter of babies outnumbering corpses. . . .

. . . With brides marrying young and widows remarrying promptly, a high proportion of the population was, at any given time, currently married and busily engaged in the production of biannual offspring. . . .

. . . Population growth is determined, after all, by the prevalence of death as well as by the pace of childbirth. By the large, the people of New France were healthy and well fed, and consequently, for those who survived the perils of infancy, the prospects of a long life were fairly good. Implicitly contrasting Canada with France's tropical colonies in the West Indies, one visitor wrote: "There is no climate in the world that is healthier; there are no diseases specific to the country; those that I have seen there were brought by French ships. There are nevertheless some women afflicted by goitres, which are caused, they say, by the melting of the snows." . . .

. . . All in all, then, early French Canada was spared the worst effects of both disease and famine. The absence of serious crisis mortality, coupled with colonial marriage patterns favouring high fertility, largely explains why this population grew so much faster than other pre-industrial populations, most notably that of old-regime Europe.

James Horn

English Colonization
of the Chesapeake

Of the half-a-million people who left England in the seventeenth century for all transoceanic destinations, about four-fifths emigrated to America. Most went to colonies which produced the major staples of colonial trade, tobacco and sugar; some 200,000 went to the Caribbean, 120,000 to the Chesapeake, and the remainder to New England and Middle Colonies. The peak period of English emigration occurred within a single generation, from 1630 to 1660, but the rapid growth of the tobacco industry created a continual demand for cheap labour in the Chesapeake throughout the century. During the 1630s and 1640s immigration averaged about 8,000–9,000 per decade and from 1650 to 1680 surged to 16,000–20,000 per decade. Highly sensitive to the social composition of new arrivals and closely attuned to demographic and social changes in the home country, Virginia and Maryland depended on large-scale emigration from English provinces to maintain their populations and support economic growth. Without sustained immigration they would have collapsed.

Settlers came from a broad range of regions and communities: from London and the Home Counties, southern and central England, the West Country, and, in smaller numbers, from northern counties. At least half were from urban backgrounds: small market towns (little more than oversized villages), decayed county towns, growing provincial capitals, bustling ports, and great cities. London dominated colonial trade throughout the century, and the great majority of emigrants, rich and poor alike, began their long journey to the colonies from the city's busy docksides. Like Charles Parker from Staffordshire, who lived in Aldgate 'halfe a yeare' before emigrating in 1685, many migrants

James Horn, "Tobacco Colonies: The Shaping of English Society in the Seventeenth-Century Chesapeake." Copyright © Oxford University Press 1998. Reprinted from *The Origins of Empire: British Overseas Enterprise to the Close of the Seventeenth Century*, edited by Nicholas Canny (Oxford: Oxford University Press, 1998), pp. 176–183, by permission of Oxford University Press.

were not natives of the city but had moved to London a few months or years earlier. Emigration was typically a two-stage process, involving first the move to the city and subsequently the decision to take ship for the colonies. Consequently, large numbers of settlers had already experienced the upheaval of leaving their home parishes and settling in unfamiliar surroundings long before they moved to Virginia and Maryland.

Not less than 70 to 80 per cent of English immigrants arrived in the Chesapeake as indentured servants, and served usually four to five years in return for the cost of their passage, board and lodging, and various freedom dues. They were drawn principally from the impoverished and unemployed of urban slums, poor rural workers from southern and central England, women domestic servants, and men from semi-skilled and, in fewer cases, skilled trades who had decided that prospects were brighter in the colonies. Age at emigration confirms their relatively humble social standing. Most were between 15 and 24 (with 20 and 21 predominating), but servants who were not registered at their port of departure, and who consequently served according to the "Custome of the Country" in the Chesapeake, were younger. About 90 per cent of those arriving without indentures in Lancaster County, Virginia, between 1662 and 1680 were less than 19 years old. The median age was 16. Generally, the youthfulness of servants implies that when they left England they had little stake in society, little substance of their own, and, in many cases, little to lose by leaving home.

Free emigrants, who paid their own passage, shared a number of similarities with servants. The majority were young, male, and single, and came predominantly from the same regions: London, the South-East, and a broad band of counties stretching from the Thames Valley to the West Country. They were a diverse group, ranging from men who had little more than the cost of their passage, fleeing from creditors or misfortune and hoping for better luck in the colonies, to wealthy merchants, gentry, and royal officials. The close connections that developed between merchants and mariners in the two major colonial ports, London and Bristol, and planter-merchants in the Chesapeake should be emphasized. Atlantic commerce, unrestricted by mercantile monopolies and regulated companies, allowed all sorts of petty traders — retailers, wholesale merchants, ship captains, seamen, and victuallers — to dabble in the tobacco trade. Small and middling traders, and mariners — such as James Turpin, a tobacconist of the Liberty of the Tower of London, who went to Virginia in 1675, and Edmund Goddard, citizen and cooper of London, originally from Suffolk—constituted the backbone of the planter-merchant class in the Chesapeake.

Sons of gentlemen and minor gentry comprised another important category of free emigrants. Promoters of colonization and colonial leaders actively encouraged the gentry to move to the New World, believing them the natural rulers of society and finding it inconceivable that the colonies could be brought under orderly rule without persons of rank to govern them. With an eye to creating a Maryland aristocracy, Lord Baltimore offered lordships and manors, "with all such royalties and priviledges" usual in England, to anyone transporting five or more men at their own expense. The *Relation of Maryland* of 1635 contained a list of "Gentlemen adventurers that are gone in person to this Plantation," which was doubtless intended to encourage others to do the same. The majority of gentry, however, did not emigrate with the ambition of becoming part of a permanent *officier* class in the colonies. Provincial politics was important, but more important was earning money from tobacco plantations, merchandizing, and other entrepreneurial activities. From this perspective, colonial gentry are hard to distinguish from merchants. County rulers, such as John Carter of Lancaster County and Thomas Willoughby of Lower Norfolk, Virginia, were both. Their gentle origins gave them an immediate introduction into the higher echelons of colonial society, yet first and foremost they were tobacco merchants and active managers of large plantations.

Black slaves from the Caribbean and Africa were a final category of immigrants, albeit reluctant ones. The size of the black population was initially small, no more than a few hundred before 1650, but from the 1680s, as the supply of indentured servants began to decline, numbers increased rapidly to about 13,000 by 1700 (13 per cent of the total population). Apart from emigrants from London or Bristol, most settlers probably encountered blacks for the first time in the Chesapeake, and in this context made the indelible connection between slavery and race. Yet the response to blacks on an everyday basis was more complex than the general framework of prejudice and the institution of slavery might imply. Especially in the early years of settlement, when numbers were small and blacks worked alongside servants and masters to bring in the tobacco crop, relations between the two races may have been relatively relaxed. Occasionally slaves were freed or purchased their liberty, and some acquired property and were able to live peaceably side-by-side with their white neighbours. The limited opportunities for blacks, slave or free, to improve their condition in this period should not be exaggerated, however. From the 1660s, when Virginia began legislating "stringent racial laws" designed to regulate white–black relations, conditions for blacks began to deteriorate sharply. Mass shipments after 1680 and the changing origin of slaves (brought directly from Africa rather than from the Caribbean) served to intensify discriminatory legislation and further debase the status of blacks.

As the white population increased rapidly—from less than a thousand in 1620 to 8,000 in 1640, 25,000 in 1660, 60,000 in 1680, and 85,000 by 1700—so the spread of English settlement pushed back local Indian populations and opened up hundreds of thousands of acres for tobacco cultivation. By the mid-seventeenth century substantial migration had taken place northward beyond the York River to the Gloucester–Middlesex peninsula and the Northern Neck. Large numbers of Virginia settlers crossed the Potomac into Maryland, the Chesapeake frontier of the 1650s and 1660s, moving up the Western Shore to Providence on the Severn River (Anne Arundel). The axis of population had shifted decisively from the older-settled region of the James River basin to the more northerly rivers of the York, Rappahannock, and Potomac, as well as across the Bay. Expansion came to a halt about the same time as the flow of immigrants from England dried up, and by the beginning of the long tobacco depression (around 1680) settlement had virtually reached its seventeenth-century limits. In the rest of the century less desirable land was taken up in the interiors of established counties and there was a drift of population westwards across the fall line, foreshadowing the major impulse of the following century. . . .

All along the tobacco coast, the formation of local societies was conditioned by the mixture of settlers from different parts of England coming into contact with one another, as well as, to varying degrees, with Indians, blacks, and other Europeans. Early settlers of York County came from London, Kent, Surrey, Essex, Middlesex, Bedfordshire, East Anglia, Wiltshire, Gloucestershire, Devon, Somerset, and Yorkshire. A group of colonists who settled in Westmoreland County, Virginia, in the middle years of the century came from Bristol, Plymouth, Somerset, Shropshire, Bedfordshire, Middlesex, and London. In a period when local customs and traditions were a vibrant force in shaping daily life and experience in England, the formation of communities in the Chesapeake, which suddenly brought together men and women from a multitude of different English backgrounds, constituted an abrupt break with the past. Unavoidably, much of the particular richness of immigrants' own provincial backgrounds was lost, but contact with other English settlers and other peoples provided an equally rich source for forging a new regional culture. . . .

In terms of first impressions, it is worth stressing that to English eyes what was missing in Virginia's and Maryland's landscape was as significant as what was present. Immigrants, whether from urban or rural backgrounds, were used to living in a society where there was a hierarchy of interdependent communities: village, market town, provincial capital, and city. Few people in England lived more than a few miles from a local town—an hour, if that, by road or across country. Along the tobacco coast, only the colonies' capitals resembled small towns and for most of the century even they were nearer in size, if not character, to English villages. Missing, too, was the bustle of fairs and market days, crowded taverns and inns (thick with the smell of smoke, ale, and stale bodies), and busy thoroughfares bringing people and goods to trade. Approximations existed, but nothing that could compare to the press of people and places familiar to English men and women in their native "countries."

Getting used to the absence of important aspects of daily life, taken for granted in England, posed one of the most difficult challenges to settlers adapting to conditions along the Bay, but certain realities, faced by all colonists, proved equally challenging. Arriving in summer, they would have been struck by the heat (as 'hot as in Spaine'), humidity, and swarms of biting insects. "The Natural Temperature of the Inha[bit]ed part of the Country," Robert Beverley remarked, "is hot and moist." Climate and health were closely related in the minds of colonists, and the heat and "Moisture . . . occasion'd by the abundance of low Grounds, Marshes, Creeks, and Rivers" were believed harmful. As early as the 1620s, the region was well known for its high mortality, and its insalubrious reputation persisted throughout the century. Colonists, George Gardyner opined, were subject to "much sickness or death. For the air is exceeding unwholesome, insomuch as one of three scarcely liveth the first year at this time." Up to 40 per cent of new arrivals may have died in their first couple of years, commonly of a variety of ailments associated with malaria and intestinal disorders. Malaria occasionally reached epidemic proportions among settlers and frequently left survivors in poor health, easy prey to a variety of other diseases. Even if the outcome was not fatal, most immigrants experienced a period of sickness or "seasoning" in their first year. Moving to Virginia and Maryland, like moving from the provinces to London, was risky and amounted to a calculated gamble on survival. For those who survived and lived long enough the rewards could be considerable, but that very success was predicated in part on a rapid turnover of population caused by the high death rate.

Natural population growth was retarded also by the considerable sexual imbalance that existed throughout the century. Besides being an immigrant society, the Chesapeake was emphatically a male society. Responding to the demand of the tobacco industry for labourers, six times more men than women emigrated in the 1630s, and although greater numbers of females took ship after 1650, men continued to outnumber women by nearly three to one throughout the rest of the century. The highly skewed sex ratio restricted family formation, severely limited numbers of children per household, and dictated that as many as 20–30 per cent of men went to their graves unmarried. The problem was exacerbated by the relatively late age at which immigrant women married. Since the great majority of women (like men) arrived in the Chesapeake as indentured servants and were usually obliged to finish their term of service before marrying, they were unable to take a husband until their mid-twenties, which was about the same age they would have married in England. A shortage of women did not, therefore, lead to a lower age of marriage which would have increased their reproductive lives and the birth rate. Any one of these things — high rates of mortality and morbidity, sexual imbalance, and late age at first marriage — could have severely restricted natural increase, but acting in concert "demographic failure along the tobacco coast was inevitable". Not until the final years of the century did the white population of Virginia and Maryland become self-sustaining.

V

Revolutions: The Great Transformation

The age of empire in the Atlantic world suffered a tremendous body blow in the half-century from 1775 to 1825. The empires that had created ties of authority, trade, and culture stretching across the Atlantic were fractured and largely demolished. Europe's American colonies rose up in rebellion and won revolutions and wars of independence. Many of these struggles were the consequence to some degree of revolutions in Europe itself, particularly the French and Spanish revolutions. Africa, however, remained within the imperial system and, in the last decades of the nineteenth century, entered a new age of empire with the formation of vast territorial colonies located not only on the coast but throughout the interior of the continent. For the Atlantic as a whole, the age of revolution was a great, but not total, transformation.

The historian Robert R. Palmer has called this time "the age of democratic revolutions." It is the ideological consistency of the revolutionary movements, more than their social and economic causes or political consequences, that marks them as an Atlantic phenomenon. Their democratic, or perhaps better still, liberal, roots are found in the theories of the great political philosophers of the late seventeenth and eighteenth centuries. John Locke, C. de Montesquieu, David Hume, Jean-Jacques Rousseau, and others reacted against monarchical absolutism and the long-held assumption that man was basically an evil being who needed to be restrained by government. The new emphasis on man's rationality and the idea of enlightened self-interest gave rise to the fear of the unrestrained power of government and a need to constrain not men so much as the state itself. Government should be based on the consent of the governed; the powers of government should be divided in order to protect against despotism; men should be equal in law and their natural rights protected; the people should be sovereign; and the individual should be free: these ideas and others related to them became the fundamental principles of the revolutionaries of the late eighteenth and early nineteenth century.

Each revolution, of course, was unique, due to the particular conditions and events which gave rise to it. Each revolution developed in a singular political culture that emphasized different elements of the relatively new and radical liberal tradition. Each revolution faced different challenges and military struggles. For these reasons and despite their common commitment to liberal principles, each revolution produced different courses and results.

The commonalities and differences are explored in the following set of readings. The first Atlantic revolution, the American Revolution, according to Jack P. Greene, was both conservative and radical at the same time. American revolutionaries sought to conserve their existing liberties and system of self-government, but unlike the other revolutions of the age it was produced by the most egalitarian society in the world, an egalitarianism that shaped the revolution as much as inequality shaped the revolutions of France, Saint Domingue, Spain, and Spanish America.

Susan Dunn compares the "sister revolutions" of America and France and considers the intriguing contrast between the ideals of American political conflict and French political unity. In the American colonies, the rights and liberties the revolutionaries acclaimed existed for the most part in practice. In France, on the other hand, revolutionaries sought to create—not protect—liberty and equality. It is harder, Montesquieu wrote, to release a nation from servitude than to enslave a free nation.

Franklin W. Knight discusses the influence and intervention of the French Revolution in the revolution of Saint Domingue in the

1790s. This Caribbean revolution, the only successful slave rebellion in history, was a complicated social and political struggle, which nevertheless was profoundly influenced by the liberal principles of liberty and equality. These principles, Knight shows, held different meanings and demanded different actions for planters, mulattos, and slaves. Although the revolution freed the slaves of Saint Domingue and created the second independent republic in the New World, its political consequences were far from liberal. The war itself—and the post-independence insecurity of Haiti—created and prolonged a powerful military caste and a tradition of dictatorship and despotism.

The revolutions of the Spanish world are considered by Jaime Rodríguez O. The revolutions and wars of independence in Spanish America often overshadow in modern historiography the Spanish Revolution. Rodríguez shows the common Hispanic liberal principles that influenced the Spanish and Spanish American revolutions. As in France, the Spanish Revolution ultimately ended in the restoration of monarchy. And, as in the United States, the Spanish American revolutions led to the creation of independent republics. The success of liberal government, however, was undermined by the rise of a military caste, as in Haiti, as well as a rival political tradition that emphasized a powerful executive.

The Atlantic revolutions of the late eighteenth and early nineteenth century were all based on liberal principles. Liberty, however, noted Bolívar who quoted Rousseau "is a succulent morsel, but one difficult to digest." North Americans, French, Dutch, Haitians, Portuguese and Brazilians, and Spaniards and Spanish Americans found liberal principles tasty. Their culture and history, the nature of each society, the relationship between colony and metropolis, and other particularities led revolutionaries to see "liberty" in different ways, to seek it by employing different methods, and to ensure it by building different kinds of governments. Liberty was "difficult to digest"; naturally, it went down easier in some revolutions than others.

Jack P. Greene

The American Revolution

In the United States, historians and the broader public have, for most of the past two centuries, looked at the American Revolution principally as the first step in the creation of the American nation. They have stressed the process of nation building epitomized by the creation of a republican political regime in each state and the subsequent establishment of a federal system for the distribution of power between the states and the nation. They have emphasized the centrality of the drive for national self-realization that, beginning during the revolutionary era, provided the foundation for an American national identity. From the national-state perspective that has largely shaped the writing of United States history, such an emphasis makes considerable sense. For developing an understanding of *why* a revolution occurred in North America during the late eighteenth century and *what* that revolution was, however, it is, in at least two major respects, seriously deficient. First, it obscures the extraordinary extent to which the American Revolution was very much a British revolution. Second, it seriously underestimates the powerful continuities between the colonial and the national eras and thereby significantly overestimates the revolutionary character of the revolution.

In this essay, I will argue that the American Revolution can be most fully comprehended by viewing it as the first step in the still incomplete process of dismantling the imperial structures created during the early modern era to bring newly encountered areas of the globe into political, economic, and cultural association with the new nation-states of Europe. The first of many such events, the American Revolution differed somewhat from many of those that followed it. I will sketch out some of the more important of these differences, differences that defined and accounted for the particularity of the American Revolution. In doing so, I will focus on three subjects: first, the nature of the British imperial polity in which the revolution occurred; second, the

Jack P. Greene, "The American Revolution," *American Historical Review*, 105, no. 1 (2000): 93–102. This document can also be found in Jack P. Greene and J. R. Pole, eds., *Colonial British America: Essays in the New History of the Early Modern Era*, pp. 195–215.

character of the political societies that participated in it; and, third, the nature of the republican polities created during it.

With regard to the first subject, the early modern English or, after 1707, British Empire was not held together by force. England may have been one of the earliest and most centralized and efficient of the nation-states that emerged in western Europe during the fifteenth, sixteenth, and seventeenth centuries. Like all the rest of those states, however, it was, for much of the two centuries after 1560 and more especially after the union with Scotland, a composite state characterized by indirect governance, fragmented authority, an inchoate theory of national sovereignty, and limited fiscal, administrative, and coercive resources. These conditions dictated that the new extended transatlantic polity we now call the British Empire would not be characterized by a devolution of authority outward from an imperial center to new American peripheries. Rather, authority in that empire would be constructed from the peripheries outward, in two phases. The first involved the creation in America, through the activities of participants in the colonizing impulse, of new arenas of local and individual power. The second involved the actual creation of authority through negotiation between these new arenas and the metropolitan representatives of the center that aspired to bring them under its jurisdiction and to which they desire to be attached. In the earliest stages of this colonizing process, the English state, lacking in revenue, had no choice but to farm out the task of colonization to private groups organized into chartered trading companies or to wealthy individuals known as proprietors. But none of these entities was able to mobilize on its own the resources necessary to establish a successful colony. Hence, they had no choice but to seek cooperation and contributions from settlers, traders, and other individual participants in the colonizing process.

Efforts to enlist such cooperation acknowledged the fact that the actual process of establishing effective centers of English power in America was often less the result of the activities of colonial organizers or licensees than of the many groups and individuals who took actual possession of land, built estates and businesses, turned what had previously been wholly aboriginal social landscapes into partly European ones, constructed and presided over a variable system of economic arrangements, created towns, counties, parishes, or other political units, and subjugated, reduced to profitable labor, killed off, or expelled the original inhabitants. By dint of their industry and initiative, tens of thousands of immigrants created social spaces for themselves and their families and thereby manufactured for themselves status, capital, and power.

Throughout early modern English/British America, independent individual participants in the colonizing process, English and other Europeans, were thus engaged in what can be described as a deep and widespread process of individual self-empowerment. In the contemporary Old World, only a tiny fraction of the male population ever managed to rise out of a state of socioeconomic dependency to achieve the civic competence, the full right to have a voice in political decisions, that was the preserve of independent property holders. By contrast, as a consequence of the easy availability of land and other resources, a very large proportion of the adult male white colonists acquired land or other resources, built estates, and achieved individual independence.

This development gave rise to strong demands on the part of the large empowered settler populations for the extension to the colonies of the same rights to security of property and civic participation that appertained to the empowered, high status, and independent property holders in the polities from which they came. In their view, colonial government, like metropolitan government, should guarantee that men of their standing would not be governed without consultation or in ways that were patently against their interests. Along with the vast distance of the colonies from Britain, these circumstances powerfully pushed those who were nominally in charge of the colonies toward the establishment and toleration of political structures that involved active consultation with local settlers. Consultation meant that local populations would more willingly both acknowledge the legitimacy of the authority of private agents of colonization and contribute to local costs. The earliest stages of colonization thus resulted in the emergence in new colonial peripheries of many new and relatively autonomous centers of English power effectively under local control.

Once these centers of local power had been established, agents of metropolitan centralization found it exceedingly difficult to bring them under regulation. Even after the crown had assumed responsibility for all but a few of the colonies, royal officials found themselves having to govern large populations of independent property holders who insisted on living under political arrangements that provided them with extraordinary local autonomy *and* with the fundamental guarantees of Englishness, including especially government by consent, rule by law, and the sanctity of private property, defined as property in individual legal and civil rights as well as property in land and other forms of wealth.

Combined with the scarcity of fiscal and coercive resources and the reluctance of the metropolitan government to spend money for imperial purposes, settler expectations inevitably meant that authority in the early modern British Empire would not be concentrated at the center but, instead, distributed between the center and the peripheries. More specifically, these conditions meant that the metropolitan government would lack the means unilaterally to enforce its will and authority in distant peripheries, that central direction in the British Empire would be minimal, that metropolitan authority in the colonies would be consensual and heavily dependent on provincial opinion, and that effective power in distant colonial polities would be firmly situated in provincial and local governments, which were widely participatory and solidly under the control of large, broadly based, and resident property-owning settler classes. The early modern British Empire was thus a loose association of largely self-governing polities. What was legal, what was constitutional, was determined not by fiat but by negotiation.

The self-made, possessing settler classes of these polities acknowledged metropolitan authority not because it was imposed on them or, primarily, because, as some contemporaries wrote, it afforded them a degree of protection in a war-prone world and gave them access to wider markets and cheaper manufactures. Rather, they accepted that authority because it brought with it incorporation into a larger system of national identity that guaranteed their Englishness, their inheritance in the form of English legal and political traditions, and their continuing control over the polities they had helped to create and to which they were committed. Predominantly reflecting a respect for the extensive empowerment and high degree of corporate and individual liberty of landowning classes, British imperial governance, like British internal governance, functioned in the colonies to preserve that empowerment and liberty and the property on which it was founded.

A similar case in reference to the role of the peripheries in the construction of authority can be made concerning all early modern European empires, but contemporary British commentators had no doubt that Britain had "dealt more liberally with her colonies than

[had] any other nation." No other European state seemed to have extended its colonies so much "liberty to manage their own affairs their own way." "In every thing, except their foreign trade," noted Adam Smith, "the liberty of English colonists" was "complete. It is in every respect equal to that of their fellow-citizens at home, and is secured in the same manner, by an assembly of the representatives of the people." "The government of the English colonies," he observed, "is perhaps the only one which, since the world began, could give perfect security to the inhabitants of so very distant a province."

If the British Empire was a consensual empire composed of a loose association of essentially self-governing polities in which authority and effective power were distributed between the center and the peripheries, the settler societies that emerged in colonial British America were, both socially and politically, certainly the most radical in the contemporary Western world. Colonial enterprisers and many of the earliest settlers hoped to establish hierarchical social orders and authoritative institutions of state and church of the kind they had known in England. From the beginning, however, social and economic conditions in America operated to prevent them from realizing their aspirations. The wide availability of land and the scarcity of labor incited individual settlers to industry, activity, and schemes of improvement, and they built societies that were radically different from most societies in the Old World. These new settler societies had, among the free segments of the population, significantly higher proportions of property holders, higher rates of family formation, broader opportunities for achieving economic competence and personal empowerment, less poverty, fewer and less rigid social distinctions, and far less powerful and obtrusive political and religious establishments.

The fundamental social barrier that in the Old World separated the genteel from the common sort who worked with their hands was far more permeable and far less formidable in America. In the expansive world of colonial British America, a world characterized, especially during the six decades just before the American Revolution, by extraordinary territorial, demographic, and economic growth and social development, the more or less continuous process of social elaboration in older areas and community formation in newer regions meant the more or less continuous creation of new opportunities, new property, and new authority. From the beginning of settlement, ambitious men and women seized the opportunities available to them to acquire substance and to demand a share of that public authority that throughout the English-speaking world had long been an attribute of substance.

As a result, the settler societies of colonial British America never developed the social foundations necessary for either an aristocracy or a social system of legally established ranks. Social differentiation proceeded apace, as some families outdistanced others in the drive for material success and social achievement. But social hierarchies were always open to infiltration or challenge from below: elite authority was tenuous, deference was weak, social relations exhibited a deeply egalitarian cast, gentility coexisted uneasily with commonality, and the combinations of older and newer gentlemen who dominated public life on the eve of the revolution did so at the sufferance of their less wealthy neighbors. From time to time and place to place, some members of these largely self-created and always continuously circulating and reformulating elites aspired to unify social, political, cultural, and economic authority in themselves, but few of them were ever able to do so to a significant degree over a long period. In contrast to the complex and highly stratified world of early modern Europe, these settler societies were thus essentially rankless societies in the sense that all free people occupied the same status before the law and enjoyed the same opportunity to strive for social respect. The profoundly egalitarian social orders of the free segments of these settler societies would provide a sturdy foundation for the limited egalitarian impulses of revolutionary and early republican America.

If these settler societies were exceptional in terms of their abundant life chances for free individuals and social elasticity, they were also latently republican. Long before they formally became republican in 1776, the British colonies in America, as Adam Smith pointed out in *The Wealth of Nations*, were "republican" in "their manners . . . and their governments." With economic competence and political empowerment so widely distributed, government rested on a broad, popular base. Political leaders, increasingly drawn from a narrower band of those ambitious to shine in the public realm, could retain power only by catering to the wider interests they shared with this larger citizenry.

In the remarkably popular polities they created, settlers dominated both the legislatures that enacted and the courts and civil offices that enforced the laws, laws that principally expressed settler concerns to preserve the property they were creating through their individual pursuits of happiness.

Compared with that of England, the public realm in these settler polities was relatively inexpensive and unobtrusive. Civil or bureaucratic establishments were small and largely volunteer. With little poverty, there were few expenses for maintaining the poor. With either weak church establishments and practical toleration or full religious freedom, there were small or no tithes. With no standing armies, defense costs were slight except during the last intercolonial wars from 1739 to 1763. All of these conditions meant that, compared to the polities of the Old World, taxes were inconsiderable and the proportion of private income that went for public expenditures was very small. Serving a citizenry that exhibited an unusual degree of political enlightenment and a warm attachment to their identities as freeborn Britons, the leaders of these settler republics stood for not only inexpensive but also locally autonomous government. Deeply suspicious of any intrusions of external power from the metropolis, they were determined to keep authority in local hands.

In these essentially self-regulating societies, as the Scottish emigrant and Pennsylvania lawyer James Wilson pointed out, society was evidently not "the scaffolding of government," but government was "the scaffolding of society." The purpose of government and law was to "protect and to improve social life" by making sure that the lands, goods, chattels, and rights "collected by the labour and industry of" settlers remained, inviolably, "their property," and the measure of a good government was the extent to which it promoted "the peace, happiness, and prosperity, the increase, and the affections of the people."

Colonial British Americans thus subscribed to the ideas that society was anterior to government; that the functions of laws, governments, and constitutions were to promote the ends of civil society, especially the great end of facilitating the pursuit of happiness by the individuals who composed that society; and that that pursuit would be, for most people, conducted far more satisfyingly in the society of the family, the neighborhood, or local civic institutions than in the small public arenas at the provincial level. Within these settler republics, as within the broader British imperial polity, much effective power remained within and radiated upward from the localities. Everywhere by the middle decades of the eighteenth century, well-articulated provincial creole identities sustained this deep and abiding localism. These identities were derived out of the nature of the specific physical spaces occupied, the societies constructed in those spaces, and the experiences—the histories—shared by several generations of inhabitants of those spaces.

Throughout the colonial period and beyond, however, the radical character of these social polities always existed in tension with another and perhaps an even deeper social impulse, the impulse to create in America cultural spaces and societies that were recognizably English. Settlers thought of themselves as involved in a great social and cultural transformation of the territories they occupied. In this transformation, individual European settlers and African slaves and their creole descendants slowly substituted a European for an indigenous landscape and system of political and cultural arrangements. Beginning on the European seaboard, they replaced the extensive agricultural villages, hunting camps, and paths of the Amerindians with intensive agricultural settlements laced with roads, country market towns tied to sizable coastal trading posts, and increasingly sophisticated commercial and social infrastructures, including stores, towns, courthouses, and churches. In the process, they inscribed the landscape with property lines and created civil polities to enforce property divisions.

Those involved in this process—settlers, land developers, merchants, and artisans—conceived of it as a massive civilizing project. Deeply aware of the profound transformative effects of what they were doing, they thought of themselves as engaged in a laborious and noble effort to conquer the wilderness by felling forests, creating new fields, orchards, and pastures, substituting domestic for wild animals, and otherwise bringing the land under their mastery. In the process, they changed indigenous landscapes that to them appeared rude, uncultivated, and under-utilized into spaces that were civil, cultivated, and productive: improved spaces that represented the outermost extensions of those Old World places on which they relied for their norms and standards of a civil society. From the beginning of English settlement in 1607, this story of the transformation of the wilderness was the principal story that informed, connected, and gave meaning to the lives of the millions of people who participated in it.

Along with their ancient bonds of consanguinity, culture, traditions, and language, their close ties of economic interest, their continuing need for metropolitan military and naval protection, and their enjoyment of the laws and liberties of Britons, the obvious achievements represented by this ongoing transformation powerfully reinforced, throughout the late colonial era, settler attachment to Britain. Simultaneously, however, the continuing gap between those achievements and the standards of the metropolitan center, between the relatively undifferentiated and simple agricultural societies settlers had created in America and the increasingly refined and cultivated world of metropolitan Britain, as well as their extensive use of African slavery rendered their claims to Britishness problematic and stimulated a profound yearning for metropolitan recognition of the validity of those claims.

From the perspective of later political revolutions, the revolution that occurred in this particular empire on the part of these particular societies was distinctive. It was not the result of internal tensions, social, religious, or political. Although the southern and middle colonies were wealthier than New England and although high military expenditures during the Seven Years' War created short-term economic problems for some colonies, all of them were broadly prosperous on the eve of the American Revolution. Throughout the 1760s and 1770s, the colonies continued to exhibit the territorial expansion, the economic and demographic growth, and the social elaboration that had long characterized them. What may make the American Revolution different is that the origins of the revolution lay not in America but in Britain. As metropolitan officials increasingly began to appreciate the growing economic and strategic importance of the colonies to British prosperity and national power in the 1740s and 1750s, they more and more began to worry lest the weakness of metropolitan authority and the extensive autonomy enjoyed by the colonies might somehow lead to their loss.

Moved by such fears and developing a new sense of imperial order that would only reach full flower in the nineteenth century, they undertook a series of measures, the combined effects of which would have been to change the British Empire from the loose federal polity it had long been into a more unitary polity with authority more clearly fixed at the center. Such measures directly challenged the autonomy of colonies over their local affairs. By subjecting the colonies to legislation and other directives to which the settler populations of those colonies had not given their consent, those measures also called into question settler claims to a British identity, the central element of which was the capacity of colonists, as Britons, to enjoy the traditional rights of Britons. Not surprisingly, these measures, interpreted by the vast majority of the broadly empowered settler populations in the colonies as an effort to subject them to a far more intrusive imperial order, elicited a powerful defense of the local corporate rights of the colonies and a rising demand for explicit metropolitan recognition of settler entitlement to the British liberties and the British identity settlers associated with those local rights.

Along with the intense settler resistance to these new measures, the stridency of their demands wounded metropolitan pride and provoked counter and highly condescending assertions of metropolitan superiority that suggested that colonists, far from being true Britons, were a kind of Others whose low characters, rude surroundings, and barbarous cruelty to their African slaves rendered them, on the scale of civilization, only slightly above the Amerindians they had displaced or the Africans among whom they lived. Such attitudes powerfully informed the measures that elicited the broad-based and extensive settler resentment and resistance of 1774–1775 and the decision for independence in 1776. The American Revolution can thus best be understood as a settler revolt, a direct response to metropolitan measures that seemed both to challenge settler control over local affairs and to deny settler claims to a British identity.

In rejecting monarchy and the British connection and adopting republicanism, the leaders of these settler revolts did not have to preside over a wholesale, much less a violent, transformation of the radical political societies that colonial British Americans had constructed between 1607 and 1776. In the words of one later commentator, "when the people of the United Colonies separated from Great Britain, they changed the form, but not the substance of their government." In every state, peculiar social, religious, economic, and political tensions shaped the course of revolutionary development. Indeed, these local tensions primarily account for the substantial differences in the revolutionary experiences from one state to another. Wherever during the late colonial era there had been abuses of executive authority, judicial or civil corruption, unequal representation, opposition to a state church, or other political problems, the new republican state constitutions or later legislation endeavored to address those problems. Against the background of the deepening political consciousness generated by the extensive political debates over the nature of British imperial constitution after 1764, the creators of those constitutions also experimented, in limited ways, with improvements to their existing political systems. The widespread political mobilization that occurred after 1764 and especially in 1775–1776 also resulted, in many states, in an expansion of legislative seats and public offices and a downward shift in political leadership that brought more settlers of somewhat less, though still substantial, property into active roles in the public realm. With astonishingly few exceptions, however, leaders of late colonial regimes retained authority through the transition to republicanism, and the republican regimes they created in 1776 and after bore a striking resemblance to the social polities they replaced.

Everywhere, political authority remained in the hands of the predominant groups among the existing settler population. As during the colonial period, the central government, an unintended consequence of the union of colonies that had come together to resist metropolitan aggression, was weak. In contrast to the French Revolution, the American Revolution did not produce a unitary national state. Effective power remained in the states, even, for a century or more, after the strengthening of the national government with the Federal Constitution in the late 1780s. For at least another century, provincial or state identities remained more powerful than the continental, or American, identity that only began to develop during the 1760s and 1770s. At the state and local levels, government remained an instrument of settler desires. Although it was somewhat more broadly participatory, it continued to rest on a limited conception of civic competence, which extended only to independent people, and on equality, that is, civil or religious equality among such people. The exigencies of war stimulated an extraordinary expansion of the public realm, and, at least during the earliest decades, republican government turned out to be far more intrusive than colonial government had ever been. Yet settler leaders continued to prefer inexpensive and small government. As during the colonial era, they kept bureaucracies small, refused to pay for permanent peacetime military and naval establishments, and were cautious in supporting public works. Like their colonial counterparts, these republican polities everywhere continued to be instruments of the predominant settler classes, principally concerned with the maintenance of orderly social relations, the dispensing of justice, and, most important of all, the protection of private property.

Nor did the new republican regimes preside over a large-scale social reconstruction. The pursuit of individual domestic happiness in the private realm remained the central cultural imperative. The social order continued to be open, social relations continued to be fundamentally egalitarian, wealth remained the primary criterion for social standing, and aspiring elites continued to decry the absence of deference from those of less wealth. With no restraints on the accumulation of private wealth, social differentiation continued unabated. Despite their own frequent, albeit often unintentional, transgressions against private property, republican state settler regimes continued to reaffirm the sanctity of private property. Land titles remained secure, except for some of those who opposed the revolution, some of whose land was confiscated and sold to pay public expenses. Next to land, slaves were the most valuable form of property in the states as a whole, and notwithstanding the emergence of a powerful antislavery movement after 1760, the institution of slavery persisted in every state in which it retained its economic viability and represented a substantial investment. As Chief Justice John Marshall later observed, "all contracts and rights, respecting property, remained unchanged by the Revolution." In effect, the decision to retain or abolish slavery was, like so much else in the new American republic, a matter for local option.

So intent have some scholars been on assimilating the American Revolution to the great European revolutions, on emphasizing its revolutionary character and radical discontinuity with the American past, that they have by and large neglected to explore the bearing of earlier American political and social experience on the events and developments of the American Revolution. A comprehension of the important implications of American social experience on contemporary understandings of that experience powerfully suggests that the colonial and revolutionary eras were much of a piece. The most radical result of the revolution was the steady and substantial reconception of political and social relations that occurred over the following half-century. In my view, however, this conceptual discontinuity needs to be understood for what it was: an elaborate working out of the logic of some of the tendencies long characteristic of the loose imperial polity of the early modern British Empire and the radical political societies of colonial British America, societies that, precisely because of their radical character, could make such a profoundly conservative revolution.

Susan Dunn

Sister Revolutions: America and France

Indeed, there was much to admire during the 1780s and early 1790s, as the American Revolution was proceeding healthily from stage to stage, accomplishing its goals. The war of the 1770s had brought independence. The Philadelphia Convention of 1787 created stable democratic institutions and a venerated Constitution, to which the founders added a Bill of Rights in 1791. Throughout the 1790s, political parties were slowly evolving, preparing the political terrain for the watershed election of 1800, when the defeated incumbent party, the Federalists, would peacefully turn over the reins of government to their adversaries, the Jeffersonian Republicans, a transfer of power rare in the history of modern revolutions.

But could Americans reasonably expect the French to learn and profit from their example? Or were the lessons the Americans had to offer and the requirements of the French "hopelessly different" from each other, as some historians contend? The French seemed to face a far more complex challenge than had the Americans. Americans, after all, were content with their legal system; they had no feudal heritage to extirpate, no hereditary social orders to combat, no privileged leisure-class aristocracy to democratize and integrate into society, no tradition of religious intolerance to oppose, no wretched poverty to eliminate, and few domestic insurrections to quell.

According to Lord Acton, both Jefferson and Madison admitted that a few seats for the Americans in both houses of Parliament in England would have set at rest the whole question of revolution. As Jefferson made clear in the Declaration of Independence, Americans wanted to return to the rights and freedoms they had long enjoyed before Parliament and King George III violated them. In this sense, their revolution signified a *return*, as the literal astronomical meaning of the word "revolution" suggests — "a circuit around a central axis, ending at the point from whence the motion began."

But for some in France, revolution denoted not return but total transformation. The goal of French radicals was to reconceive and reorganize the political, legal, and social structure of the nation, to overthrow the nation's institutions, to break with a thousand years of history.

And yet, as different as the historical, military, and social circumstances were, as different as the size of their populations — 24 million people in France, fewer than 4 million in the thirteen colonies — the two revolutions shared significant features. The whole Atlantic civilization, the historian R. R. Palmer commented, "was swept in the last four decades of the eighteenth century by a single revolutionary movement that shared certain common goals." In America and in France, revolutionary leaders wanted to install representative governments based on popular sovereignty and the will of the majority. They called for conventions and drafted constitutions. They composed Declarations or Bills of Rights that posited the same inalienable human rights — life, liberty, and the pursuit of happiness — and upheld the principle of citizens' equality before the law. The purpose of government, they declared, was to protect the rights and freedom of citizens.

Leaders in both countries were convinced that they were constructing a "new order for the ages." The French created a new calendar in 1792, beginning time with the year of the abolition of the monarchy and the crowning of the people as sovereign. They were convinced that they could "regenerate" humanity. Americans too conceived their revolution as a radical beginning, not just for America but for the entire world. "Happily for America, happily we trust for the whole human race," Madison trumpeted in *The Federalist* No. 14, we "pursued a new and more noble course . . . and accomplished a revolution that has no parallel in the annals of human society."

The American model was France's for the taking—after all, she had paid for it, and her officers and soldiers had fought and died for it. When the French set about drafting a constitution and establishing unfamiliar political and judicial institutions, advice and wisdom from thoughtful Americans might not have been unseasonable. Lafayette, for his part, was intent on following as closely as possible lessons from America. At one Paris dinner party in June 1789, he listened to Gouverneur Morris's suggestions. "I [took] the opportunity to tell him," Morris wrote in his diary, "that if the [Third Estate] are now very moderate they will probably succeed, but if violent must inevitably fail."

But mostly Lafayette listened to Jefferson. In the summer of 1789, Lafayette brought his friends to Jefferson's spacious town house on the Champs-Elysées, where, over dinner and port, they debated the makeup of the new government. Aware of the diplomatic necessity of appearing "neutral and passive," Jefferson listened, saying little. But in private Lafayette and Jefferson spent hours together discussing their ideas for a constitution and a Charter of Rights for France. Eager to assist, Jefferson sketched out his recommendations, advising the creation of a representative body that, with the consent of the king, levied taxes and made laws, and an independent judiciary. In lieu of an itemized Bill of Rights, he offered some general principles of freedom and legal process.

"I have never feared for the ultimate result," Jefferson wrote to the young marquis the following spring, "tho' I have feared for you personally. Take care of yourself, my dear friend, for tho' I think your nation would in any event work out her salvation, I am persuaded were she to lose you, it would cost her oceans of blood, & years of confusion & anarchy." Jefferson was convinced that Lafayette had a major role to play and that, more than anyone else, he was the Revolution's American anchor. Without Lafayette, the Revolution might fail. Jefferson had always admired the Frenchman's "zeal," "good sense," and "sound genius." If Lafayette had a "foible," it was his "canine" appetite for popularity and fame, but Jefferson believed that he would get over this.

Jefferson was buoyantly optimistic about the prospects for change in France. To his friend Maria Cosway he admitted that the cutting off of heads was so "*à la mode*" that he was happy, upon awakening, to feel his own head attached to his shoulders. Nevertheless, even mobs roaming through the streets scarcely diminished his enthusiasm for the Revolution. Agreeing with their goals, he congratulated himself on having slept quietly through the night, as peaceably as ever. "So far it seemed that your revolution has got along with a steady pace," he confidently wrote to Lafayette in the spring of 1790, though reminding him that "we are not to expect to be translated from despotism to liberty in a feather-bed."

On July 15, 1789, the day after the storming of the Bastille, Lafayette was asked by the National Assembly to command the National Guard. Though his task was to assure law, order, and security in Paris, he always stressed his own view that the overriding function of the Guard was to unify the people. The oath of loyalty that he swore promised that the Guard's members would "remain united with all Frenchmen by the indissoluble bonds of brotherhood."

Lafayette proved adept at calming angry mobs, restoring order, and saving lives. His talent for finding just the right mediating gesture defused many incendiary situations. He astutely ordered the demolition of the Bastille, the hated prison that symbolized the feudal past. Once, when the king's guards were threatened by a mob, Lafayette handed one of the guardsmen the revolutionary ribbon from his own hat, appeasing and delighting the crowd. The insignia he had chosen for the National Guard was also a diplomatic masterstroke; it combined blue and red, the colors of Paris, and the white of the Bourbons, a marriage of revolution and monarchy. Remembering the skill with which Washington had carefully created his public persona of disinterested leader, he too declined any salary.

And yet, Lafayette failed in his mission. His paramount wish had been to unite all revolutionary factions around a constitutional monarchy that embraced revolutionary values of equality and freedom. But unity proved an elusive dream. On the right, royalists condemned him for insulting the royal family and tolerating mob demonstrations. On the left, radicals attacked him for quelling popular demonstrations, defending the king, and seeking power for himself. His popularity was completely destroyed in 1791 when he ordered the Guard to fire on demonstrators demanding the abolition of the monarchy. "I verily believe that if M. de La Fayette were to appear just now in Paris unattended by his army," Gouverneur Morris wrote to George Washington a few weeks later, "he would be torn to pieces. Thank God we have no populace in America." Resigning from the Guard, Lafayette accepted the king's appointment to head the army in the north. But when the monarchy was abolished in the fall of 1792, knowing that his situation was hopeless, Lafayette fled France. He hoped to reach the Belgian coast, from where he could sail to America, but Austrian troops refused to allow him free passage and had him arrested. Lafayette was imprisoned in Austria for five harsh years.

While Lafayette languished in one lugubrious, damp prison after another, his health steadily deteriorating, the Revolution in France was plunging into a downward spiral, devolving into Terror, devouring its children and its leaders. Devastating news of the guillotining of the pitiable monarch and Queen Marie Antoinette as well as frightening reports of summary arrests, mass drownings, and the decapitation of thousands of French men and women trickled in to him. When his wife, Adrienne, visited him in his dungeon, she recounted the hideous details of the guillotining of her cherished mother.

Americans, still grateful to Lafayette for his role in their revolution, followed his misfortunes with deep sympathy. During the decade of the 1790s, the young American government displayed considerably more appreciation toward the valiant marquis than toward the French nation that had played a decisive role in the American victory over England—and this despite the Treaty of Amity and Commerce that the Americans and French had signed in 1778. Indeed, the treaty, which had stipulated that France and the United States would defend each other against England and that neither nation would conclude a formal truce with England without the consent of the other, had become an embarrassment. Despite the enthusiasm of many Americans for the French revolutionary cause, Washington's policy of neutrality, buttressed by his own immense prestige and by Federalists' antipathy for regicide in France and commonsensical reluctance to plunge their country back into war with England, succeeded in relegating the treaty to oblivion.

In 1793, Washington, though reluctant to intervene officially in European politics, instructed Gouverneur Morris, the minister to France, to express "informally the sentiments and the wishes of this country regarding M. de La Fayette." Again in 1796 Washington made his objections about Lafayette's imprisonment known to the Austrian ambassador in London, and finally he wrote to the emperor himself, all to no avail. Only when the new moderate Directory government in France demanded Lafayette's release was the prisoner finally freed. The fragile Directory, which had been set up in 1795, a year after the "Thermidorean" counterrevolution had finally put an end to the Revolution and the Terror, feared Lafayette's return to France but felt strongly that the world-famous French citizen should no longer be arbitrarily imprisoned in Austria. Thus the Directory asked Citizen General Napoleon Bonaparte, fresh from his victory in Rivoli, to negotiate for Lafayette's freedom, on condition that he not live in France.

Forty years old, worn, drained from his suffering, most of his fortune confiscated, Monsieur Lafayette (he had given up his noble title and the aristocratic "de") and his wife waited for two more years in Prussia and Holland before it was safe for them to return to France. The great French writer Chateaubriand wrote of Lafayette, "This man has lived."

When he could finally reenter France in 1800, Lafayette found a country transformed by many of the Revolution's accomplishments. Virtually all the vestiges of feudalism had been abolished. Citizens were equal before the law; the aristocracy was no longer a privileged elite exempt from taxes; the right of all children to share equally in inheritance had replaced primogeniture; Church property had been confiscated and sold; Jews and Protestants had been granted civil rights; illegitimate children had won full legal status; married couples could divorce; a meritocracy had replaced the hegemony of the aristocracy; and the principles of the "rights of man" were universally respected.

And yet Lafayette also found an exhausted people for whom the term "republic" had become a smear word. In a plebiscite in 1799, the people of France had voted for the constitution that guaranteed the autocracy of Napoleon. The vote was 3,011,007 to 1,562. The nation wanted, first and foremost, order and the rule of law, and Napoleon and then the Restoration Bourbons would supply them in their ways. France would not know republican government until 1871.

And how had the American Revolution fared in French opinion? Preceding Lafayette's flight and the downfall of the French Revolution came the eclipse of the American "beacon." The Revolution that had been extolled by the French as the model and hope for humanity had soon lost its authority and radiance. Perhaps that model was not perfect after all, the French began to muse. Maybe they could improve upon it, maybe even surpass it. The Americans, they pointed out, had ratified in 1787 a constitution that did not contain a Bill of Rights, and they still tolerated slavery. And were they not setting the clock back by retaining a Senate that mirrored the English hereditary House of Lords? Perhaps the Americans' esteem for English tradition was the problem. The French wanted no part of a system of checks and balances that thwarted the people's will. The French representative Lanjuinais mocked "the Anglo-American Mr. Adams, the Don Quixote of nobility," asserting that American Anglophiles "have lost their influence over us; they impose upon us no longer." The philosopher Mably joined the chorus, expressing disappointment with an America preoccupied with wealth and commerce.

So would it be the French and not the Americans who were destined to dazzle the world with perfection? Duke Mathïeu de Montmorency, a veteran of the American Revolutionary War, acknowledged that the Americans had created a worthy precedent, but, he grandly added, "they have given a great example to the new hemisphere. Let us give it to the universe!" For Condorcet, another French *philosophe*, the American Revolution had merely paved the way for the French Revolution, which would be based on truer, purer, and more profound principles. "Why speak of the best that exists?" the *philosophe* Dupont asked in 1788. "Why not speak of the best that is possible?"

Many people dreamt of a clean sweep of tradition, a government founded solely on Enlightenment truths. "O nation of France, you are not made to receive an example, but to set it!" declared loftily the representative Rabaut Saint Etienne. The tables had quickly turned. Jacobin leaders believed that France no longer needed to look to America for guidance. Saint-Just pitied the American "federal" nation. Why, it was not even a republic, he scoffed, but a hopelessly fragmented conglomeration. Anacharsis Cloots, the self-styled "representative of humanity" from Prussia, triumphantly divulged that the Americans were secretly envious of the French system of government and reproached themselves daily for lacking the political insight of the French!

Prey to increasingly grandiose notions, the French began to claim that America should look to France for her own salvation. Whereas Jefferson, with a certain generosity of spirit, had written to his friend George Mason that he "consider[ed] the establishment and success of the [French] government as necessary to stay up our own," Robespierre chose a different tone: "And you, brave Americans, your freedom was won with our blood and is protected by your alliance with us. What would be your fate if we no longer existed? You would crumble once again under the yoke of your enemy!" The marriage of revolutions ended in divorce. The French abandoned American theories of government. Neither the institutions of the young republic nor the thoughtful ideas behind them held any attraction for revolutionaries in France.

Lord Acton wrote that "what the French took from the Americans was their theory of revolution, not their theory of government—their cutting, not their sewing." The cutting—whether colonial war or regicide, declaration of independence or tennis court oath—is the easy part. The art is in the sewing. . . .

Jefferson knew that as Americans pursued their happiness, they would disagree on all manner of social, political, and economic issues and would engage in partisan conflict. After all, he himself had been the principal leader of the earliest opposition party. And as President he had presided over a government whose checks and balances—the collision of the different branches of government—made unity all but impossible. The unity that Jefferson prized was based neither on ideological consensus nor on fraternal communion. For the third President of the United States, unity meant citizens' allegiance to the political and moral principles expressed in the nation's founding documents. Jefferson never confused this kind of shared commitment to institutions that aspired to guarantee life, liberty, and the pursuit of happiness for citizens with citizens' ideological unanimity.

Unity for Jefferson could only mean a shared commitment to core democratic values and to a republic that, though "indivisible," permitted political fragmentation and unruly—though moderate—ideological division. Lafayette's presence in America could enable all Americans to remember and celebrate the quasi-mythic founding epoch when those luminous political and moral principles were first declared.

And what did Lafayette mean by "unity"? The "reconciliation between the political parties" that he wished to promote may have signified a temporary respite from party war, or perhaps a sense of harmony and good feeling as people experienced the fellowship of their common participation in the American political experiment. Lafayette certainly did not harbor any hidden, nefarious motives in wishing to be a unifying national figure during the French Revolution or in relishing that same role in the United States of the 1820s.

And yet the term "unity" had earned the darkest of reputations during the French Revolution. "The republic, one and indivisible," was the shibboleth on every French citizen's lips for four years. Unity represented the Revolution's highest goal but also explained its calamitous descent into repression and terror.

The kind of unity cherished by the French was something quite alien to the American mentality. After centuries of the wrenching inequality of a rigid, elitist caste system, revolutionaries in France hungered first and foremost for equality. While the Americans' driving passion was for freedom, in France people longed for a nation of equal citizens. And was it not logical, revolutionaries reasoned, that equal citizens would share the same revolutionary ideals and goals? What would propel and guide the Revolution if not the people's oneness and unanimity? Their unity constituted the motor, the sine qua non, of radical political and social change. But unity could not be achieved as long as division and opposition persisted. Divisions of any kind became anathema, so many reminders of the prerevolutionary society deeply divided along class, or rather caste lines.

Tumult, division, and competing interest groups in the United States vs. concord, unity, and community in France. Here were the antithetical concepts of democracy and nationhood that shaped the core values of both revolutions, influencing, as we shall see, their notions of individual rights and freedoms, coloring their political discourse and style, and setting the stage for the success or failure of the two revolutionary projects. during the next two centuries, those divergent revolutionary traditions and visions would galvanize leaders of liberation movements around the world, inspiring some to install a system of adversarial political parties, imbuing in others the idea of "one-party democracy."

We live in a world shaped by—sometimes still reeling from— the political ideas of a generation of eighteenth-century revolutionary leaders. Throughout much of the twentieth century, the French revolutionary vision of the nation as a unitary and organic whole has colored French political culture. "Since the dawn of our history," Charles de Gaulle declared in 1947, "our misfortunes occur in proportion to our division; but good fortune has never betrayed a unified France." De Gaulle's message of unity never varied, not during World War II, not during the Fourth Republic, and not during the Fifth Republic. It was also a message with which any radical revolutionary leader in France in 1793 would have been comfortable. "There is only one duty and one law," de Gaulle proclaimed, "and that is French unity. There is only one interest that counts, that of France. There is only one duty that exists for us, and that is to unite and rally around her."

In the United States, tumult and conflict have been as American as baseball and town meetings. The American system has always worked best when stimulated by the creative tension of sharply adversarial politics. Jefferson could define and defend his vision in contrast with a Hamilton, Lincoln with a Douglas, Roosevelt with a Hoover. In 1936, FDR, railing against the New Deal, declared to a tumultous Madison Square Garden crowd, "They are unanimous in their hate for me, and I welcome their hatred!" Conflict, not consensus, produced the meaningful change and progress that occurred in the 1930s.

Franklin W. Knight

The Haitian Revolution

The Haitian Revolution represents the most thorough case study of revolutionary change anywhere in the history of the modern world. In ten years of sustained internal and international warfare, a colony populated predominantly by plantation slaves overthrew both its colonial status and its economic system and established a new political state of entirely free individuals—with some ex-slaves constituting the new political authority. As only the second state to declare its independence in the Americas, Haiti had no viable administrative models to follow. The British North Americans who declared their independence in 1776 left slavery intact, and theirs was more a political revolution than a social and economic one. The success of Haiti against all odds made social revolutions a sensitive issue among the leaders of political revolt elsewhere in the Americas during the final years of the eighteenth century and the first decades of the nineteenth century. Yet the genesis of the Haitian Revolution cannot be separated from the wider concomitant events of the later eighteenth-century Atlantic world. Indeed, the period between 1750 and 1850 represented an age of spontaneous, interrelated revolutions, and events in Saint Domingue/Haiti constitute an integral—though often overlooked—part of the history of that larger sphere. These multi-faceted revolutions combined to alter the way in-

Franklin W. Knight, review of *The Haitian Revolution*, *American Historical Review*, Vol. 105, No. 1 (February 2000): 103–115.

dividuals and groups saw themselves and their place in the world. But even more, the intellectual changes of the period instilled in some political leaders a confidence (not new in the eighteenth century, but far more generalized than before) that creation and creativity were not exclusively divine or accidental attributes, and that both general societies and individual conditions could be rationally engineered. . . .

If the origins of the revolution in Saint Domingue lie in the broader changes of the Atlantic world during the eighteenth century, the immediate precipitants must be found in the French Revolution. The symbiotic relationship between the two were extremely strong and will be discussed later, but both resulted from the construction of a newly integrated Atlantic community in the seventeenth and eighteenth centuries.

The broader movements of empire building in the Atlantic world produced the dynamic catalyst for change that fomented political independence in the United States between 1776 and 1783. Even before that, ideas of the Enlightenment had agitated the political structures on both sides of the Atlantic, overtly challenging the traditional mercantilist notions of imperial administration and appropriating and legitimating the unorthodox free trading of previously defined interlopers and smugglers. The Enlightenment proposed a rational basis for reorganizing state, society, and nation. The leading thinkers promoted and popularized new ideas of individual and collective liberty, of political rights, and of class equality—and even, to a certain extent, of social democracy—that eventually included some unconventional thoughts about slavery. But their concepts of the state remained rooted in the traditional western European social experience, which did not accommodate itself easily to the current reality of the tropical American world, as Peggy Liss shows in her insightful study *Atlantic Empires*. . . .

The intellectual changes throughout the region cannot be separated from changes in the Caribbean. During the eighteenth century, the Caribbean plantation slave societies reached their apogee. British and French (mostly) absentee sugar producers made headlines in their respective imperial capitals, drawing the attention of political economists and moral philosophers. The most influential voice among the latter was probably Adam Smith (1723–1790), whose *Wealth of Nations* appeared in the auspicious year of 1776. Basing his arguments on the comparative costs of production, Smith insisted that, "from the experience of all ages and nations, I believe, that the work done by free men comes cheaper in the end than that performed by slaves." Slavery, Smith further stated, was both uneconomical and irrational not only because the plantation system was a wasteful use of land but also because slaves cost more to maintain than free laborers. . . .

French Saint Domingue prided itself, with considerable justification, on being the richest colony in the world. According to David Geggus, Saint Domingue in the 1780s accounted for "some 40 percent of France's foreign trade, its 7,000 or so plantations were absorbing by the 1790s also 10–15 percent of United States exports and had important commercial links with the British and Spanish West Indies as well. On the coastal plains of this colony little larger than Wales was grown about two-fifths of the world's sugar, while from its mountainous interior came over half the world's coffee." The population was structured like a typical slave plantation exploitation society in tropical America. Approximately 25,000 white colonists, whom we might call psychological transients, dominated the social pyramid, which included an intermediate subordinate stratum of approximately the same number of free, miscegenated persons referred to throughout the French Caribbean colonies as *gens de couleur*, and a depressed, denigrated, servile, and exploited majority of some 500,000 workers from Africa or of African descent. These demographic proportions would have been familiar to Jamaica, Barbados, or Cuba during the acme of their slave plantation regimes. The centripetal cohesive force remained the plantations of sugar, coffee, cotton, and indigo and the subsidiary activities associated with them. The plantations, therefore, joined the local society and the local economy with a human umbilical cord—the transatlantic slave trade—that attached the colony to Africa. Economic viability depended on the continuous replenishing of the labor force by importing African slaves. Nevertheless, the system was both sophisticated and complex, with commercial marketing operations that extended to several continents.

If whites, free colored, and slaves formed the three distinct castes in the French Caribbean colony, these caste divisions overshadowed a complex system of class and corresponding internal class antagonisms, across all sectors of the society. Among the whites, the class antagonism was between the successful so-called *grands blancs*, with their associated hirelings—plantation overseers, artisans, and supervisors—and the so-called *petits blancs*—small merchants' representatives, small proprietors, and various types of hangers-on. The antagonism was palpable. At the same time, all whites shared varying degrees of fear and mistrust of the intermediate group of *gens de couleur*, but especially the economically upwardly mobile representatives of wealth, education, and polished French culture. For their own part, the free non-whites had seen their political and social abilities increasingly circumscribed during the two or so decades before the outbreak of revolution. Their wealth and education certainly placed them socially above the *petits blancs*. Yet theirs was also an internally divided group, with a division based as much on skin color as on genealogy. As for the slaves, all were distinguished—if that is the proper terminology—by their legal condition as the lifetime property of their masters, and were occasionally subject to extraordinary degrees of daily control and coercion. Within the slave sector, status divisions derived from a bewildering number of factors applied in an equally bewildering number of ways: skills, gender, occupation, location (urban or rural, household or field), relationship to production, or simply the arbitrary whim of the master. . . .

Without the outbreak of the French Revolution, it is unlikely that the system in Saint Domingue would have broken down in 1789. And while Haiti precipitated the collapse of the system regionally, it seems fair to say that a system such as the Caribbean slave system bore within itself the seeds of its own destruction and therefore could not last indefinitely. . . .

The local bases of the society and the organization of political power could not have been more different in France and its overseas colonies. In France in 1789, the political estates had a long tradition, and the social hierarchy was closely related to genealogy and antiquity. In Saint Domingue, the political system was relatively new, and the hierarchy was determined arbitrarily by race and the occupational relationship to the plantation. Yet the novelty of the colonial situation did not produce a separate and particular language to describe its reality, and the limitations of a common language (that of the metropolis) created a pathetic confusion with tragic consequences for metropolis and colony.

The basic divisions of French society derived from socioeconomic class distinctions. The popular slogans generated by the revolution— Liberty, Equality, Fraternity and the Rights of Man—did not express sentiments equally applicable in both metropolis and colony. What is more, the Estates General, and later the National Assembly, simply could not understand how the French could be divided by a common language. And yet they hopelessly were.

The confusion sprung from two foundations. In the first place, the reports of grievances (*cahiers de doléances*) of the colonies represented overwhelmingly not the views of a cross-section of the population but merely those of wealthy plantation owners and merchants, especially the absentee residents in France. Moreover, as the French were to find out eventually, the colony was quite complex geographically. The wealthy, expatriate planters of the Plain du Nord were a distinct numerical minority. The interests and preoccupations of the middling sorts of West Province and South Province were vastly different. In the second place, each segment of the free population accepted the slogans of the revolution to win acceptance in France, but they then particularized and emphasized only such portions as applied to their individual causes. The *grands blancs* saw the Rights of Man as the rights and privileges of bourgeois man, much as the framers of North American independence in Philadelphia in 1776. Moreover, *grands blancs* saw liberty not as a private affair but rather as greater colonial autonomy, especially in economic matters. They also hoped that the metropolis would authorize more free trade, thereby weakening the restrictive effects of the mercantilist *commerce exclusif* with the mother country. *Petits blancs* wanted equality, that is, active citizenship for all white persons, not just the wealthy property owners, and less bureaucratic control over the colonies. But they stressed a fraternity based on a whiteness of skin color that they equated with being genuinely French. *Gens de couleur* also wanted equality and fraternity, but they based their claim on an equality of all free regardless of skin color, since they fulfilled all other qualifications for active citizenship. Slaves were not part of the initial discussion and sloganeering, but from their subsequent actions they clearly supported liberty. It was not the liberty of the whites, however. Theirs was a personal freedom that undermined their relationship to their masters and the plantation, and jeopardized the wealth of a considerable number of those who were already free. . . .

With the colonial situation far too confusing for the metropolitan legislators to resolve easily, the armed revolt in the colonies started with an attempted coup by the *grands blancs* in the north who resented the *petits blancs*–controlled Colonial Assembly of St. Marc (in West Province) writing a constitution for the entire colony in 1790. Both white groups armed their slaves and prepared for war in the name of the revolution. When, however, the National Assembly passed the May Decree enfranchising propertied mulattos, they temporarily forgot their class differences and forged an uneasy alliance to forestall the revolutionary threat of racial equality. The determined desire of the free non-whites to make a stand for their rights—also arming their slaves for war—made the impending civil war an inevitable racial war.

The precedent set by the superordinate free groups was not lost on the slaves, who comprised the overwhelming majority of the population. If they could fight in separate causes for the antagonistic free sectors of the population, they could fight on their own behalf. And so they did. Violence, first employed by the whites, became the common currency of political change. Finally, in August 1791, after fighting for nearly two years on one or another side of free persons who claimed they were fighting for liberty, the slaves of the Plain du Nord applied their fighting to their own cause. And once they had started, they refused to settle for anything less than full freedom for themselves. When it became clear that their emancipation could not be sustained within the colonial political system, they created an independent state in 1804 to secure it. It was the logical extension of the collective slave revolt that began in 1791.

But before that could happen, Saint Domingue experienced a period of chaos between 1792 and 1802. At one time, as many as six warring factions were in the field simultaneously: slaves, free persons of color, *petits blancs*, *grands blancs*, and invading Spanish and English troops, as well as the French vainly trying to restore order and control. Alliances were made and dissolved in opportunistic succession. As the killing increased, power slowly gravitated to the overwhelming majority of the population—the former slaves no longer willing to continue their servility. After 1793, under the control of Pierre-Dominique Toussaint Louverture, ex-slave and ex-slaveowner, the tide of war turned inexorably, assuring the victory of the concept of liberty held by the slaves. It was duly, if temporarily, ratified by the National Assembly. But that was neither the end of the fighting nor the end of slavery.

The victory of the slaves in 1793 was, ironically, a victory for colonialism and the revolution in France. The leftward drift of the revolution and the implacable zeal of its colonial administrators, especially the Jacobin commissioner Léger Félicité Sonthonax, to eradicate all traces of counterrevolution and royalism—which he identified with the whites—in Saint Domingue facilitated the ultimate victory of the blacks over the whites. Sonthonax's role, however, does not detract from the brilliant military leadership and political astuteness provided by Toussaint Louverture. In 1797, he became governor general of the colony and in the next four years expelled all invading forces (including the French) and gave it a remarkably modern and democratic constitution. He also suppressed (but failed to eradicate) the revolt of the free coloreds led by André Rigaud and Alexander Pétion in the south, captured the neighboring Spanish colony of Santo Domingo, and freed its small number of slaves. Saint Domingue was a new society with a new political structure. As a reward, Toussaint Louverture made himself governor general for life, much to the displeasure of Napoleon Bonaparte. . . .

The reality of a semi-politically free Saint-Domingue with a free black population ran counter to the grandiose dreams of Napoleon to reestablish a viable French-American empire. It also created what Anthony Maingot has called a "terrified consciousness" among the rest of the slave masters in the Americas. Driven by his desire to restore slavery and disregarding the local population and its leaders, Napoleon sent his brother-in-law General Charles Victor Emmanuel Leclerc with about 10,000 of the finest French troops in 1802 to accomplish his aim. It was a disastrously futile effort. Napoleon ultimately lost the colony, his brother-in-law, and most of the 44,000 troops eventually sent out to conduct the savage and bitter campaign of reconquest. Although Touissant was treacherously spirited away to exile and premature death in France, the independence of Haiti was declared by his former lieutenant, now the new governor general, Jean-Jacques Dessalines, on January 1, 1804. Haiti, the Caribbean, and the Americas would never be the same as before the slave uprising of 1791.

The impact of the Haitian Revolution was both immediate and widespread. The antislavery fighting immediately spawned unrest throughout the region, especially in communities of Maroons in Jamaica, and among slaves in St. Kitts. It sent a wave of immigrants flooding outward to the neighboring islands, and to the United States and Europe. It revitalized agricultural production in Cuba and Puerto Rico. As Alfred Hunt has shown, Haitian emigrants also profoundly affected American language, religion, politics, culture, cuisine, architecture, medicine, and the conflict over slavery, especially in Louisiana. Most of all, the revolution deeply affected the psychology of the whites throughout the Atlantic world. The Haitian Revolution undoubtedly accentuated the sensitivity to race, color, and status across the Caribbean.

Among the political and economic elites of the neighboring Caribbean states, the example of a black independent state as a viable alternative to the Maroon complicated their domestic relations. The predominantly non-white lower orders of society might have admired the achievement in Haiti, but they were conscious that it could not be easily duplicated. "Haiti represented the living proof of the consequences of not just black freedom," wrote Maingot, "but, indeed, black rule. It was the latter which was feared; therefore, the former had to be curtailed if not totally prohibited." The favorable coincidence of time, place, and circumstances that produced a Haiti failed to materialize again. For the rest of white America, the cry of "Remember Haiti" proved an effective way to restrain exuberant local desires for political liberty, especially in slave societies. Indeed, the long delay in achieving Cuban political independence can largely be attributed to astute Spanish metropolitan use of the "terrified consciousness" of the Cuban Creoles to a scenario like that in Saint Domingue between 1789 and 1804. Nevertheless, after 1804, it would be difficult for the local political and economic elites to continue the complacent status quo of the mid-eighteenth century. Haiti cast an inevitable shadow over all slave societies. Antislavery movements grew stronger and bolder, especially in Great Britain, and the colonial slaves themselves became increasingly more restless. Most important, in the Caribbean, whites lost the confidence that they had before 1789 to maintain the slave system indefinitely. In 1808, the British abolished their transatlantic slave trade, and they dismantled the slave system between 1834 and 1838. During that time, free non-whites (and Jews) were given political equality with whites in many colonies. The French abolished their slave trade in 1818, although their slave system, reconstituted by 1803 in Martinique and Guadeloupe, limped on until 1848. Both British and French imperial slave systems—as well as the Dutch and the Danish—were dismantled administratively. The same could be said for the mainland Spanish-American states and Brazil. In the United States, slavery ended abruptly in a disastrous civil war. Spain abolished slavery in Puerto Rico (where it was not important) in 1873. The Cuban case, where slavery was extremely important, proved far more difficult and also resulted in a long, destructive civil war before emancipation was finally accomplished in 1886. By then, it was not the Haitian Revolution but Haiti itself that evoked negative reactions among its neighbors.

Jaime E. Rodríguez O.

The Spanish and Spanish American Revolutions

During the second half of the eighteenth century and the early nineteenth century, the Spanish world underwent a major transformation. The reigns of Carlos III and Carlos IV (1759–1808) witnessed the development of modern political thought—which emphasized liberty, equality, civil rights, the rule of law, representative constitutional government, and laissez-faire economics—among a small but significant group of Spaniards and Americans. As long as the Crown governed effectively, these ideas remained largely intellectual pursuits. But the French invasion of Spain and the collapse of the Monarchy in 1808 provided the liberal minority with an unprecedented opportunity to implement its goals.

The disintegration of the Crown triggered a series of events that culminated in the establishment of representative government in the Spanish world. The initial step in that process was the formation of local governing juntas in Spain and America that invoked the Hispanic legal principle that sovereignty, in the absence of the king, reverted to the people. Although the Peninsular provinces made that transition easily, the American kingdoms faced the opposition of royal officials, resident Europeans, and their New World allies. The creation of the Junta Suprema Central Gubernativa del Reino appeared to provide a solution to the crisis of the Monarchy. That body not only recognized the rights of Spanish provinces but also acknowledged that the American kingdoms constituted integral and equal parts of the Monarchy and possessed the right to representation in the government.

The decisive French victories of 1809, however, destroyed the fragile balance established by the Junta Central. When the body dissolved itself in January 1810, appointing a Council of Regency in its place,

Jaime E. Rodríguez O., "Conclusion," in The Independence of Spanish America (Cambridge: Cambridge University Press, 1998), pp. 238–246. Reprinted with the permission of Cambridge University Press.

some provinces of Spain and several kingdoms of America refused to recognize the legitimacy of the new government. The convening of the Cortes resolved the concerns of the provinces of Spain and many parts of the New World. The Spanish parliament provided American autonomists with a peaceful means of obtaining home rule. Moreover, the extensive debates in that congress, which were widely disseminated by the press during the 1810–1812 period, significantly influenced both the Spanish Americans who supported as well as those who opposed the new government in Spain.

The deputies of Spain and America, who enacted the Constitution of the Spanish Monarchy in 1812, transformed the Hispanic world. The Constitution of Cádiz was not a Spanish document; it was as much an American charter as a Spanish one. Indeed, it is unlikely that the Constitution of 1812 would have taken the form it did without the participation of representatives from the New World. The American deputies to the Cortes played a central role in drafting the constitution. Their arguments and proposals convinced some Spaniards to embrace substantial change in America as well as in the Peninsula. Some of the important *liberal* reforms that characterized the Spanish Constitution of 1812, such as the provincial deputation, are directly attributable to New World deputies. Similarly, some transformations that Spaniards sought for their region, such as *ayuntamientos* for small towns, had a profound effect in the New World, where *ayuntamientos* had been restricted to major urban centers.

The Constitution of Cádiz abolished seigniorial institutions, the Inquisition, Indian tribute, and forced labor—such as the *mita* in South America and personal service in the Peninsula—and asserted the state's control of the Church. It created a unitary state with equal laws for all parts of the Spanish Monarchy, substantially restricted the authority of the king, and entrusted the Cortes with decisive power. When it franchised all men, except those of African ancestry, without requiring either literacy or property qualifications, the Constitution of 1812 surpassed all existing representative governments, such as those of Great Britain, the United States, and France, in providing political rights to the vast majority of the male population.

The Constitution of the Spanish Monarchy expanded the electorate and dramatically increased the scope of political activity. The new charter established representative government at three levels: the municipality, the province, and the Monarchy. It allowed cities and towns with 1,000 or more inhabitants to form *ayuntamientos*. Political power was transferred from the center to the localities as vast numbers of people were incorporated into the political process. Although the elite clearly dominated politics, hundreds of thousands of middle- and lower-class men, including Indians, mestizos, and *castas*, became involved in politics in a meaningful way and made their presence felt.

Despite the unparalleled democratization of the political system, civil war erupted in America because some groups, which refused to accept the government in Spain, insisted upon forming local juntas, whereas others, which recognized the Regency and the Cortes, opposed them. Political divisions among the elites combined with regional antipathy and social tensions to exacerbate the conflict in the New World.

The American movements of 1810, like those in Spain, arose from a desire to remain independent of French domination. Some kingdoms of the New World, as well as some provinces of the Peninsula, questioned the legitimacy of the Council of Regency and its right to speak for the Nación Española. The great difference between the Peninsula and America was that the regions of Spain fought an external enemy, whereas the New World realms grappled with internal disputes. The conflict in America waxed and waned during the first constitutional period, 1810–14. At times, when the royal authorities acted with restraint, accommodation seemed possible. The situation changed with Fernando VII's return in 1814. He abolished the Cortes and the Constitution, restoring absolutism. Unfettered by that charter, the royal authorities in the New World crushed most autonomy movements. Only the isolated Río de la Plata remained beyond the reach of a weakened Spanish Monarchy.

Fernando VII's return provided an opportunity to restore the unity of the Spanish world. Virtually every act that had occurred since 1808—the struggle against the French, the political revolution enacted by the Cortes, and the autonomy movements in America—had been taken in his name. Initially it appeared that he might accept moderate reforms, but ultimately the king opted to rely on force to restore royal order in the New World.

The Crown's repression prompted the minority of America's politically active population that favored independence to act decisively. Republicans renewed the struggle in Venezuela in 1817, and by 1819 the tide had turned against the Monarchy when a combined force of *neogranadinos* and Venezuelans defeated the royalists at Boyacá, forcing the viceroy and other officials to flee from Bogotá. In the south, José de San Martín won a decisive victory in Chile in April 1818.

The renewed conflict in South America enhanced the power of military men. Self-proclaimed generals like Simón Bolívar and former professional soldiers such as José de San Martín gained immense power and prestige as the leaders of the bloody struggles to win independence. Although civilian and clerical institutions—*ayuntamientos*, courts, parishes, cathedral chapters—continued to function, and although new governments were formed and congresses elected, military power predominated. Colombia provides the clearest example of that phenomenon.

Convened by Bolívar in February 1819, the Congress of Angostura legitimized his power and in December created the Republic of Colombia, incorporating Venezuela, New Granada, and Quito. Although Venezuela and New Granada possessed some representation at Angostura, Quito had none. Later in 1821, the Congress of Cúcuta, pressured by President Bolívar and intimidated by the army, ratified the formation of the Republic of Colombia, again without any representation from Quito. In contrast to the Spanish Constitution of 1812, written by a Cortes composed of elected representatives from all parts of the Monarchy—which granted considerable autonomy to the regions via the constitutional *ayuntamientos* and the provincial deputations, restricted the power of the king, and bestowed sovereignty on the legislature—the new Colombian constitution created a highly centralized government that granted vast authority to the president.

The military did not gain such power in the southern cone, even though the structures and processes of the Spanish Constitution of 1812 did not significantly influence either the Río de la Plata or Chile. Because the autonomists in those regions gained control early, neither area participated either in the formation of constitutional *ayuntamientos* and provincial deputations or in the popular elections established by the Constitution of Cádiz. Although Buenos Aires and Santiago experienced partisan conflicts and civil wars during the early years, the region escaped the brutal campaigns waged in northern South America. The Río de la Plata obtained its autonomy and ultimately its independence by default; the area experienced little armed conflict with the royal authorities. Similarly, Chile endured only limited warfare in its struggle for emancipation. After 1818 large military contingents left those regions to secure the independence of Peru, even though some royalist forces remained in the south. As a result, civilians dominated the governments of those regions.

By 1819 it was clear that Fernando VII would have to send more troops if he wished to retain control of America. But raising yet another expeditionary force to reconquer the New World only increased discontent in the Peninsula. The *liberales* in Spain exploited the army's disenchantment with the war in America, eventually forcing the king to restore the Constitution in March 1820. The return of constitutional order transformed the Hispanic political system for the third time in a decade.

The restoration of constitutional government elicited disparate responses from the American regions. When the news arrived in April, the people of New Spain and Guatemala enthusiastically reestablished the constitutional system. In the months that followed, they conducted elections for countless constitutional *ayuntamientos,* provincial deputations, and the Cortes. Political instability in the Peninsula during the previous dozen years, however, had convinced many *novohispanos* that it was prudent to establish an autonomous government within the Spanish Monarchy. The autonomists, the members of the national elite who ultimately gained power after independence, opted for a constitutional monarchy. They pursued two courses of action. New Spain's deputies to the Cortes proposed a project for New World autonomy that would create three American kingdoms governed by Spanish princes and allied with the Peninsula. The Spanish majority, however, rejected the proposal that would have granted Americans the home rule they had been seeking since 1808. At the same time, New Spain's autonomists encouraged and supported the royalist Colonel Agustín de Iturbide, who accepted their plan and for autonomy, which resembled the proposal presented to the Cortes. Independence was assured when Iturbide and his supporters won the backing of the majority of the royal army. Mexico achieved its independence not because the royal authorities were defeated militarily but because *novohispanos* no longer supported the Crown politically. Central America also declared independence and joined the new Mexican Empire. It seceded peacefully in 1823, after the empire was abolished, and formed a separate nation.

The newly independent Mexicans carefully followed the precedents of the Spanish constitutional system. Although they initially established an empire, they eventually formed a federal republic in

1824. They modeled their new constitution on the Spanish charter because it had been part of their recent political experience. After all, distinguished *novohispano* statesmen like José Guridi y Alcocer and Miguel Ramos Arizpe, who had participated in writing the Constitution of 1812, also served in the Mexican Constituent Congress. To many Mexicans, it was as much their Constitution as Spain's. In keeping with Hispanic constitutional practices, they also formed a government with a powerful legislature and a weak executive branch. Similarly, federalism in Mexico arose naturally from the earlier political experience; the provincial deputations simply converted themselves into states. Like Mexico, the new Central American republic established a federation based on Hispanic constitutional practices.

In South America the restoration of the Spanish Constitution provided those favoring independence the opportunity to press their campaign to liberate the continent. In contrast to New Spain, the South American insurgents defeated the royal authorities militarily. Two pincer movements, one from the south and the other from the north, eventually converged on Peru.

In 1820 the republicans began systematically to liberate Venezuela and New Granada. On October 9, 1820, Guayaquil declared independence, formed a republic, and attempted without success to free the highland provinces of the Kingdom of Quito. A mixed force consisting mainly of local troops, Colombians, and men from San Martín's army, under the command of General Antonio José de Sucre finally defeated the Spanish forces in Quito on May 24, 1822, at the Battle of Pichincha. Bolívar, who arrived from the north in June with more Colombian troops, incorporated the region into the Republic of Colombia despite opposition from both Quito and Guayaquil. Subsequently, Bolívar imposed martial law in the former Kingdom of Quito to impress men as well as to requisition money and supplies for the struggle against the royalists in Peru, the last bastion of royal power in America.

The southern forces led by San Martín landed in Lima in August 1820 with a liberating army composed of Chileans and *ríoplatenses*. Although he controlled the coast, San Martín could not overcome the royalists in the highlands. In an effort to win the loyalty of the population, Spanish *liberales* forced Viceroy Joaquín de la Pezuela to abdicate on January 29, 1821, named General José de la Serna captain general and superior political chief, and implemented the Constitution of 1812. The Spanish constitutionalists reorganized the army and nearly drove San Martín's forces from the coast. But divisions within the royalist ranks prevented them from defeating the forces of independence.

Unable to obtain the support he needed in Peru and abroad, San Martín ceded the honor of final victory to Bolívar. Although the Colombians arrived in force in 1823, they made little progress. Divisions among Peruvians, shortage of supplies, and strong royalist armies kept them pinned down on the coast. However, the royalists were also divided. In Upper Peru the absolutist general Pedro Antonio Olañeta opposed La Serna and the Spanish *liberales*. After the Spanish Constitution was once again abolished, General Olañeta took up arms against the Spanish *liberales* on December 25, 1823. Internecine warfare contributed to the royalists' defeat. For nearly a year, while Bolívar and his men recovered, royalist constitutional and absolutist armies waged war in the highlands. Ultimately, General Sucre defeated the royalist constitutional army in the decisive battle of Ayacucho on December 9, 1824. Olañeta's absolutist forces, however, retained control of Upper Peru. Political intrigue finally ended the struggle: Olañeta was assassinated in April 1825. The death of the absolutist officer marked the end of royal power in Upper Peru. Subsequently, General Sucre formed the new republic of Bolivia. By 1826, when the last royal forces surrendered, Bolívar dominated South America as president of Colombia, dictator of Peru, and ruler of Bolivia.

Two competing political traditions emerged during the independence period: One, forged in more than a decade of war, emphasized strong executive power; the other, based on the civilian parliamentary experience, insisted upon legislative dominance. They epitomized a fundamental conflict about the nature of government. New Spain, which achieved independence through political compromise rather than by force of arms, is representative of the civil tradition. There the Spanish constitutional system triumphed and continued to evolve. Despite subsequent *golpes* by military men, civilian politicians dominated Mexican politics.

In contrast, military force ultimately liberated northern South America. Unlike Mexico, in Colombia, Peru, and Bolivia, the men of arms dominated the men of law. The Hispanic constitutional experience exerted little influence in the region. The three newly independent South American nations established strong centralist governments with powerful chief executives and weak legislators. In 1830, Colombia—sometimes called *Gran Colombia*—splintered into three countries: Venezuela, New Granada, and Ecuador. The preponderance of the men of arms, however, was harder to eradicate.

The southern cone, which also had won independence by force, did not fall under the control of military men. The region endured only limited warfare with royalist forces. Most of the armed conflicts occurred between and among provinces. Although Santiago and Buenos Aires toyed with federalism, Chile eventually established a highly centralized oligarchical republic, whereas in the Río de la Plata, the various provinces formed a loose confederation. Despite vast differences in the nature of their regimes, civilians dominated both nations.

By 1826 the overseas possessions of the Spanish Monarchy, one of the world's most imposing political structures at the end of the eighteenth century, consisted only of Cuba, Puerto Rico, the Philippines, and a few other Pacific islands. Having achieved independence, the countries of the American continent would henceforth chart their own future. Most, however, entered a prolonged period of economic decline and political instability. Military strongmen—*caudillos* but not institutional militarists—dominated many nations, whose shattered institutions no longer functioned. The stable, more developed, and stronger countries of the North Atlantic—such as Britain, France, and the United States—flooded Spanish America with their exports, dominated their credit, and sometimes imposed their will upon the new American nations by force of arms.

Spain's and America's nineteenth-century experience provides stark proof of the cost of independence. Like its American offspring, the former metropolis suffered political chaos, economic decline, economic imperialism, and foreign intervention. Both the Peninsula and the nations of the New World endured civil wars and military *pronunciamientos*. In their efforts to resolve their political and economic crises, Spain and America experimented with monarchism and republicanism, centralism and federalism, and representative government and dictatorship. Unfortunately, there was no simple solution for nations whose economies had been destroyed by war and whose political systems had been shattered by revolution. Political order and economic growth would not begin to be restored in both regions until the 1870s.

Why did Spain and Spanish America decline politically and economically during the nineteenth century? Why did they not, like Britain and the United States after the latter's emancipation, enjoy political stability and continued economic growth? The answer lies in the nature of the Spanish Monarchy and the timing of Spanish American independence.

The emancipation of Spanish America did not merely consist of separation from the mother country, as in the case of the United States; it also destroyed a vast and responsive social, political, and economic system that functioned well despite its many imperfections. The worldwide Spanish Monarchy had proven to be flexible and able to accommodate social tensions and conflicting political and economic interests for nearly 300 years. The American upper class formed an integral part of the Monarchy's elite and was tied to its European counterpart through marriage and, frequently, economic associations. Tangled family and business relationships linked American autonomists to Spanish royalists and constitutionalists to absolutists. These networks, which arose as a result of the interlocking bureaucracy that anchored the Monarchy, grew as the population and economy expanded. They provided the social, political, and economic space required to resolve conflicts and maintain the system in operation. Despite inefficiencies and inequities, the Spanish Monarchy functioned as an economic system and, as a unit, possessed the strength to participate effectively in the world economy. In the postindependence era it became apparent that, individually, the former Spanish Monarchy's separate parts were at a competitive disadvantage. In that regard, nineteenth-century Spain, like its American offspring, was just one more newly independent nation groping for a place in an uncertain and difficult world.

In contrast to the United States, which obtained its independence in 1783, just in time to benefit from the insatiable demand for its products generated by the twenty years of war in Europe that followed the French Revolution of 1789, the Spanish world achieved emancipation *after* the end of the European wars. Not only did the new nations have to rebuild their shattered economies, but they also faced a lack of demand for their products. Instead, Europe and the United States were eager to flood Spanish America with their own goods. The new countries did not enjoy prosperity during their formative years, as the United States had. Rather, the Spanish American states had to face grave internal and external problems with diminishing resources.

After independence, Spanish and American *liberales* advanced similar solutions to the fundamental socioeconomic problems their nations faced. They proposed abolishing privileges, primarily the clerical and military *fueros*. They also stripped the Church of its landed wealth and forced communal villages to establish private landholding. *Liberales* in all countries perceived these actions as necessary to creating the vibrant economies and modern societies they desired. Conservatives, who also favored economic growth, viewed the reforms as attempts to destroy religion, order, and morality. Similarly, most former Indian communities and many other *campesinos* did not consider beneficial the *liberal* efforts to modernize the countryside. These conflicts were not easily resolved; *liberal*—conservative, Church—state, and urban—rural struggles consumed Spain and America during the nineteenth century.

Only in the last third of the nineteenth century did the nations of America and Spain begin to consolidate their states. By the 1870s and 1880s, Spain, and most Spanish American countries had established stable governments and undertaken the difficult process of economic rehabilitation. Unfortunately, the former Spanish Monarchy had languished during fifty crucial years in which Britain, France, Germany, and the United States had advanced to a different stage of economic development. In the period since the great political revolution had dissolved the Spanish Monarchy, the North Atlantic world had changed dramatically. Western European and U.S. industrial corporations and financial institutions had achieved such size and strength that the emerging economies of Spanish America and Spain simply could not compete. Consequently, the members of the former Spanish Monarchy were forced to accept a secondary role in the new world order. The failure of either Spanish absolutists or *liberales* to reach an accommodation with America had indeed proven costly to both sides.

As a result of the great political revolution that led to the dissolution of the Spanish Monarchy, however, Spain and the new nations of America developed a unique political culture based not on foreign models but on their own traditions and experience. After independence in America and after Fernando VII's death in the Peninsula, the old absolute Monarchy disappeared. The people of the Spanish-speaking world ceased being subjects of the Crown and became citizens of their nations. During the nineteenth century, the new political systems of Spain and Spanish America were consolidated on the basis of the liberal tradition of constitutional government and political representation that had emerged in the Cortes of Cádiz and its rival regimes in America. Despite power struggles, such as those between monarchists and republicans, centralists and federalists, and parliamentarians and *caudillos*, a liberal, representative, constitutional government remained the political ideal of the Spanish-speaking nations. Indeed, even *caudillos* and dictators have been forced to acknowledge, at least in principle, the supremacy of the rule of law and the ultimate desirability of civilian, representative, constitutional government.

Suggestions for Further Reading

The Atlantic World

The only general survey of the Atlantic region to date is Paul Butel's *The Atlantic* (London: Routledge, 1999), although it focuses more on strictly European oceanic developments, exploration, and trade than on colonization, imperial rule, and the interactions of peoples in Africa and America. Connections among Europe, Africa, and the Americas are discussed and placed in even wider context in Philip D. Curtin, *The World and the West: The European Challenge and the Overseas Response in the Age of Empire* (Cambridge: Cambridge University Press, 2000); and Bernard Waites, *Europe and the Third World: From Colonization to Decolonization, c. 1500–1998* (New York: St. Martin's Press, 1999). A concise introduction to this vast topic is provided by David Richardson's fine essay, "The Rise of the Atlantic Empires," in Anthony Tibbles, ed., *Transatlantic Slavery: Against Human Dignity* (London: National Museums and Galleries on Merseyside, 1995), pp. 17–28; and by J. H. Elliot's equally fine summary "The Atlantic World," in Elliot, *The Old World and the New, 1492–1650* (Cambridge: Cambridge University Press, 1970), pp. 79–104. Alan L. Karras discusses the Atlantic world as a field of historical analysis in "The Atlantic World as a Unit of Study," in *Atlantic American Societies* (London: Routledge, 1992), pp. 1–15; as does John Thornton in the introduction to his impressive history, *Africa and Africans in the Making of the Atlantic World, 1400–1800*, 2d ed. (Cambridge: Cambridge University Press, 1998), pp. 1–9.

Origins

The classic study of the Mediterranean Basin and a good point of reference for thinking about the Atlantic and the shift from the Mediterranean to the Atlantic is Fernand Braudel's *The Mediterranean and the Mediterranean World in the Age of Philip II*, 2 vols., trans. Sian Reynolds (New York: Harper and Row, 1972). James S. Romm presents a fascinating account of the geographical knowledge of Greco-Roman antiquity in *The Edges of the Earth in Ancient Thought* (Princeton: Princeton University Press, 1992). For the development of cartography and navigation, see George Fadlo Hourani's *Arab Seafaring in the Indian Ocean and Early Medieval Times* (Princeton: Princeton University Press, 1995); and Tony Campbell's "Portolan Charts from the Late Thirteenth Century to 1500," in *The History of Cartography, Volume*

One: Cartography in Prehistoric, Ancient, and Medieval Europe and the Mediterranean, J. B. Harley and David Woodward, eds. (Chicago: University of Chicago Press, 1987), pp. 371–463. Specialized map collections are now increasingly available on the Web, but especially recommended for scope, description, and imagery of various cartographic traditions is the website of the Bodleian Library's Map Room at Oxford University (www.Bodley.ox.AC.UK/BODHOME.htm). For deciphering the Portuguese aspirations, see L. N. Gumilev, *Searches for an Imaginary Kingdom: The Legend of Prester John* (Cambridge: Cambridge University Press, 1987). On the Portuguese "voyages of discovery," see Brian Johnson Barker's *Dias and de Gama: The Portuguese Discovery of the Cape Sea-Route* (Cape Town: Struik, 1989). The early transition of European exploration, seafaring, and colonization from the Mediterranean to the Atlantic is superbly examined by Felipe Fernández-Armesto in *Before Columbus: Exploration and Colonization from the Mediterranean to the Atlantic, 1229–1492* (New York: Oxford University Press, 1987). The Spanish side of exploration is discussed in an excellent biography of the mariner, Felipe Fernández-Armesto, *Columbus* (New York: Oxford University Press, 1992). Also see William D. Phillips, Jr., and Carla Rahn Phillips, *The Worlds of Christopher Columbus* (Cambridge: Cambridge University Press, 1992). For analyses of language and European thought, see Mary B. Campbell, *The Witness and the Other World: Exotic European Travel Writing, 400–1600* (Ithaca: Cornell University Press, 1988); and Stephen Greenblatt, *Marvelous Possessions: The Wonder of the New World* (Chicago: University of Chicago Press, 1991).

Encounters

The past two decades have witnessed an outpouring of rich new scholarship on the diverse series of cultural encounters among various groups of Africans, Amerindians, and Europeans during the first three centuries of contact in the Atlantic world. The best introduction to the entire topic is Stuart B. Schwartz's edited collection of twenty essays entitled *Implicit Understandings: Observing, Reporting, and Reflecting on the Encounters Between Europeans and Other Peoples in the Early Modern Era* (Cambridge: Cambridge University Press, 1994). A good overview for North America is Gary B. Nash, *Red, White, and Black: The Peoples of Early America*, 4th ed. (Englewood Cliffs, N.J.: Prentice

Hall, 1999). Richard White's *Middle Ground: Indians, Empires, and Republics in the Great Lakes Region, 1650–1815* (Cambridge: Cambridge University Press, 1991) explores interaction among French, English, and Amerindians in the Great Lakes, while Daniel H. Usner's *Indians, Settlers and Slaves in a Frontier Exchange Economy: The Lower Mississippi Valley before 1783* (Chapel Hill: University of North Carolina Press, 1992) explores similar dynamics in the region of the lower Mississippi. Ramón A. Gutiérrez provides an insightful analysis of interaction and cultural change between Spanish and Pueblos in his *When Jesus Came, the Corn Mothers Went Away: Marriage, Sexuality, and Power in New Mexico, 1500–1846* (Stanford: Stanford University Press, 1991). James Lockhart explores cultural interaction and change in the Valley of Mexico in his *The Nahuas After the Conquest: A Social and Cultural History of the Indians of Central Mexico, Sixteenth Through Eighteenth Centuries* (Stanford: Stanford University Press, 1992). There are a number of good regional studies of European interactions with Africans, such as John Vogt's *Portuguese Rule on the Gold Coast, 1469–1682* (Athens: University of Georgia Press, 1979). The best comprehensive analysis is found in Philip D. Curtin's *The World and the West: The European Challenge and the Overseas Response in the Age of Empire* (Cambridge: Cambridge University Press, 2000). Jerald T. Milanich and Susan Milbrath provide a well-illustrated overview of early Caribbean encounters in their *First Encounters: Spanish Explorations in the Caribbean and the United States, 1492–1570* (Gainesville: University of Florida Press, 1989). The best study of Portuguese-Amerindian interaction is John Hemming's *Red Gold: The Conquest of the Brazilian Indians, 1500–1760* (Cambridge, Mass.: Harvard University Press, 1978). A good recent overview of African cultural adaptation to the New World is Michael L. Connif and Thomas J. Davis, eds., *Africans in the Americas: A History of the Black Diaspora* (New York: St. Martin's Press, 1994). For British North America, see Philip D. Morgan, *Slave Counterpoint: Black Culture in the Eighteenth-Century Chesapeake and Lowcountry* (Chapel Hill: University of North Carolina Press, 1998). For the African Caribbean, Hilary Beckles and Verene Shepard, eds., *Caribbean Slave Society and Economy: A Student Reader* (New York: The New Press, 1991) provides an excellent anthology of recent scholarship. Richard Price's *Maroon Communities: Rebel Slave Communities in the Americas*, 3rd ed. (Baltimore: Johns Hopkins University Press, 1996) explores one facet of slave resistance in the Caribbean and other regions of the Americas. A. J. R. Russell-Wood's *The Black Man in Slavery and Freedom in Colonial Brazil* (London: The Macmillan Press, 1982) provides an excellent analysis of black society in Portuguese America.

Trades

The classic survey of the Atlantic economy is Ralph Davis, *The Rise of the Atlantic Economies* (Ithaca: Cornell University Press, 1973). An interesting and well-illustrated book on ships and sailing is by Roger Morris, *Atlantic Seafaring: Ten Centuries of Exploration and Trade in the North Atlantic* (Aukland, New Zealand: International Marine/McGraw-Hill, 1992). Timothy R. Walton focuses on the Spanish transatlantic commercial system in *The Spanish Treasure Fleets* (Sarasota, Fla.: Pineapple Press, 1994). The fur trade and French-Indian relations are the subjects of Denys Delâge, *Bitter Feast: Amerindians and Europeans in Northeastern North America, 1600–64* (Vancouver: UBC Press, 1993). The "plantation complex", the economic system of commercial agriculture based on slave labor, is analyzed by Philip D. Curtin, *The Rise and Fall of the Plantation Complex: Essays in Atlantic History* (Cambridge: Cambridge University Press, 1990). The best recent summary of the slave trade is by Herbert S. Klein, *The Atlantic Slave Trade* (Cambridge: Cambridge University Press, 1999). For a more exhaustive treatment of the subject, see Hugh Thomas, *The Slave Trade: A History* (New York: Alfred A. Knopf, 1998). An analysis of the silver, fur, and slave trades is given by Eric R. Wolf in *Europe and the People Without History* (Berkeley: University of California Press, 1982). Scholarly papers on commercial European expansion are found in James D. Tracy, ed., *The Rise of Merchant Empires: Long-Distance Trade in the Early Modern World, 1350–1750* (Cambridge: Cambridge University Press, 1990), and Tracy, ed., *The Political Economy of Merchant Empires: State Power and World Trade, 1350–1750* (Cambridge: Cambridge University Press, 1991).

Newcomers

An essential starting point for understanding the process of depopulating and repeopling the Americas is Alfred W. Crosby's *Ecological Imperialism: The Biological Expansion of Europe, 900–1900* (Cambridge:

Cambridge University Press, 1986). Francis Jennings provides a survey of North America's Amerindian population, the movement of native peoples before and after conquest, their decline and eventual revival in his *Founders of America: How Indians Discovered the Land, Pioneered in It, and Created Great Classical Civilizations; How They Were Plunged into a Dark Age by Invasion and Conquest; and How They are Now Reviving* (New York: W. W. Norton, 1993). The essays collected in Ida Altman and James Horn, eds., *To Make America: European Emigration in the Early Modern Period* (Berkeley: University of California Press, 1991) explore aspects of European migration and settlement throughout the Americas. Bernard Bailyn provides a good overview of the diverse process of peopling of England's North American colonies in his *The Peopling of British North America: An Introduction* (New York: Vintage Books, 1986). Good studies of specific British American regions include David Cressey, *Coming Over: Migration and Communication between England and New England in the Seventeenth Century* (Cambridge: Cambridge University Press, 1987), and James Horn, *Adapting to a New World: English Society in the Seventeenth-Century Chesapeake* (Chapel Hill: University of North Carolina Press, 1994). The peopling of Spanish America is examined in a collection of essays edited by David J. Robinson, *Migration in Colonial Spanish America* (Cambridge: Cambridge University Press, 1991). Philip D. Curtin's *The Atlantic Slave Trade: A Census* (Madison: University of Wisconsin Press, 1969) sparked a lively and ongoing debate on the volume of African forced migration to America, yet most subsequent estimates of the slave trade's volume have fallen within Curtin's own margin of error, and his book remains the essential starting point on this subject more than three decades after its first publication. Recent revisions of Curtin's estimates along with discussions of the population history of the African Diaspora in the Americas can be found in David Eltis and David Richardson, eds., *Routes to Slavery: Direction, Ethnicity, and Mortality in the Transatlantic Slave Trade* (London: Frank Cass, 1997).

Revolutions

The historiographies of the American, French, Haitian revolutions, and the rest are seemingly inexhaustible. Studies that offer a comparative perspective are far fewer. R. R. Palmer is the pioneer with *The Age of Democratic Revolutions: Political History of Europe and America,*

1760–1800, 2 vols. (Princeton: Princeton University Press, 1959–1964). A forum entitled "Revolutions in the Americas" in *The American Historical Review* (Volume 105: 1, February 2000) includes comparative-oriented essays on the American, Haitian, Mexican, and Spanish American revolutions. A recent study of the American and French Revolutions is by Susan Dunn, *Sister Revolutions: French Lightening, American Light* (New York: Faber and Faber, 1999). A recent history of the Saint Domingue Revolution is by Carolyn Fick, *The Making of Haiti: The Saint Domingue Revolution from Below* (Knoxville: University of Tennessee Press, 1990). A classic study, first published in 1938, that is still in print is C. L. R. James, *The Black Jacobins: Toussaint Louverture and the San Domingo Revolution* (London: Allison and Busby, 1980). Views of the Caribbean in the age of revolution have been put together by David Barry Gaspar and David Patrick Geggus, eds., *A Turbulent Time: The French Revolution and the Greater Caribbean* (Bloomington: Indiana University Press, 1997). The only study that puts the Spanish American revolutions within the context of the Spanish Revolution is Jaime E. Rodríguez O., *The Independence of Spanish America* (Cambridge: Cambridge University Press, 1998). An account of the American, Haitian, and Spanish American Revolutions, although not a comparative study, is Lester D. Langley, *The Americas in the Age of Revolution, 1750–1850* (New Haven: Yale University Press, 1996).